The Mothers of American Presidents

The
MOTHERS
of AMERICAN
PRESIDENTS

Doris Faber

THE NEW AMERICAN LIBRARY

The author gratefully acknowledges the permission of the publishers to reprint material from the following works:

A Family Album by Rebekah Baines Johnson, published by the McGraw-Hill Book Company. Copyright © 1965 by the Johnson City Foundation.

A Puritan in Babylon by William Allen White, published by The Macmillan Company. Copyright © 1938 by The Macmillan Company.

Diary and Autobiography of John Adams edited by Lyman H. Butterfield, published by the Belknap Press of the Harvard University Press. Copyright © 1961 by Massachusetts Historical Society.

"Honey Fitz": Three Steps to the White House by John Henry Cutler, published by The Bobbs-Merrill Company. Copyright © 1962 by John Henry Cutler.

The Papers of Woodrow Wilson, Vols. I and II, edited by Arthur S. Link, published by the Princeton University Press. Vol. I, Copyright © 1966 by the Princeton University Press. Vol. II, Copyright © 1967 by the Princeton University Press.

First Printing
Published by The New American Library, Inc.
1301 Avenue of the Americas, New York, New York 10019
Library of Congress Catalog Card Number: 68-23843
Printed in the United States of America

246047

*It may be said that the most
important feature in a woman's history
is her maternity.*

　　　　　　　　　—Mrs. Trollope

In Appreciation

To THANK all of the librarians and Presidential relatives and experts in a variety of endeavors who have generously helped me during the preparation of this book would take many pages. Although my gratitude is profound, I would rather forego any such lengthy catalog and merely say that I am most indebted to the following: Eugene Aleinikoff, Gertrude Ball, Willa Beall, Robert R. Bolton, Lillian H. Brown, Elizabeth Carpenter, Rose A. Conway, Janet Dakin, Margaret Truman Daniel, Roland Doty, Lloyd A. Dunlap, Dorothy Eaton, Dwight and Milton Eisenhower, Mr. and Mrs. J. Earl Endacott, Florence Etherington, John Fenton, Mr. and Mrs. Max Frankel, Stella Gliddon, Paul Greenfeder, Robert A. Gutwillig, Virginius Hall, Betty Hein, Sylvia C. Hilton, Helen Howe, Henry Jameson, Mrs. Lyndon B. Johnson, Irwin Karp, Mrs. Joseph P. Kennedy, Hannah Kessel, Peggy Kienast, Edward Kuhn, Jr., Philip D. Lagerquist, Kittie Clyde Leonard, Chester Lewis, Raymond Link, Mr. and Mrs. Stuart Long, Helen MacLachlan, Watt P. Marchman, Elizabeth R. Martin, Mrs. George R. Mercer, Dwight M. Miller, Mary Stribling Moursund, Edgar N. Nixon, Richard L. Ottinger, William G. Ray, Nan Robertson, Robert R. Rodger, Ishbel Ross, Stanley Schachter, J. Duane Squires, Kate M. Stewart, Charles P. Taft, Mary L. Thomas, Mary Jane Truman, Herbert S. Turner, Gregory C. Wilson, and Ernest L. Wright, Jr. To those whose patience and encouragement merit a much warmer expression of appreciation, I can only add that I am well aware of what I owe to them. Beyond all others, though, my husband and daughters deserve my deepest thanks, which I hereby proffer to Hal and Alice and Margie. But as is only right and proper, I dedicate the pages that follow to my mother.

D. F.

Contents

An Opening Note

Back when this book was not yet thought of, I stopped in at the New York Public Library on Fifth Avenue to browse through the *Dictionary of American Biography*. And I found that Abigail Adams was the only Presidential mother who had been dignified by a separate listing under her own name; the others were merely mentioned briefly in the articles about their sons. What a shame, I murmured; they should have been included.

"Why?" demanded the young man on duty at the reference desk. "What did they do?"

"They produced Presidents."

"Pure accident," said he.

Now I doubt it. For these mothers are, by and large, an awesomely strong group, both physically and mentally. "When woman's field widens, Mother, you must become President of a Railroad Company," Will Taft once wrote home from law school, and some similar comment could have been addressed to many of them. Yet they all concentrated on the one career which the old and the new orthodoxy join in presenting as the salvation of females.

What is more, they all made good at it—even Phoebe Harding. Thus far only thirty-five women have given the United States a chief executive; to do so is no common feat. In effect, these ladies are the heroines of true American success stories, the feminine equivalent of the Horatio Alger tales.

It is certainly possible to dispute the proposition that maternal pluck and luck can make a President without other help, and I would dispute it myself. But these women must have done more than they are generally given credit for—just about every major figure among the tenants of the White House was his mother's firstborn male child.[1] I do not mean to be facetious in bringing up this odd little statistic.

Over the last century or so, investigators of various persuasions have tried to discover why first sons have a better chance for achieving distinction than do younger siblings; and at least part of the answer seems to be that first sons often are given superior educational opportunities.[2] But I would suggest that maternal prodding may bear serious looking into—George Washington and Franklin Roosevelt and Will Taft, in the bargain, had older half-brothers, but they themselves were the first sons of remarkably strong-minded second wives.

Yet apart from the kind of homage newspaper editorial writers compose on Mother's Day, the female parents of Presidents have attracted few admirers besides a delightfully Victorian clergyman from Staten Island. The Reverend Doctor William Judson Hampton made a hobby of writing to Presidents and their relations, asking leading questions about the role of maternal religion in shaping Presidential character, and he finally published a devout little volume in 1922 entitled *Our Presidents and Their Mothers*. In this he patiently went down the roster of chief executives, demonstrating that every one of them had been raised by a deeply religious woman. Even Anna Pierce, who reputedly drank and wore red ribbon bows around her ankles, sturdily went to church.

Surprisingly enough, Doctor Hampton's thesis stands up under close scrutiny. But on second thought it is not strange that these mothers should be devoted to religious observance, for their faith

[1] Jackson is a possible exception, and so, at least for his military leadership, is Eisenhower. Altogether twenty of the thirty-five Presidents to date have been their mother's first boy: Washington, Adams, Jefferson, Madison, Monroe, J. Q. Adams, Polk, Fillmore, Buchanan, Lincoln, Grant, Arthur, T. Roosevelt, Taft, Wilson, Harding, Coolidge, F. D. Roosevelt, Truman, and Lyndon Johnson. While a strict constructionist might exclude Taft because his mother bore one boy before him who died in infancy, the very liberal might even include John Kennedy who became the oldest boy in his family rather later.

[2] See "Birth Order, Eminence and Higher Education," by Professor Stanley Schachter of Columbia in the *American Sociological Review* (October, 1963); "Birth Order and Its Sequelae," by Professor William D. Altus of the University of California in *Science* (January 7, 1966); and "Presidential Scholars: What Shapes Their Talent?" by Walter A. Coyne in *American Education* (June, 1967).

was the cornerstone of their universe—the reason why they never considered any career except motherhood; perhaps in an age of doubt, psychiatry had to be invented to perform the same service.

However, when ambitious and capable individuals voluntarily vow to seek only vicarious satisfaction of their own ambitions, quite a charge of energy pours into the career of maternity. This raises a point which escaped William Bullitt when he was assembling data on the youth of Woodrow Wilson to feed Freud for analysis, just as it seemingly has escaped most otherwise conscientious and learned historians, as well as Philip Wylie when a decade ago he was damning American mothers for viperishly smothering their sons. Almost without exception, in the cases where sufficient evidence survives to permit any verdict at all, the Presidents of the United States have been, in the forthright parlance of the playground and no matter if they did or did not engage in sporadic fist-fighting, Mama's boys.

Some accepted domination meekly, others fought it all of their lives. Even George Washington, who stayed as far away from his mother as he possibly could, was profoundly influenced by her, and thus can be included among this company. If so, Lyndon Johnson has something in common with him.

Still I must emphasize that I am not attempting to glorify Mary Ball Washington or Rebekah Baines Johnson. Countless other women have worked along similar lines without achieving similar results, and even these two were surely not infallible, for they could not repeat anything like their first triumph with their other sons. In fact, a rather startling number of Presidents seem to have had younger brothers who became serious drinkers.

Although the intensity of the effort lavished on one particular son may have some bearing on this black sheep phenomenon, there is no way of proving it. Nor is there any way of explaining why one son—usually, yet not always, the firstborn—acquires a special status in his mother's eyes. There may even be a chance that superior ability has a little to do with this process of selection, and thus that nature and nurture combine to exalt the chosen vessel. Of course, no such favoritism is supposed to be displayed by a properly saintly parent of either sex, but traditionally fathers have received ample leeway when it comes to singling out a first son.

Now as to these Presidential fathers, beyond any question many of them were worthy citizens who made a mark in their own communities; half a dozen attained some wider eminence.[3] But from colonial days to the present, even in the home of so positive a male parent as Joseph P. Kennedy, the bringing up of a man's children has been largely his wife's work—the boys as well as the girls were Rose Kennedy's department for the first ten or twelve years of their lives. I would not think of contending that fathers are unimportant, and yet at least in Presidential families their influence seems to have been felt most on the matter of their sons' predilection for politics.

Predictably, quite a number of these mothers wanted their sons to become preachers; only a few openly pressed the case for public service. But even here, a more subtle conditioning may be involved. Erich Fromm has suggested [4] that men who seek political careers may be unconsciously trying to substitute mass adulation for the uncritical maternal adulation they received in boyhood, and that immature though such a reaction may appear, these men do not suffer any severe personality disorder—if, in addition, they are able to find wives who take over the deeper reassuring formerly offered by their mothers. A provocative theory in the light of several Presidential examples, not all in the distant past.

Be that as it may, the basic training of any child is said to occur before adolescence, when fathers often find themselves with a *fait accompli* on their hands. Excepting Theodore Roosevelt, Sr., whose commanding presence cannot be overlooked, most Presidential fathers appear to have made no very strong impress before then; and some never did. The incidence of early death among these men is higher than among their wives, as is the incidence of chronic failure in the worldly sense.

3 John Adams, of course; and the Benjamin Harrison who was an early governor of Virginia as well as the father of William Henry; the John Tyler who was also a governor of Virginia and father of the President of the same name; Benjamin Pierce, a governor of New Hampshire and father of Franklin; Alphonso Taft, judge and cabinet member and father of William Howard; and Joseph P. Kennedy, capitalist extraordinary.

4 See Fromm's *The Art of Loving* (New York: Harper, 1956), p. 96.

So there are grounds for concluding that the main contribution made by a number of them was indirect, to put it kindly, in that they gave their wives and sons an unacceptable example which had to be surpassed. Others certainly operated on their sons' ambition in a more straightforward manner, as will, I hope, be obvious in the ensuing chapters.

For if I have come at all close to my own objective, these maternal portraits will not seem to be drawn out of unreasonable perspective. Nor will they show how a woman goes about raising a son to be President, but rather what manner of woman has already done so. Anybody looking for a guidebook, as it were, will have to be contented by a few not very helpful hints—mothers of Presidents tend to be better educated than the female average, they tend to marry later than usual, and they have an intense interest in seeing that their sons get the best possible schooling. It might be added that so far none of them has produced her famous son in a hospital, which certainly simplifies the task of turning Presidential birthplaces into tourist shrines.

Otherwise, a few of these mothers were rich but most were not; some had sunny dispositions and some were glum indeed; they do not lend themselves to easy generalizations. But only a very small number of women have in the course of the American experience lived the kind of lives that ordinarily become the focus of biographical inquiry—there just is not enough to say about the vast majority to fill a chapter, let alone a whole volume. Because these thirty-five women share a special distinction, and because documentary evidence pertaining to Presidential families does get saved, it has been possible to assemble this book. Perhaps it is even possible that something of the truth about American women as they really are, and not as they are supposed to be, may have thus been preserved.

The Mothers of American Presidents

Rebekah Baines Johnson

A GENTLE LADY

Rebekah Baines Johnson

I<small>T WAS A SIMPLER ERA</small> when Miss Rebekah Baines reached
the age for marrying. At least in her part of the world, the rising
and the setting of the sun seemed no more natural than a somewhat similar arrangement pertaining to girls. Even the brightest
were supposed to concentrate their energies on hemstitching pil-
lowslips and whipping up spoonbread and becoming the mothers
of possible Presidents. Miss Rebekah was exceptionally bright, but
she was also a realist and saw no sense in trying to upset nature;
instead she won exactly what she wanted without ever stepping
beyond the proper place for a woman.

What she wanted so urgently did differ, of course, from a man's
ambition. No matter if he does crave power and riches to vindi-
cate a principle, sooner or later a man is going to enjoy the power
for its own sake. Rebekah Baines Johnson's goal, on the other
hand, had not the slightest tinge of ego to it. She was driven to
make something of her son—in order to reflect glory in another
direction. The person she meant to honor was her father.

Joseph Wilson Baines was the third in an eventual total of six
sons sired by a Baptist pastor with the wanderlust; from North
Carolina down and around to Texas, the family kept right on

moving and growing till the Civil War. As a slender, wavy-haired lad, young Joe served two years as a soldier in a Texas company. He came home with a droopy moustache and an interest in studying law.

That fit in with the Baines pattern to the extent that it involved working with the head rather than the hands. There were Baines reverends traceable in a direct line all the way back to Scotland, not just the general run of itinerant preachers but educated men, likely to edit a newspaper on the side, teach school, or struggle to get a backwoods college started. Joe Baines felt no uncertainty about his own religious faith—but he was hankering after a career in politics.

"I am a Baptist and a Democrat," he would introduce himself, and how could he go wrong in Texas? Alas, he was not rugged enough to survive when the going got rough. He won a term in the legislature, and owing, one suspects, to a harmless sort of deal, he was appointed to serve four years as the Texas secretary of state; the *quid pro quo* apparently was his promise to write campaign biographies of a few Democratic stalwarts, which task must have come easy to him because he had been putting out a rural weekly along with practicing law. But he was thwarted at every turn when he tried to run for Congress.

Although doubtless Joe Baines was a good man with decent, Populist instincts, the evidence that he was a great man does not exist—except in the testimony of his adoring daughter Rebekah. She was born on June 26, 1881, in the town of McKinney, to the north of Dallas, and between this father and his firstborn there immediately began to grow a remarkable bond. But let Rebekah herself testify:

> At an incredibly early age, my father taught me to read. . . . He taught me how to study, to think and to endure. . . . He taught me that "a lie is an abomination to the Lord" and to all real people the world over. . . . He was the dominant force in my life as well as my adored parent, reverenced mentor and most interesting companion.

But this was not the whole story. Had Joe Baines been content to grow old serenely in McKinney, basking in the moderate regard of his neighbors and the love of his family, quite possibly the recent course of American history might have been rather different. But he could not help thirsting for something stronger. Congress was his goal—and he failed to reach it. He also lost the tidy little fortune he had managed to make during his middle years by some judicious land-speculating. As a result, he was a defeated man when he died in 1906, at the age of sixty. And Rebekah was so shaken by anguish that she all but consciously dedicated the rest of her own life to repaying him for his suffering. It is not fanciful to suggest that her father's frustration built up such pressure on her mind and heart as to become the central fact of her existence; she suggested it herself, as shall appear in due course.

Rebekah was twenty-five already and not yet married when her father died, although she had had suitors aplenty. Besides a finer grain than usual in central Texas, she was blessed with a cameo purity of feature and coloring—azure blue eyes and ash blond hair which she brushed ever so deftly into a soft frame for her face. For she owed much to her mother, too. That lovely, sweet-tempered daughter of a country doctor had been a child of not quite fifteen on her own wedding day, and then had waited twelve years more for the joy of fondling her first baby; after Rebekah, she had given birth to a boy and then another girl, but like her husband she could scarcely help favoring the first. In return, Rebekah took her sunny, friendly mother as a model—up to a point.

If there were any deeper reasons why Rebekah did not marry sooner, they need not be dwelt on because she had quite adequate surface grounds for delaying beyond her maternal example. To a degree that was unusual but not unnatural, she yearned for an education before settling down; and at least one other girl from the same town had the same notion, for they went off to Baylor together. Then after a few semesters, there was the sad duty of having to help nurse her failing father. Only nine months elapsed between his death and her marriage. In fact, as his last gift to his cherished daughter, Joe Baines himself sent Rebekah to make the acquaintance of Sam Ealy Johnson, Jr.

Not that matchmaking impelled him. Home for the Baineses during this unhappy period was a humble cottage in Fredericksburg out in the hill country to the west of Austin, instead of the two-story stone mansion some fifty miles closer in to the capital where they had lived till the price of cotton plummeted. They had moved in the hope that law business would be more active in this thriving German settlement, but Lawyer Baines no longer had the stamina to seek out clients. Perhaps as much to do her bit financially as to keep busy, Rebekah had started giving elocution lessons and writing for newspapers; she was mailing accounts of hill country happenings to several dailies off in Dallas, San Antonio, and Austin. What her father did suggest was that she go interview Mr. Sam.

For that young man had recently been chosen as the district's representative in the state legislature, and it seemed possible that his thoughts on drought relief might make lively reading. Nevertheless, the interview produced nothing much journalistically—at the time. "I asked him a lot of questions," Rebekah recalled later, "but he was pretty cagey and I couldn't pin him down. I was awfully provoked at that man." She was also fascinated.

He was earthy and coarse, yet clever; a big, brash creature of contradictions. Although almost thirty, he still had some of the gangling look of a fifteen-year-old whose knees and elbows just will not stop extending longer and longer distances from the rest of him, but his boisterous laugh was a man's and so were his eyes. For all his rough ways, there was a winning tenderness in his glance.

Of course he was a different breed from the Baines menfolk. His people had been rip-roaring trail drivers—it was Sam's father and uncle, coming out from Georgia to try their hand at driving Texas longhorns up the Chisholm Trail toward Kansas, who had built the first cabin on the site of nearby Johnson City. Still he did not lack schooling, and had even done a stint of teaching before going in for politics, meanwhile farming the old family place on the side. To say that Rebekah immediately saw in his tougher fiber exactly the ingredient for guaranteeing political success, if he were to have the help of someone like herself, would probably be exaggerating. But on a less cerebral level she was certainly attracted by him.

For his part, the attraction of an opposite pulled equally. Yet soft as she struck him, Miss Rebekah did startle him, too, by her appetite for politics. Finding repeated opportunity to visit in her locality, he took her to a Confederate reunion at which they both thrilled to the oratory of "Silver-toned Joe"—Senator Joseph W. Bailey, one of the prides of Texas. And he drove her to Austin when William Jennings Bryan himself addressed the legislature. Possibly their acquaintance might not have ripened further if Rebekah's emotions had not been in a rare state of upheaval during these months just after her father's death. As it was, Sam grasped the chance her bereavement offered. On August 20, 1907, they were married.

How long it took Rebekah to find out that she had overestimated her husband's political potential nobody can say; most likely the suspicion arose well before a year passed. But if Sam's bragging and bluster masked an inner uncertainty that ensured he would never amount to much in politics, she felt no despair. To her he was just as tender and grateful as his eyes had promised, and she possessed in full measure the Southern wifely gift of seeing only the bright side. Without ever uttering a word of complaint, she would serve him and bear with him for thirty years and consider their union happy; but it was not the core of her existence. One year and seven days after marrying, she discerned the reason why she had been brought forth on this earth. In her own words:

> It was daybreak, Thursday, August 27, 1908, on the Sam Johnson farm on the Pedernales River near Stonewall, Gillespie County. In the rambling old farmhouse of the young Sam Johnsons, lamps had burned all night. Now the light came in from the east, bringing a deep stillness, a stillness so profound and pervasive that it seemed as if the earth itself were listening. And then there came a sharp compelling cry—the most awesome, happiest sound known to human ears—the cry of a newborn baby; the first child of Sam Ealy and Rebekah Johnson was "discovering America."

With her first glance into the eyes of her infant son, Rebekah Baines Johnson beheld—this is what she wrote—"the deep purposefulness and true nobility" that had shone in her own father's eyes. And at that moment she embarked on a loving, driving, ruthless exercise in anthropomorphism that may have been matched on a few occasions but has surely never been surpassed. It is not facetious to call the project to which she consecrated herself the creation of a god in a man's image; and if in the larger sense she failed, as any such effort must fail, one can only be awed by what she did accomplish.

To see Johnson City and its environs is to marvel at the boldness of her venture, let alone its outcome. This is not a landscape to nourish optimism about man's destiny. The town of some four or five hundred souls which was to be the principal setting for her life could scarcely be more dreary—a surviving photograph of Main Street about 1906 depicts a scene from a horse opera in the lowest budget category. Instead of high drama, it brings to mind dust. As to those hills amid which it straggles in the heart of what Texans call the hill country, they too are a disappointment. They dip and climb no higher than the rolling terrain encountered in little Connecticut, with the prevailing color in this case the dun yellow of pebbly desert sand; it is heart-breaking country for the man who lacks the money to pay for irrigating his land. Sam Johnson lacked any such stake.

But the grubbiness of it all, the puny scale of everything that man had put his hand to beneath so infinitely wide a sky, the almost total absence of the graces of civilization—none of this stopped Rebekah. Whatever was missing she would provide. To begin with, she spent quite some effort on arriving at a name suitable for her special baby. Naturally, she would have preferred Joseph but it was impossible. Joe Johnson? That would never do, indeed not. It was Sam who at last suggested naming the boy for his own lawyer friend, W. C. Linden, and Rebekah agreed, provided, she held out, that she could change the spelling. "Lin*den* isn't so euphonious as Lyn*don* Johnson would be," she said.

In fairness, Sam's part in shaping his son cannot be overlooked but it must not be emphasized either. Being by nature one of the most competitive men alive, he would shake the boy awake before sunrise, and holler at him: "Get up, Lyndon, every boy in town already has gotten an hour start on you and you never will catch up!" The plain fact was, though, that if Sam could not help making a contest out of everything, he could not manage to take many prizes. He failed at farming before Lyndon was five; then on moving into Johnson City, he latched onto real estate trading as a likely outlet for his high charge of energy. It suited his temperament to whip around talking up deals of all sorts. One evening he came home with the deed to the local weekly and said: "Honey, I want you to get this paper out." For several years, Rebekah did just that, writing all the copy and assembling the ads; Lyndon cranked the old hand press. As for politics, Sam won another few terms in the legislature, receiving five dollars a day for attending in Austin two months a year, but wider opportunity failed to present itself. Optimistic as he always would be, still he was sometimes reduced to selling off sections of Grandpa Johnson's original claim in order to pay for groceries, and such an example could hardly inspire a sharp-witted son. The piece Lyndon spoke at the exercises ending school the year he spent in the third grade was an opus entitled: "I'd Rather Be Mama's Boy."

And he was. Before he was two, she had taught him the alphabet; she had him reciting Longfellow by his third birthday and attending school a year later. The conviction that this child had the mark of greatness was not hers alone. "I have a mighty fine grandson, smart as you find them," white-bearded Grandpa Johnson wrote to one of his daughters out West. "I expect him to be United States Senator before he is forty." But if a few others shared at least a portion of Rebekah's obsession, it was his mother who convinced the boy himself.

Should he let slip at breakfast that he had neglected to memorize a multiplication table he was supposed to have by heart, she would drill him relentlessly through the rest of the meal, follow him out onto the porch, walk with him to the road, even start toward school with him, letting him go on alone only when she was satisfied that he had mastered the lesson thoroughly. But her pursuit still remained worshipful. She never disparaged him, she merely implored him to live up to the best that was in him; no wonder her Lyndon became more accustomed to homage than criticism, for she would not allow him the least doubt that he was destined for leading.

Every two years, give or take a few months, she was bearing another baby—little Rebekah, then Josefa, then Sam Houston Johnson, and finally Lucia. Rebekah thought she loved them all alike, finding exceptional qualities in each, but when it came to labeling snapshots in the family album, for instance, the antics of

Lyndon commanded more attention than anything the others did. "Notice Lyndon's protective air," she wrote beneath a picture of him hugging his little brother; the special charm of the infant and his sisters went uncelebrated. "He was always bossy," one of his sisters would say many years later. "I think he thought he was papa."

But Rebekah Baines Johnson never struck her neighbors as unnatural, except in the breadth of her patience. Remembering just how meager Johnson City was in providing nutriment for the human spirit, perhaps one may grasp at least a partial appreciation of the value placed there on the simple virtues. Patience, kindness, humility are cherished as precious commodities in so limited an environment, and Miss Rebekah's portion of each distinguished her. Beyond the call of duty, she also gave Johnson City a vision transcending the parched reality of life there. She sent to Dallas for patterns, and kept herself and her little girls dressed in what passed for elegance. Her pale gold hair would gleam long afterward in the memory of the generation that learned to recite "The Village Blacksmith" in her parlor, as would the roses she somehow made to flourish over a trellis against her front porch. Teaching her elocution pupils or coaching a church pageant, she was always quicker to praise than to scold. "She was a gentle lady," they would insist.

But she never relaxed her pressure on Lyndon. Even the direction in which she was driving him was carefully planned; from an early date, her parlor bookshelf boasted a full set of *The Writings of Thomas Jefferson*. And she sent to Dallas constantly for other books, no matter how she had to scrimp and serve chili to pay these bills. Nor did it disturb her to see her dear boy develop a rowdy streak as he progressed on through high school, somewhat in the manner of his own father. Anybody could tell Lyndon was growing tall and rangy like Sam, and some of Sam's raw strength would never hurt him. As for the boy's mind and heart, she was satisfied; here he took after her father.

So Rebekah felt no envy of any other woman alive. Her old friend who had gone with her to Baylor had also married a Johnson City man. "Rebekah," Miss Mary would tease her, casting an eye at the cranky dragon of a kitchen stove with which Rebekah did battle daily, "we should have married those preachers!" But the thought that she might have done better in a worldly sense could not trouble Lyndon's mother. Exactly as he was, he was perfection to her—or would be, with her help. What other position could compete with hers? Sharing this opinion, those closest to her would in later years add their own further information.

On television and many times in interviews, occasionally with tears in his eyes, Lyndon Johnson would tell how his mother bore with his rebellion after high school, when he cut out for California and then came back to work on a road gang; how she subtly steered his thoughts back to higher goals, then stayed up all night drumming geometry into his head so he could pass the entrance examination at the Southwest State Teachers College in San Marcos; and how she ceaselessly poured out a stream of loving, prodding letters that gave him the courage to aim for Washington.

Less melodramatically but with a warmth only rarely displayed by any daughter-in-law, Mrs. Lyndon Johnson would speak her own praise for her husband's mother. If the prospects for friction seem overwhelming when such a mother must part with her son, it appears that this transfer in 1934 was managed with a minimum of difficulty, almost as though by a prearrangement in which the male was skillfully passed from one protecting, supporting, adoring woman to the other. To note that the bride of the thirty-fifth President strongly resembled his mother in outer grace as well as inner steel is not to belittle the latter's feat of accepting displacement with composure.

Does it not all add up, then, to a triumphant endorsement of the old wives and the new psychiatry? It does indeed, if the personal fulfillment of any one individual be taken as the ultimate goal. Growing old calmly, so nearly at peace with her universe that she was able to retire without regrets, Rebekah Baines Johnson could read the Twenty-third Psalm and smile. As she watched Lyndon's rise in Washington, she knew the supreme joy of having her cup run over. Yet the psychiatrists, if not the old wives, might have second thoughts.

For a person obsessed is still a person beset by an evil spirit, and although Rebekah Johnson could never have knowingly done evil to anybody, she was a woman obsessed. She proved this with a letter she wrote to her first son in 1937 when he won his first election to Congress—a letter dashed off in a rush of emotion.

> My darling Boy:
>
> Beyond "Congratulations, Congressman," what can I say to my dear son in this hour of triumphant success? In this as in all the many letters I have written you there is the same theme: I love you; I believe in you; I expect great things of you.
>
> To me your election not alone gratifies my pride as a mother in a splendid and satisfying son and delights me with the realization of the joy you must feel in your success, but it in a measure compensates for the heartache and disappointment I experienced as a child when my dear father lost the race you have just won. My confidence in the good judgment of the people was sadly shattered then by their choice of another. Today my faith is restored. How happy it would have made my precious noble father to know that the first born of his first born would achieve the position he desired! It makes me happy to have you carry on the ideals and principles so cherished by that great and good man. I gave you his name. I commend to you his example. You have always justified my expectations, my hopes, my dreams. How dear to me you are you cannot know, my darling boy, my devoted son, my strength and comfort.
>
> Take care of yourself, darling. Write to me. Always remember that I love you and am behind you in all that comes to you. Kiss my dear children in Washington for me.
>
> My dearest love,
> Mother

The most extraordinary thing about this letter is an omission. Sam Ealy Johnson, the man who had fathered the new Congressman and who had been her husband for nearly thirty years, was even as she wrote enduring the hardest contest of all. Two years earlier, he had been almost overcome by a severe heart attack and then rallied, but his spirit and his body were still pitifully weak; he needed every possible consolation prize. So the total absence of any reference to Sam is rather chilling.

Just a few weeks after Lyndon's victory in a special spring election to fill an unexpired term, his father was felled by another attack. Sam lingered through the summer, only to die in October. Then at her leisure during the two decades remaining to her, years spent by her own choice in her own small, cozy house in Austin, Rebekah wrote glowing words about her husband for the family history she took pleasure in compiling, along with her collecting of antique pressed glass goblets. Still, her previous unstudied neglect suggests that she may have been less than candid in retrospect. But even in the unlikely event that her husband had failed to suffer from her helpless preoccupation with two other men, her image as a good wife must certainly be affected.

Furthermore, some heed must be paid to the fact that Rebekah Baines Johnson had two sons. One of them became the President of the United States, although she did not survive to see his ascent beyond the post of Senate Majority Leader. But it would be distorting her portrait to ignore her other son, Lyndon's younger brother Sam Houston Johnson; if his mother is to receive some measure of credit for the success of one son, she can hardly escape some measure of censure for the failure of the other.

It is, of course, too pat to say that Sam Houston every day of his childhood was oppressed by the sure knowledge that no achievement of his could ever attract the attention that Lyndon got. Their three sisters labored under a similar disadvantage and survived it better (eventually marrying and producing or adopting a child apiece), but girls are taught to be more philosophical about taking second place. By the testimony of Johnson City, Sam Houston was a bright, likable boy on the quiet side, the one who would leap up out of bed without complaint to start the fire in the kitchen stove. He did not seem defeated then, and after attending college in San Marcos he studied law at Cumberland University in Williamsburg, Kentucky. But he never practiced; by that time, Lyndon had got into Congress, and intermittently for twenty years Sam Houston worked in his Washington office. Then there was a crippling accident, after which he was seen no more in the capital. Thereafter, Lyndon went on to the Vice Presidency, then possibly by some mystic Bainesean predestination, into the White House itself.

But the judging of such mysteries is not really man's business, nor are any of us wise enough to separate out the individual strands that make up the web of any life. How much Rebekah Baines Johnson influenced either of her sons, after all, can only be estimated. When she died in Austin at the age of seventy-seven, on September 8, 1958, and was laid to rest in the family plot out beside the Pedernales River, Lyndon Johnson spoke his own assessment. "She was quiet and shy," he said. "But she was the strongest person I ever knew."

2

"SHE WAS THE GLUE..."
Rose Fitzgerald Kennedy

Even an ordinary man, when he is ready to marry, may have some trouble finding a female he deems worthy of becoming the mother of his sons. In the case of an extraordinary man like Joseph Patrick Kennedy, the quest can be much more difficult. But luck was with him, and he had the wit to take advantage of it—he never engaged in any shrewder maneuver than his courtship of Miss Rose Fitzgerald.

They met at Old Orchard Beach in Maine as high school boy and girl, and there ought to be a plaque marking the spot. For no matter if one thinks of the Kennedy saga as Shakespearean or merely frightening, its impact on at least one generation has been immeasurable. Perhaps some enterprising clam bar proprietor will in due course apply for landmark status, but meanwhile the first act of the drama can still be savored.

It has distinct elements of *Romeo and Juliet*. To start with, the two young people involved already had that indefinable quality setting them apart from their peers: Rose was not just a pretty, dark-haired colleen, she was remarkably pretty and thoughtful, too; Joe was a big, freckle-faced redhead who could make blue-blooded Yankees elect him to class offices. But beyond what he and she could do on their own at this early date, there was the matter of their families.

While the Boston Irish around the turn of this century hardly resembled the Veronese of old, a bit of a feud did exist between Joe's father and Rose's. Being realistic gentlemen, they forgot quite often that they disliked each other, and cooperated for the greater good of their city's Democracy; and even when they were on the outs, words and not swords would, of course, be their weapons. Yet their antipathy was constantly feeding—with a splendid irony, considering what was to come—on the disparity in the style with which they both practiced politics.

Otherwise, these fathers had a lot in common. Both were the sons of famine-driven immigrants, and both had a fierce urge to better themselves. The obvious thought that they were personal rivals for power can be dismissed, because over the years there were too many other competitors to justify such a claim. But Joe's father, Patrick Joseph—the P.J. on the behind-the-scenes Board of Strategy which more or less ran Boston—was a listener, a string-puller, a hardheaded man of some dignity. On the other hand, Rose's father, John F. Fitzgerald, although he was far from a fool, had found that it paid to play the buffoon. His antics definitely failed to amuse P.J., but they won Fitz a seat in Congress fifty years before their mutual grandson Jack made the same race. By the time Rose and Joe met, Fitzie was mayor of Boston.

Thus Rose was the good catch, as far as the worldly could see. Only an insignificant few years of her infancy had been spent in the slum clamor of her father's "dear old North End"—he used the phrase so often in invoking the glory of Erin transplanted that an organization calling itself the "Dearo's" helped him mightily when he set his sights on City Hall. But even before then, Fitzie made sure his firstborn had the best of everything; whereas P.J. liked the idea of his son learning the value of a dollar, and kept his family right in the old neighborhood, albeit in a somewhat better house, when saloonkeeping and his assorted other interests—by reliable account, all legitimate—began yielding a fairly comfortable income.

It is not equally clear that Fitzie's activities honored the spirit as well as the letter of the law. But to blink at the stuffing of

Rose Fitzgerald Kennedy

ballot boxes was a prevalent tic in the Boston of the day, and if he displayed such a reflex, he had plenty of company. Yet the topic here is Honey Fitz as the father of Rose, and what a doting parent he was! Nobody could be safe from his fond efforts to extend the circle of her admirers. President Cleveland took the proffered opportunity rather coldly, but President McKinley was courtesy itself as he was presented to Rose and her younger sister Agnes. These White House visits occurred when Fitzie brought his family down to Washington briefly—en route to winter holidays in Florida. Let it be remembered that before she even met Joe Kennedy, Rose had shaken hands with two Presidents and repeatedly visited Palm Beach.

Not that the Fitzgeralds lived lavishly, by her future standards. While Fitzie served his three terms in Congress, the family stayed most of the year in a relatively modest house right outside Boston, but then when he became mayor, they moved into a more suitable dwelling in the Dorchester section of the city. Indoors and out, this afforded ample space for Fitzie's growing family. Rose's little brothers had all the room they needed for playing baseball; she had her own tennis court. Yet she was not above going to Dorchester High—and Old Orchard Beach.

Some say that Rose and Joe met even before both families spent a season at the Maine seashore, but neither of them remembered any such occasion. Yet a prior meeting is entirely plausible, because practically from the day of her birth in July of 1890 (for some reason, Rose never liked to advertise the exact date), Fitzie had delighted in showing off his darling to the voters and his cronies. So her familiarity with political ritual was almost as awesome as her sons later claimed. "Now I'm grateful to Mother," Jack used to tell predominately female audiences after his mother had taken a bow and said a few words, "but of course she's been doing this sort of thing for seventy years and she ought to be good at it . . ." When Bobby came to campaigning later, he embroidered on the same theme. "Come on, Mother, who was in the White House when you started? Wasn't it Abraham Lincoln? Come on, wasn't it?"

Rose's precocious initiation into politicking was not solely her father's idea. As much as he adored the limelight, his wife shunned it. She was a lovely, shy country girl Fitzie had come across when he led a political club on a berry-picking outing beyond the city limits; how he went about charming Josephine Mary Hannon is immaterial, but she made him a loyal, sensible helpmate who managed for the most part to stay out of the newspapers during a very long life—she was ninety-nine when she died in 1964. "I want my home to be a place of inspiration and encouragement to all my family," she told a magazine writer on one of the rare occasions when she consented to be interviewed. "I am a home woman in every way, and my one ambition is to make the home the most happy and attractive place for my husband and children." Unlike various other political wives who have made the same protestation, Josephine Fitzgerald meant it; and thus her daughter Rose had a second reason for coming on stage early.

At ship launchings and ribbon cuttings, at all manner of ceremonial occasions, when Honey Fitz bustled forward, there beside him, smiling brightly, would be little Rose, standing in for her mother. Although this was some decades before the woman's vote became an accepted factor in political computation, Fitzie already appreciated the importance of appearing as a happy family man. So by the time Rose was in her teens, she already had proved that she had that magic inner light which flashes on in the presence of crowds—charisma, they called it when her son Jack arrived on the political scene.

But even if Rose flourished under the gaze of the multitude, she certainly was not unfeminine. She took after her father in having a lively curiosity about almost everything, yet she was even more significantly her mother's daughter. From her mother, Rose absorbed that profound and abiding religious faith which, in turn, secured her from all temptation to tamper with nature's laws. Endowed with a mind so potentially probing that she graduated from high school at the age of fifteen, Rose Fitzgerald might have cherished her own personal ambitions, intellectual or political, had she been born a boy; but having been created female, she never doubted that her only ambition must be for her menfolk. Her mother and her church set up a framework for her future which was absolutely indestructible.

And so the girl Joe Kennedy met on the beach up in Maine was glowingly pretty, and poised beyond her years; she was already a sharp political realist, and yet she was also immune to egotism. Now was he not an indecently lucky young man?

He thought so then, nor is there any reason to suspect that he ever changed his mind. For over and above all the rest, Joe fell in love with Rose, and she with him. To contemplate the record of their life together is to perceive that this, in the long run, was really the secret of their success. Without exceptional talents which complemented each other almost unbelievably aptly, love alone could never have achieved what these two did; but without love, the whole game would have been lost.

In the first place, their path to the altar had more than a few obstacles. Long after these had been surmounted, when Rose was asked if there had been family objections to the match, she would smile inscrutably and say: "Not exactly." But nine years elapsed between the time she and Joe danced at her senior prom and the autumn day when they married. During those years she grew into a young woman who quite startlingly suggests another dark-haired beauty chosen as a Kennedy wife; it is probably pure coincidence that Rose Fitzgerald and Jacqueline Bouvier were both twenty-four when they became brides, and various differences besides the mere matter of a generation distinguished each of them, but still there are uncanny similarities.

At fifteen, when Rose's father handed her her high school diploma, she was already a personage in her own right. She was graduating with honors, although she was the youngest graduate in the school's history, and her classmates had voted her Boston's prettiest high school senior. To show those stiff-necked Yankees that the Irish could produce a real lady, the initial plan was for her to enter Wellesley in the fall, and the faint tinge of regret in her tone when she spoke of it long afterward suggests that the plan was Rose's own. But she accepted the parental verdict that she was too young gracefully; instead there were music lessons at the New England Conservatory, a few terms at the Convent of the Sacred Heart on Commonwealth Avenue, and then Manhattanville in New York. The relative merits of secular *versus* parochial schooling does not seem to have been debated—from grade school on, she had alternated without the least diminution of her religious fervor.

Her father's main goal was to give her a high-toned polish, and she was more than willing; but she still appreciated "Sweet Adeline," along with serious music. In fact, her father learned the song from her—once, just before a rally, he heard her strumming it on the piano, and asked her to teach him the words, which he had the notion of singing from the platform that evening. To comprehend the response of the audience, it is helpful to recall the opening lines of a verse current in Boston then:

> *Honey Fitz can talk you blind*
> *On any subject you can find . . .*

Fitzie had the sagacity to yield to popular request thereafter, and sing instead of making speeches; he sang "Sweet Adeline" so often that it became his trademark. He even sang it from the bridge of the steamer on which he embarked with Rose and Agnes when he determined to give them the cultural benefits of the Old World. His exuberance not only failed to daunt his daughters—one particularly outlandish coup he pulled off in England positively enthralled them.

It seems that Sir Thomas Lipton had visited frequently in Boston, and, being Irish-born, the millionaire tea packer and yachtsman felt quite at home with Fitzie. There had even been rumors that the sixty-year-old Sir Thomas was going to marry Rose, which gossip was groundless but not in any way irksome; it did not prevent the traveling Fitzgeralds from going down to the sea when they read about an English regatta in which Sir Thomas was to test his *Erin*.

From the wharf, they spied Sir Thomas's yacht out in the harbor, and while they stood gazing seaward, a launch came in—inspiring Fitzie to behave exactly as he would have in Boston. He proclaimed that he and his daughters were friends of Sir Thomas who desired transportation out to the *Erin*. It dismayed him not the least to learn that this launch was known to the benighted British as royal, belonging as it did to the King of England, and the nonplussed deck officer allowed the Boston party aboard.

Out on the *Erin*, great excitement stirred when Sir Thomas saw in his glass that the royal launch was approaching. He quickly had his crew brought forward to receive the King and Queen, and several anxious American guests demanded impromptu lessons in curtsying. While Sir Thomas was trying to explain the etiquette to be followed when Their Highnesses came aboard, the launch drew close enough for him to spy the three figures standing at the rail. "My heavens!" he cried. "It's my friend John Fitzgerald of Boston, with Rose and Agnes."

After that, attending a continental convent school with the daughters of Europe's minor aristocracy might have been something of an anticlimax, but Rose did not find it so. Although she would have preferred enrolling at a French convent, these were closed owing to some church-and-state difficulties, so she and Agnes were deposited instead with the Sisters of the Sacred Heart in Germany. Ever after, Rose could make a creditable little speech in either French or German; she also won a gold medal for her piano playing and acquired a taste for opera, to which the convent students were exposed in more than one way—when the chaperone shepherding a group on a Christmas holiday tour of cultural centers discovered that she had booked seats for an evening on which the Imperial Kaiser would occupy the royal box, that dour spinster doggedly scissored the front of every girl's dress because in the presence of the Imperial family, high necklines were *verboten*.

So Rose learned a lot in Europe, and Agnes must have, too, but poor Agnes appears to have been destined to remain forever in Rose's shadow. On one occasion she emerged, for President McKinley was said to have thought her the prettier of the two; and yet he was, of course, a Republican, and thus not to be trusted. Not that Rose herself ever gave any sign of seeking to diminish her sister, but the process had an air of inevitability about it. Agnes was shy like her mother, she married only after Rose did, and she died before the Second World War; perhaps the best clue to their relationship is the fact that the Miss Ann Gargan who would patiently attend Joe Kennedy during the difficult years after his stroke many decades later was Agnes's daughter.

But even Agnes must have gained confidence from that first

sojourn in Europe, for most of the other students at the convent were thick-ankled daughters of Prussian colonels. However, a sprinkling represented France, and among these girls Rose had a little more competition; it did not faze her, though. She acquired some expertise in the art of looking chic in the lumpy black school uniform, then en route home she stopped in Paris to pay the first of many, many visits at the salons of the *haute couture*.

Thus by the time Rose returned to Boston, there could be no doubting that she had accomplished the family objective. She looked stunning in her feathery French hats, and she had a superb assurance. "Pink teas bore me," she pronounced. Instead she devoted herself to teaching catechism classes for North End slum children, she became the youngest member of the Boston Public Library's book selection committee, she visited settlement houses. Of course, to the Back Bay backbone of old Yankee society, she was still merely the surprisingly stylish daughter of an Irish politician, and nobody invited her to join the Junior League. Nevertheless, the city's Catholics understood that she was "high Irish" and then some—she and her escort generally led the grand march at the best of the Irish balls.

That the escort was usually not Joe Kennedy signified no change in his heart or hers. But a clear grasp of reality would always be a strong point they had in common, and reality in their romance dictated biding their time till Fitzie could be convinced that P.J.'s boy was a comer. Although it is not likely that Joe had ever for an instant felt any uncertainty about his chances for breaking out of bush leagues, he needed a few years to get started.

His own parents had done their part by sending him to Harvard, which was not overly hospitable then to the son of a saloonkeeper; but Joe was more than a match for the snobs he met, and he managed to make the kind of friends who were in a position to provide helpful hints when he graduated. Many of them were going into banking—a profession which appealed to Joe by virtue of its opportunities for close study of big money. What with these connections, plus his own father's friends, he conceived a neat plan.

Although the conventional entrances to a banking career were barred to him because of his religion, he found a back door; he spent a year and a half as a state bank examiner, privileged to inspect the books of dozens of banks for the non-princely remuneration of $1,500 per annum. But by the end of that period, he knew the ins and outs of banking so thoroughly that he was able to maneuver a deal affecting the control of a small bank in East Boston. At twenty-five, Joe Kennedy became the youngest bank president in Massachusetts—"in the world" was how he put it.

That sounded impressive enough to Fitzie. Since Rose had already turned down a candidate or two backed by her father, and it was time she had a husband, the parental blessing was at last forthcoming. On October 7, 1914, she and Joe were married by Cardinal O'Connell in the private chapel attached to his residence. They spent a two-week honeymoon down in White Sulphur Springs, then Mr. and Mrs. Joseph P. Kennedy moved into the small house at 83 Beals Street in the Brookline area, where their first four children were born.

Compared with the grandiose complexities of their later life, the years the Kennedys spent on Beals Street have a pastoral simplicity. At the time, the neighborhood was pleasantly uncrowded, with empty lots beside and directly across from their gray frame dwelling. It was a five-minute walk to church or to the electric streetcar line; they paid a maid seven dollars a week, and when a baby nurse was also needed, they paid her about half of that. Newspapers were only a penny apiece, and evening dresses for Mrs. Kennedy cost a couple of hundred dollars instead of a couple of thousand—these were her own nostalgic comments when she was asked more than fifty years later about what life in this little house had been like. "We loved it," she added.

Not that she or her husband just marked time serenely. Without benefit of jet transport or the quiver of urgency that would later attach itself to the mere sound of his name, the man of the household was soon ranging high and wide in his financial dealings; the big money soon was pouring into his eager hands. Even with the assistance of a nursemaid, his wife had her hands full, too. Within a year of her marriage, she gave birth to a lusty boy who was named after his father, and Joe Jr. carried the intense hopes of both parents from that instant. His mother spent more effort on training him than on any of her other children. "My theory is if you bring up the oldest the way you want the others to go, invariably they'll all follow," she explained much later, when her second son had amply justified her faith in her own maxim.

John Fitzgerald Kennedy was born two years after Joe Jr., on May 20, 1917; Rosemary arrived in 1919, Kathleen in 1920. On pleasant days, their mother would take them all for a walk, wheeling the smallest in a carriage while the others toddled along on foot. "I made a point each day to take them into church for a visit," she recalled afterward. "I wanted them to form a habit of making God and religion a part of their daily lives, not something to be reserved for Sunday." But that was only one phase of her program. "You have to tend to the roots as well as the stems," she elaborated in one of her more solemn moments, "and slowly and carefully plant ideas and concepts of right and wrong . . . and social implications and applications." Translated into practical terms, to her that meant taking the children on little trips to Plymouth Rock, to Concord Bridge, to Bunker Hill. Grandpa Fitzgerald took them to ride on the swan boats in the Public Gardens, and to see the Red Sox. Their father sometimes took them out, too; he dragged them through the neighborhood in snowy weather on a homemade orange-crate sled.

But circumstances conspired to put an end to this homey idyll after only five or six years. Then the constant aggrandizement of Joe Kennedy's income and the advent of more babies dictated a move to a larger house. Eunice was born in 1921; Patricia in 1924; Robert in 1926. These Kennedys would never remember a time when there had been no chauffeur and limousine, or when there had been neighbors up and down the block with clotheslines flapping across their little backyards. In this new period, Rose Kennedy worked out an efficient filing system to keep track of which children had already had the measles, or needed a vaccination. If the file came in handy during the 1920's, it came in even handier when she unearthed it during the 1950's; Jack was running for the Senate then, and his mother's friendly little talks using the cards as her text may have turned the tide for him.

However, there is no need to bank on any such extravagant claim. Despite all of the propaganda picturing Joe Kennedy as an insatiable Svengali of a father—"Second best is a loser," and "When the going gets tough, the tough get going," and so on—the

plain truth is that during his children's formative years, he was
away from them much more than he was home. The children were
Rose's department; making money was his. In 1927, when his
absences became so prolonged as to prove beyond any question
that he had outgrown Boston, he moved his family up to New
York, first to the affluent Riverdale area of the Bronx and then to
the even more affluent Westchester preserve of Bronxville. But by
this time, Wall Street itself could not contain him; he was deeply
involved in the movie business, and spent most of the year in
Hollywood. It was his wife who preserved the family unity. "She
was the glue," Jack later testified. "She's not as forceful as my
father, but she was the glue."

Yet she did more than merely bind nine children into a marvelous solidarity (Jean was born in 1928, and Edward in 1932).
Rose Kennedy, no less than Joe, had no use for second best, and
she worked at bringing up winners just as hard as her husband
worked at amassing his millions. She had a taste for splendor, and
she could have spent her evenings at the opera while her husband
was squiring Gloria Swanson to parties on the West Coast; but
instead she dined at home, twice each evening. There was one
sitting for the younger children, then another for the older. Suiting her choice of subject to the age level, she would lead the
conversation.

"Why are those cities out in California named Santa Monica
and Santa Barbara?" she would ask. Or why had the priest worn
purple vestments that morning? Or why did it get dark during an
eclipse? There was no particular plan about all this, or any mysterious skill; she was simply doing what any good teacher does, but
she certainly accomplished more than most mothers do.

She kept down the uproar, for one thing, but the children had
plenty of opportunity along these lines and they were constantly
pummeling each other outside the dining room; that did not disturb her, though. She merely kept a ruler handy for when any of
them got overly rambunctious. She was strict, too, when it came to
allowances—much stingier with the pennies than the children's
father, who was supposed to be so tough. But if Joe Kennedy
found grasping little hands held out on his arrival home, he also

found an atmosphere wonderfully rich in affection—that was Rose Kennedy's signal achievement.

Beneath the hard shell that he showed the world, Rose's husband had the same priceless brand of warmth; his fury in the money markets was, of course, fed by his hopes for his sons. As they advanced into their teens, he took over from their mother—at least on such matters of high policy as the schools to which they should be sent. She had come around to the belief that Catholic schools were to be preferred for all the children, but he overruled her in the case of the boys; he thought they should have the broadening experience of Harvard, just as he had. He also modified her stand in favor of a foreign educational overlay, such as she herself had enjoyed—she wanted to send the boys on to Oxford or Cambridge, and he picked the socialistically tinged London School of Economics. "When they grow older, they're going to have a little money," he said. "I'd like them to know what the have-nots are thinking."

Yet there is an old saw that only three things parents can do will have any influence on their offspring—"Example, example and example." It appears that Joe Jr. favored his father's example to a notable extent. Bigger and stronger than Jack, even allowing for the two-year difference in their ages, he was also a more compelling personality; he overpowered all of the other children. But they idolized him instead of resenting him, after he survived adolescence. His mother once explained that the other boys had never envied Joe Jr. when he was the first to go off to school or win a letter or make an exciting trip because they always understood that Jack would be next, and then Bobby, and then Teddy. Thus it is not altogether surprising that the family should apply the same logic later in larger issues.

When it did tragically happen that Joe Jr. was killed while serving as a Naval pilot during the Second World War, the fact that Jack took rather more after his mother than his father became of some moment. His distinctive way of speaking, for instance, was really hers. Said an old friend of the family: "When Jack spoke, I could hear his mother's voice." More significantly, the stoic silence with which Jack bore the pain of his injured back was following his mother's example. Joe Kennedy recognized her valor hand-somely. "In all the years that we have been married," he com-mented forty-six years after their wedding, "I have never heard her complain. Never. Not even once. That is a quality that chil-dren are quick to see." But before the world suspected her courage, Rose Kennedy had a grand opportunity to display the winning charm Jack inherited from her.

It took Franklin Roosevelt's puckish sense of humor to come up with the notion of sending an unreconstructed Irishman over to England as the United States Ambassador to the Court of St. James's. Joe Kennedy thought the idea was pretty cute, too. "Well, Rose," said he, as they were dressing for dinner with the King and Queen at Windsor Castle, "this is a helluva long way from East Boston, isn't it?" Of course the appointment owed more to politics than mere puckishness, for Joe Kennedy had worked hard to get F.D.R. elected and then reelected in 1936; Joe Kennedy, the stock manipu-lator, had also done a good job of policing Wall Street as the first chairman of the Securities and Exchange Commission. How his isolationist views hexed him in London during those tense years just before Hitler invaded Poland is irrelevant here, but Rose Kennedy made a magnificent ambassadress. Gowned by Molyneux and trained by Honey Fitz, she and her brood of attractive children enchanted photographers on both sides of the Atlantic. She was still a trim size eight despite her nine pregnancies, and when F.D.R.'s son-in-law stopped off at the American Embassy in London, he said: "At last I believe in the stork."

But if hobnobbing with royalty enthralled her, the fates were not to be denied a cruel revenge. In a speech about the fearful menace of war, Joe Kennedy reminded his audience in 1940 that he and his wife had given nine hostages to fortune; within the next decade, they lost three of them.

Rosemary was the first to leave them, but it was not death that took her. From babyhood, Rosemary had never learned as quickly as the others, but her parents had refused to take the word of doc-tors that there was no hope for her. As she grew up physically, her mental retardation became inescapably clearer, till in London the strain of having to watch her every minute brought her mother to surrender. So they sent Rosemary to a Catholic institution in the

Midwest in 1941, without any publicity at all. It was vaguely indicated that she had embraced the religious life.

Three years later, Joe Jr. was killed in action.

Then in 1948, the sweet, spirited Kathleen—who had pained her parents a few years previously by marrying a handsome but Protestant British marquis, only to become a war widow within three months—Kathleen was killed in an airplane crash.

Like Jack, who took after her, Rose Kennedy kept doing what had to be done under the circumstances. When Jack made what would prove to be his crucial move, daring to try for a Senate seat at the age of thirty-five instead of comfortably holding onto his grandfather's old place in the House of Representatives, his mother flew home from Paris to do her share of handshaking. Sister Eunice has been credited with thinking up the idea of holding tea parties in every Massachusetts city and town, and Jack's sisters all turned out to help; but nobody outdid Mrs. Joseph P. Kennedy in that campaign.

It was later related by a Boston ward leader that Ambassador Kennedy had called him in during the final weeks of the drive to ask for some help. "I told him that he was right about Boston," said this gentleman. "I said to him, 'Joe, the fight's falling off and it needs something to pick it up.' I asked him for permission to use Mrs. Kennedy. He answered, 'But, Johnny, she's a grandmother!' 'That's all right,' I told him, 'she's a Gold Star mother, the mother of a war hero and a Congressman, the wife of an ambassador, the daughter of a mayor . . . and she's beautiful and she's a Kennedy. Let me have her.' And he thought it over and finally said, 'Well, take it slow with her.' "

She was, of course, sensational. She drove around town in a limousine equipped with the props she needed—a mink stole for an audience of rich suburban matrons, a simple strand of pearls for the less affluent ladies, an assortment of hats. She told every audience that she knew her son better than anybody and she knew what kind of a Senator he would be. Then out came those file cards.

Thereafter, the difference was only that she talked more and more to strangers far away from Boston. Down in North Carolina to drum up Presidential votes for Jack in 1960, she improved an idle moment by walking briskly into a college dining hall, where

she stopped at a table occupied by a professor drinking coffee.
"Hello, I'm John Kennedy's mother," she said. Looking up somewhat quizzically, the professor replied: "I'm sorry. I don't believe
   No woman who had already passed her seventieth birthday had
I have him in my class." She told the story herself.
any right to look as gorgeous as Mrs. Joseph P. Kennedy looked at
her son Jack's Inauguration Ball—to which she wore the same lace
gown embroidered with silver and gold paillettes that she had worn
twenty-three years earlier on being presented at the British Court;
and not a jot of alteration was needed, either. But surely no
woman anywhere, let alone her elegant young daughter-in-law,
minded the implication that such a feat could be possible.

After Jack entered the White House, it became his mother's role
to speak out on mental retardation; that was the Kennedy way of
trying to make it up to Rosemary. Now Rosemary's mother could
say openly: "We had a daughter born about a year and a half after
our second son, who later became President . . ." Numerous other
philanthropic interests also occupied her, as did all manner of
social and political fêtes, and she came in for her share of the
Kennedy-directed quipping that distinguished this period. At a
banquet to raise money for a New York hospital, Adlai Stevenson
blandly introduced her as "the woman who started it all—the head
of the most successful employment agency in America."

On the Riviera or in Rome, at Palm Beach every winter, at Cape
Cod every summer, the President's mother still lived a life strenuous enough to exhaust almost anybody else only half her age.
Around noon on November 22, 1963, she was playing golf at the
club near the large white house on the Cape that had for many
years been the family's main base of operations; soon the house
would be full of commotion as children and grandchildren all flew
in for Thanksgiving. Although her husband had been piteously
invalided by his stroke almost a year earlier, Rose Kennedy would
have much to be thankful for . . .

On her return from the golf course, her niece Ann Gargan told
her the news that had just burst onto the radio.

Yet from this, too, she recovered. Thereafter, she rarely spoke
of Jack except as "the President," and she referred to his death as
"the tragedy." Doubtless her religion provided solace; wherever

she happened to be, she would always manage to start her day by attending Mass. But in time she was back on a platform, saying a few words on behalf of Bobby, or Teddy. "I used to say," she told an interviewer in 1967, "that a lot of women have been the mothers of one President, but there's never been a woman who's been the mother of two or three Presidents—so get busy!" That, she quickly added, was just a joke. Now was it really?

CINDERELLA
IN KANSAS

Ida Stover Eisenhower

SHE WAS BORN ON MAY 1, 1862, near the Shenandoah in western Virginia, so the smell of burning haystacks became one of her first memories. War scorched her valley, it wrecked the orchards and charred the barns, and she would always believe that it also killed her parents. Ida Stover's opportunities for taking a bleakly tragic outlook were exceptional, but a happier person never lived.

Apparently, girl babies did not run in her family. She had seven brothers—ranging in age from three to seventeen—when her mother died in 1867; Ida was then scarcely five years old. But her notion that anguish over the senseless destruction of the Civil War had caused her mother's death may have had some basis in fact. No matter whether it did or not, though, Ida grew up feeling sure warfare was the worst evil afflicting mankind. That one of her own sons became a soldier would have made her miserable if anything could, but she had no talent at all for suffering.

Had she been gifted in that direction, her childhood offered plenty of scope. Although her father did not die for another sev-

Ida Stover Eisenhower

eral years, he could not deal by himself with his children and his ruined farm, and he sent them a few miles up the road to their maternal grandparents. Ida's memories of the period she spent with these frugal old relatives sounded rather like a tale told by the Brothers Grimm.

"Because I was a girl," Ida Eisenhower remarked nearly eighty years later, "I was told I must listen, not talk, and not expect to go to school much." Instead, she was expected to do most of the cooking for her brothers. There was a big brick oven; this became her nemesis. "If I burned anything or took it out underdone, I was punished."

Yet she did have good times when she was allowed to go out riding with her brothers—"We would make for the woods, get off our horses and sit around, making plans." After her father's death, a small inheritance was set aside to be distributed as they each reached legal age, and so these orphaned children holding conclave beneath some favorite tree could do more than just dream about a better future. When they got their father's money, they decided, they would seek their fortune in Kansas.

Nowadays with good and evil not quite as easily identifiable, such a homespun history may arouse mixed emotions. But even though Ida Eisenhower was old enough when she told it to have some trouble, which did not bother her a bit, about remembering exactly what she had just heard on the radio, she appears to have preserved a clear picture of the distant past; this is, of course, not unusual. Perhaps her narrative was colored too starkly—at least one of her sons thought this was the case—and yet in its essentials it was accurate. Gravestone markings prove that.

The mere facts, in any event, have less significance than the moral of this story. Probably the only purely time-passing occupation Dwight Eisenhower's mother ever indulged in was playing solitaire—after her sons grew up to the point when she sometimes had a spare half an hour, she might look for a deck of cards. But maybe the game was not frivolous, after all, because from it she drew one of her favorite sayings, which she often repeated to Dwight with a twinkle in her eye. "The Lord deals the cards; you play them." It was what her childhood taught her.

The Lord was a real presence to her. If a girl was not supposed to be spoiled by schooling, even Ida's grandfather saw the necessity of letting her learn to read the Bible. That no other literature was made available to her at least partly explains the avid way she went at reading Scripture; parish records kept by a little Lutheran church outside the Virginia hamlet of Mount Sidney disclose that once Ida Stover was cited for memorizing 1,365 verses during a six-month period. But it must also be recognized that the Bible spoke to her need as no other voice could. Her Bible told her everything was going to be all right with the world when the proper time came, and she believed it absolutely.

Still there had to be more than faith alone to make anybody as cheerful as she was; dour true believers can easily be found among the ranks of many sects. Faced with Ida Eisenhower, one must fall back on the old idea that some people have naturally sunny dispositions. She certainly did—and common sense, too. Instead of waiting on her grandparents' farm for a prince with a glass slipper to come and rescue her, or just waiting for her twenty-first birthday so she could take her inheritance and join her older brothers in Kansas, she thought she ought to go to high school. Somehow she had concluded that she would like college, and she must also have already been collecting the supply of handy maxims from which she would always be able to draw an appropriate piece of advice; first things first fit this situation, impelling her to run off to the county seat of Staunton when she was about sixteen.

In this quiet town where Thomas Woodrow Wilson had been born twenty years earlier, she had no difficulty finding a family willing to take her in if she would cook dinner and help with the chores in exchange for room and board while she went through high school. After that, she got a job teaching the three R's out in the country; at twenty-one, she took the money coming to her, lavished six hundred dollars of it on an immense ebony piano, and then she set out for Kansas.

She went with an aunt of hers—together they accompanied a group akin to the Mennonites who were organizing a mass migration. These Brethren in Christ, more frequently called the River Brethren because they favored river baptizing, were methodical and efficient pioneers. They arranged for household property to be sent ahead by freight cars, and Ida had no problem about trans-

porting her prized piano. She had also made some arrangements of
her own, for one of her brothers had settled in Topeka, and he
would welcome her. He had assured her, in addition, that the college the River Brethren had founded in nearby Lecompton would
accept female students. In the fall of 1883, Miss Ida Stover appeared there with her piano to begin studying music, history,
literature—anything the college would teach her.

The breadth of learning she was offered may not have been very
wide, nor its depth very deep, but that long-since-departed institution in Lecompton served humanity well. It introduced the delighted Miss Stover to David Eisenhower.

He was a serious young man, just as standoffish as she was
friendly. Even their coloring was opposite, his being about as dark
as hers was golden. While Ida lacked the classic features that are
required if a girl is to be credited with beauty—her nose was too
insignificant and her mouth rather disproportionately large—the
effect when she smiled, which she did almost constantly, captured
David. Fortunately, he did not even have to smile to look appealing—he had the wonderful gift some diffident boys have of word-
lessly being able to bring out the mothering urge in women of
almost any age. As it happens, he was sixteen months younger than
Ida, and at first it may have been his boyish need for reassurance
that attracted her to him. But these two were really much better
suited than appearances indicated.

In their heritage, they were surprisingly alike. Like Ida's forbears, David's people were originally and stubbornly German;
both families were descended from thrifty farmers who had arrived
in Pennsylvania before 1750—it is a matter of record that the first
Eisenhauers to settle there had their children baptized by a Stoever
farmer-pastor whose progeny later moved down the Shenandoah
Valley to Virginia. But whether Pennsylvanian or Virginian, both
families had stayed close to their own kind and kept to German
ways. One generation back, owing to intermarriage with a River
Brethren family, the Eisenhowers had left the Lutheran fold to
adopt the Mennonite style of worship, but this could be no impediment. At the prospect of an escorted trip to Kansas, Ida had
willingly made the same change—although she never went so far
as to wear the Brethren's plain gown and sedate bonnet. Nor, for

that matter, did David grow the flowing beard the Brethren's men wore. In their own way, they were both too independent-spirited to accept any rigid dictation on such matters.

Nevertheless, they both had the same unclouded perspective on right and wrong—to do good was right, and to do harm was wrong. Furthermore, after two years at college they also agreed that education, important as it was, must give way to a higher goal. On September 23, 1885, when Ida was twenty-three, they were married in the college chapel.

For David more than for his wife, the step marked a decisive compromise; but he had already learned to do that. He had wanted to be an engineer, he had seized on this fine-sounding profession as the answer to his quest for something besides following the plow. To his father any such ambition was incomprehensible—David's father had put his whole life's quota of questioning into the single rashness of moving from Pennsylvania to Kansas, where he immediately proceeded to duplicate his stolidly prosperous agricultural past, modified only by the vagaries of the new climate. Since his experience totally excluded the possibility of sending a son back East to engineering college, David had already settled for the lesser boon of Lecompton.

Here by the banks of the Kaw River, in a three-story building originally intended to be the first capitol of Kansas, one laboratory room and four recitation rooms comprised the basic instructional facilities of the institution hopefully christened Lane University; the name was in tribute to Kansas's first United States Senator, who had pledged one thousand dollars toward equipping the abandoned capitol site for educational purposes. With much enthusiasm and little money, the Brethren had gone about adding what they could. But some of the students who turned up could pay only a dollar or two a week for their tuition and board, so the campus as well as the curriculum remained rather spartan. Finding higher mathematics and anything but a smattering of science out of Lane's range, David studied Greek instead.

As a result, he would awe neighbors for the rest of his life when they stopped by to chat with Ida—and found her husband poring over a Bible printed in Greek. But far more importantly, David Eisenhower never forgot how he had felt about having to give up the chance of studying engineering. So he made it a major article of his own faith that he would not try to influence any son of his for or against a particular career; and he and Ida both held to this despite the most painful provocation either of them could imagine.

David's private struggle before he decided to marry—and thus give up engineering for good—can only be imagined; he never spoke of it. But his father certainly expected him to renounce oddity at this crucial moment in a young man's maturing, and to take up farming as any sensible fellow would. Treating David as no different from the rest of his children, his father deeded over one hundred and sixty acres to him, along with two thousand dollars in cash to get him started with livestock and a house. If David argued not, he acted out his meaning—with Ida's loyal assent, he sold the land and then put every penny he had into a partnership in a general store. This was located in a Kansas crossroads auspiciously named Hope.

Many years later, several of the sons Ida almost immediately began giving David would bristle at the suggestion that their father had no head for business; what he did have was a short-fused temper, which several of them got from him. Yet the most charitable thing one can say about David's storekeeping was that he lacked the experience to understand how long farmers had to be carried on credit while they waited payment for a cash crop—and how sly it was of his own partner to pack up while the going was good. So David was stuck with a sheaf of bills from suppliers demanding their money, without any prospect of collecting from his customers until a good long spell of rain produced a decent wheat crop.

By the time his plight became clear to him, Ida had already produced one baby—Arthur, who would be the banker—and she was pregnant again. There was no more help to be looked for from David's father. The only way out he could think of was to give the whole sorry mess into a lawyer's hands, then take the best job he could find. That happened to be as a railroad mechanic clear down in Texas but off he went anyway, with Ida bravely staying on alone till after the second baby arrived.

Although she expected the lawyer to provide her with a fair amount of money as the accounts got untangled, it did not work out that way. His smooth explanation that nothing was coming to her, after all, failed to convince her, and for once in her life she got her dander up sufficiently to make her accuse him of trickery and say, all right, she would prove her case herself. Watching over her first boy and then having her second, whom she named Edgar— after Edgar Allan Poe, whom she admired, even if he was a drinker—kept her too occupied for carrying out her threat. But off and on for years, she kept muttering about getting around to study up on the law so that she could protect her family against thieves, embezzlers, chiselers, and other kinds of crooks.

What she did do was much harder than studying law would have been. After giving birth to Edgar—who did become a lawyer— with only friendly neighbors to help her, she set out on the railroad for Texas, one infant in her arms and his brother clutching at her skirt. Thus it was in a gabled framehouse in the Texas town of Dennison that her third son, David Dwight Eisenhower, was born on October 14, 1890—after awhile Ida decided to reverse the order of his names to avoid confusion with his father and to make sure nobody called this boy Dave. She had no use for nicknames, and once she discovered she had unwittingly brought forth an Art and an Ed, she tried thereafter to stick to one-syllable first names not susceptible to abbreviation. How much energy she spent shaking her head when she heard Dwight called Ike nobody ever measured, but she was an energetic headshaker and the expenditure must have been considerable.

If not for the circumstance of Dwight's having been born there, the Eisenhowers' stay in Texas might well have been overlooked, for they spent only about two years away from Kansas. As it is, an historical marker has had to be affixed to the unpretentious house in which they lived, but even so the mecca for Eisenhower admirers is the comfortably typical, law-abiding, God-fearing town of Abilene in Kansas. Had David and Ida Eisenhower traveled from sea to sea in search of an all-American community in which to bring up their sons, they could not have hit upon a sounder choice.

It even had an uproarious past, which is a great asset to any small town. Right after the Civil War, it had been the western terminus of the railroad that by dint of later machinations became the Union Pacific, and an enterprising cattle trader built some livestock pens beside the depot. Then a glorious decade of sin and prosperity descended on Abilene—to accommodate the cowboys who whooped into town thirsty and otherwise deprived after driving enormous herds of longhorns up from Texas, an enclave known as Hell's Half-Acre arose right beyond the cattle pens. Wild Bill Hickok was the sheriff who kept a semblance of order here. How could a town do better in the way of providing a hero for its boys?

The same Chisholm Trail which Lyndon Johnson could see the start of ended practically in Dwight Eisenhower's backyard. But the days of Abilene's glory were well over before the Eisenhowers moved there. Once the railroad was extended westward to Dodge City, the bulk of cattle moving up from Texas was aimed toward the new terminus because for man and beast both, Abilene was getting a little fussy—it began enforcing quarantine laws to keep out diseased steer, and other sorts of laws to discourage rowdy cowboys. Such was the pressure of civilizing domesticity that Abilene in the 1890's wanted no part of its own past except the memory of it, which it did a man good to contemplate every so often as an exhilarating antidote to respectability.

But if David Eisenhower felt a yearning for this sort of stimulation, it had nothing to do with his decision to make his home there. Abilene was the place his own father had chosen, and family ties drew him back as soon as he heard of a job he could have. Tinkering with tools had always appealed to him, so his sister Amanda let him know that the creamery where her husband was one of the managers had an opening for a man to take care of the machinery. Although the pay was less than fifty dollars a month, he accepted the offer.

How Ida accomplished so much with so little money is impossible to explain, no matter that prices were lower then and needs were fewer. Sink or swim was another of her favorite sayings, though, and she had no intention of sinking.

The first seven years after their return to Abilene were the hardest. Living in a tiny cottage, Ida had to fit five boys into rooms with scarcely the floor space for the necessary beds; her fourth son was Roy—who would be the druggist—and then came

Paul who heartbreakingly left them before his first birthday when he succumbed to diphtheria. But not long afterward, a relative gave them the opportunity for improving their situation without any great expenditure; he sold them a house of no imposing size, although it was grand enough to boast an upstairs, and it was set on three whole acres of land.

Then Ida came into her own. Her son Dwight's forte in the future would be the deploying of large numbers of men to the best effect, and he learned more than the rudiments from his mother. She organized and directed her own small army with the firm touch of a field marshal, but, of course, she had had a certain amount of practice already with all those brothers of hers. Now her objective was nothing less than to wield the manpower at her disposal into an almost completely self-sustaining unit.

Their property already had a large barn and some healthy apple trees; she saw to it that a good many other potentialities were realized toward the end of producing just about everything hungry boys needed to fill them up. They kept a cow, chickens, ducks, and pigs, plus two horses for nonculinary purposes; they grew vegetables for the table and feed for the animals. "They," needless to say, were the six sons she raised to maturity. Earl—the engineer— and Milton—the college president—were born in two successive years just before the turn of the century.

The way their mother arranged things, each boy alternated between outdoor and indoor chores, the latter being considered infinitely less desirable because hopping out of bed at half-past four in the morning was called for to start the kitchen fire. Dragging buckets of laundry water was not popular, either. For that matter, Dwight in his younger days had no particular liking for work of any description. "I was a great bawler," he recalled once, "because I was trying to get out of doing things. And I remember a neighbor lady coming in one day, who said, 'Ida, what are you doing to that child?' She said, 'Oh, he'll be all right as soon as he brings his kindling in.' And of course I was."

Not that all discipline problems were allowed to solve themselves, not a bit. The rod was not spared when a boy neglected a chore or his schoolwork; Ida reached for it when instant retribution struck her as imperative, but she preferred to have the culprit wait till his father came home for supper. In her mind at any rate, David was the court of last resort, and yet there are grounds for wondering if she had a true picture of her own power. Hers was a much more forceful personality than her husband's, which does not seem ever to have occurred to her.

Humming a hymn as she worked, Ida Eisenhower was demonstrably more than merely contented with her lot—like Cinderella, she was living happily ever after, Kansas style. She enjoyed baking nine loaves of bread every other day. "There's no rest for the wicked," she would aver cheerfully as she rolled up her sleeves and reached for the flour. Certainly her husband worked hard, too, and his example no doubt did its share in impressing his sons with the importance of being earnest. Yet he left them at six in the morning not to return till six at night, and after supper he generally sat reading or studying a homemade wall-sized diagram of the Egyptian pyramids—he had some abstruse theories about their construction which it pleased him to try to prove. One looks in vain amid the foliage of anecdote that always springs up around a Presidential family for some word or deed of his that bears on his relationship with his sons, apart from his role as chief wielder of the rod. He does not seem to have taken his boys hunting, or to have counseled them in any memorable way. Although they would always speak of their parents' marriage as an ideal partnership, one is forced to conclude that he was the silent partner.

This is not to say his influence was negligible. His grown sons— as Ida would have said, the proof of the pudding—were all fine, upstanding citizens, and they all agreed that their father deserved a lot of the credit. Unlike so many other Presidential cases, Dwight Eisenhower had no black sheep siblings, and he had his own explanation for this. He said: "The answer lies, I think, in the fact that our family life was free from parental quarreling and filled with genuine, if not demonstrated love." He also agreed with his mother that children usually turn out well if they are given plenty of work to do. Surely David Eisenhower contributed toward all of this but his greatest contribution must have been his refusal to emulate his own father. By refraining from any attempt to influence his boys in their planning for their future, he gave them the best gift he had to offer.

Ida, on the other hand, was a constant and easily visible influence on her sons. Dwight even looked just like her, his temperament was like hers, he laughed the way she did; allowing for the difference in their size and sex, her enthusiastic chuckle at the slightest joke was the model for his hearty guffaw. On a further debt to her, he testified once in a television interview:

> [*After explaining how, one Halloween evening when he was about ten, he was forbidden to go out with his older brothers, and went bellowing into the yard to beat his fists on the stump of an old apple tree, where his father found him and gave him a good tanning, then sent him off to bed*] . . . about a half hour later my mother came in the room and she began to talk to me and she used some Bible verses, and then she talked awhile, trying to show me how when you get so angry at someone, that you couldn't help yourself. Well, then in the meantime she began to wash my hands and get a little salve on them, and wrap them up and I think that was one of the most important moments in my life, because since then, I want to tell you this, I've gotten angry many times, but I certainly have tried to keep from showing it.

That he also followed her lead when it came to appreciating ripely familiar home truths it is not necessary to demonstrate. But although Ida Eisenhower influenced her son in many ways, she, no less than her husband, gave Dwight a free choice at the crucial moment.

While the boys were young, they had been required to take part in daily prayer sessions and round-robin Bible reading, but neither parent made any effort to compel such observance after their sons grew away from their own religious preoccupation. Cards made their appearance, and in time cigarettes were allowed; music secular as well as devotional tinkled from Ida's still-prized piano in the parlor. All of this was in a real sense preparation for what lay ahead.

Ida and David both would have liked to see all of their sons achieve the college education they themselves had only tasted. Of course the boys would have to manage the financial details on their own; up until the day he retired, David never made more than a hundred and fifty dollars a month. But their sons, being such experienced odd-job doers since early childhood, could be expected to solve this problem. However, Arthur, the oldest, was in too much of a hurry about making a success to spare the time for further schooling, and although it saddened his parents when he went right from high school to look for work in Kansas City, they did not try to change his mind. Then Edgar set himself on studying law, even though the rest of the family thought he might do better as a doctor, and again Ida and David let him go his own way with their blessing.

It was much harder when Dwight's turn came. He wanted a college education all right, and yet he had not picked out any particular goal by the time he finished high school; so he and Ed fixed it up that they would take turns helping each other. Dwight would work two years while Ed studied, sending Ed whatever he earned, and then they would reverse the arrangement. But before the first two years were ended, Dwight found an opportunity that looked pretty good to him—West Point.

Neither parent could help feeling crushed by his decision to apply, but neither of them said a word to dissuade him. To his mother, the restraint was the hardest struggle of her life, for she was deeply convinced that soldiering was a wicked business. David's pacifism was just as sincere, yet he could see the sense of Dwight's plan, which would net him a free education. Ida's emotions were too strong for any such logic to move her, but still she kept her feelings to herself. "It is your choice," she told Dwight, and that was all she said to him on the subject.

When he picked up his suitcase to walk the few blocks over to the old Union Pacific depot, she stood on the porch and waved to him; Milton, standing beside her, was positive that she did not shed a tear until Dwight disappeared from sight. Then tears flooded down her cheeks, and she ran upstairs to weep away the day alone in her room. In her own mind, she could have no doubt that Dwight was lost to her. She had raised a good boy, but she had signed him over to the government; that was how she felt then. Yet she was truly incapable of looking on the dark side for long, and although she never did learn to admire the martial spirit, she came to take pride in Dwight, after all.

Not that she ever singled him out for a special position among her boys. When Abilene was draped from one end of town to the other with his picture after he came home as the triumphant hero of the greatest military campaign in all history, and a reporter asked her if she wasn't proud of her son, she said: "Which one?" And she was genuinely puzzled. To her, all of them had turned into good men, and being good was really all that mattered.

For all his growing beyond Abilene, Dwight remained a good son to her. Plucked out of military files to be stamped "DECLAS-SIFIED" two decades after V-E Day, a sheet of the yellow message paper used at the headquarters of the Allied High Command gives evidence of the dimension of his filial devotion. The piece of paper had previously been stamped "TOP SECRET"—as was only natural for a headquarters directive dispatched in May of 1944, a scant few weeks before the invasion of France. But this particular order called for sending a Mother's Day greeting to Mrs. Ida Eisenhower in Kansas.

Throughout the war, Dwight's letters to her kept coming once or twice a month, no matter where he happened to be. Every so often, a parcel would arrive unexpectedly, containing handker-chiefs someone had given him in Scotland, or some other souvenir. As his increasing eminence brought repercussions in the form of publicity about his family, he warned her not to let photographers tire her out. But he also told her he was delighted that more people were learning what her six sons and their father always knew—that she was the greatest woman in the world!

Her letters to him were another matter. Just about the time Dwight's fame started spreading, her own life took quite a differ-ent sort of turn. After sending their sons out into the world, Ida and David Eisenhower were blessed with serene years beyond the bounty given most people. When they celebrated their golden wedding anniversary in 1935, all of the boys and their wives came home to make the occasion memorable. In his later decades, David switched over to working for a local utility company where he took charge of pension arrangements for his fellow employees, and if his own income never became very grand, still it proved ample to provide a furnace for their house, a refrigerator, even a small car. With her new leisure, Ida could lavish care on her flowers and her strawberries; she produced a phenomenal supply of crocheted doilies. After he retired, David showed a talent for handwork, too, his metier being rughooking.

Then early in 1942, when he was nearing eighty, David died. Within about a week, his wife's bewilderment gave way to an accepting calmness of spirit but she paid a price for it. From then onward, her memory almost completely failed her. She was still cheerful, she even enjoyed being teased about her lapses. When Milton, then president of Kansas State College, drove over for Sunday dinner, he often asked her as they got up from the table: "Mother, what did we have for dinner?" She would think a bit and then smile brightly. "It was good, wasn't it?" He sometimes tried another tack. "Mother, I'll bet you can't name your six sons in order." "You know them as well as I do," she would answer complacently.

To keep her from any mishap, the boys had arranged for a practical nurse companion, and it was this lady who wrote regularly to Dwight and the others. Her letters recited a placid round of preserving elderberries, potting geraniums, going out to picture shows. Yet that was not the whole extent of their activities; in her old age, Mrs. Eisenhower was led astray.

Much earlier in her life, well before Dwight had even left for West Point, Ida and David, too, had become dissatisfied with conventional church services. Assembling a small group of the likeminded, they had taken to holding weekly Bible study sessions at each other's homes; and as time went on, they had begun corresponding with similar groups elsewhere and subscribing to various periodicals. In a loose sort of way, they eventually affiliated themselves with the Jehovah's Witnesses.

Their sons knew all about this, of course; it was no secret. But they would no more have thought of trying to dissuade their parents than Ida and David thought of trying to convert their children. Although an aggressive evangelism came to characterize the sect as a whole, the Eisenhower version was different. Just as neither Ida nor David had worn bonnet or beard in their Brethren days, neither of them went out preaching the Witnesses' message after they changed their allegiance—until Ida was well past eighty.

Then it was not her own idea. Being of the same persuasion, her companion began driving her all over that part of Kansas to distribute leaflets from door to door and to smile sweetly at street meetings. While her son was leading the United States Army to victory in Europe, his mother was inciting refusal to salute the flag. Eventually, an old Abilene friend let a few of the boys know what was happening, and there ensued an immediate flurry of swift visits, the companion was fired, a respectable Presbyterian lady was hired in her stead. Mrs. Eisenhower thenceforth attended Presbyterian Bible study classes.

Yet it was not their mother's convictions her sons objected to, it was the unconscionable way in which she had been used as a living advertisement. Nor did this cease immediately. Even years later, after Dwight was in the White House, letters would arrive from many parts of the country demanding to know: was it really true that Ike's mother had been a Jehovah's Witness? And if so, how was it possible that he had never admitted it publicly? Composing diplomatic answers to such mail was one of the least pleasant tasks facing his Presidential secretariat.

If not then, at least in his reminiscent years thereafter, her son did publicly put the matter in its proper perspective. To him, his mother's personal religious feelings had been a matter of concern only to herself and her God. "Her serenity, her open smile, her gentleness with all and her tolerance of their ways"—these were the things that mattered to him. But after Ida Eisenhower died quietly in her sleep on September 11, 1946, at the age of eighty-four, her neighbors put the case in their own—and her own—way. "She was the salt of the earth," they said.

LIGHT-FOOT BAPTIST

Martha Young Truman

Nobody ever had a harder month than Harry Truman did right after he became President. It was early in April of 1945 when Franklin Roosevelt's death stunned the world, and left the winning of the most terrible war in history to his successor. But fortunately, Mother's Day rolled around as usual in May.

During those interim weeks, if it seemed utterly numbing to think of this little man from Missouri as the keeper of the keys to the arsenal of democracy, there were reasons for the difficulty. Having jauntily brushed aside tradition, F.D.R. had only recently won his fourth term; a good many adults had no clear memory of any previous White House occupant. Even Roosevelt haters conceded that a giant had perished, in which judgment Winston Churchill assented. Truman himself appeared to share the general concern. Talking to reporters the day after he was sworn in, he said: "Boys, if you ever pray, pray for me now."

Yet what he needed most, of course, was an image. As it happened, Harry Truman had the makings of a strong President, which he immediately began to demonstrate within the private confines of his office. But there was still the problem of getting the public to see him in the part. No calculated press agentry could

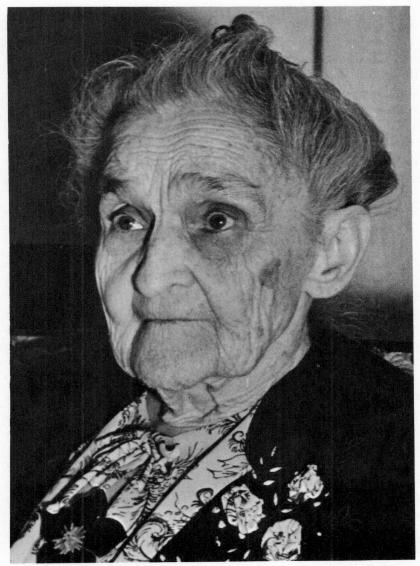

Martha Young Truman   (PICTORIAL PARADE)

have accomplished more toward this end than his ninety-two-year-old mother did all by herself.

Since her Harry was not going to be able to come out to Missouri for Mother's Day, she went to Washington instead. He sent the Presidential airplane, *The Sacred Cow*, to fetch her. When it landed, he bounded up and brought her into the doorway for the benefit of the horde of photographers who had naturally been forewarned, but for once a few words were worth more than a thousand pictures. In a peppery voice that cut right through the frenzy of picture-snapping, Mother Truman let off a snapper of her own. "Oh, fiddlesticks!" she said. "If I'd have known there was going to be all this fuss, I wouldn't have come."

So America could relax. No longer was there a sort of vacuum at the center of its government, and if it took some professional politicians much more time to get the message, that was their misfortune; the voters had the clue they needed. What is more, after such a long spell of Hudson River squiredom, they liked hearing plain talk from the Big Muddy country. "Give 'em hell, Harry!" they shouted three years later when Mother Truman's boy spoke his own blunt comments about Congress, and they defied all the experts by picking him for a full term, instead of another New Yorker.

Martha Ellen Young, as she had started life, was a sensible mixture of sugar and spice right from her girlhood. That had, of course, been a long, long while before her son could invite her to the White House, back in the troubled days when Mr. Lincoln had paced its corridors. She never got over her distaste for that man, and when Harry teased her that she could sleep in the same bed which his Illinois predecessor had used, she told him she would rather sleep on the floor. Her parents would have expected no less.

They were Solomon Young, a shrewd and successful farmer who knew how to profit from the westward urge which possessed the nation in his day; and his spunky, redheaded wife. Kentucky was their original home, then they moved out to the far reaches of Missouri where Martha Ellen, the next to last of their nine children, was born on November 25, 1852; the farmhouse she arrived in sat on land that has long since been swallowed up by Kansas

City. Although Solomon moved his family no further, he did acquire more and better acreage till he had the equivalent of a good-sized plantation; and he built a better house a few miles distant, in future shopping center territory. He amassed his capital by riding the westbound trails himself—carrying supplies to wagon trains and even driving cattle clear out to California gold rushers. On principle, not that he ever owned more than a few slaves, he took the Southern side in the great issue of the era. But being forty-five when the fighting started, he did not enlist and kept right on with his livestock trading.

In the course of one of his absences, a band of Union-sympathizing raiders crossed over from Kansas. Jim Lane's Redlegs, so-called from the red gaiters they wore, galloped into the Young farmyard one morning and forced Martha Ellen's mother to bake biscuits till her hands blistered. They butchered four hundred hogs meanwhile, then just for the fun of it shot up the chickens and set fire to the hay barn. Martha Ellen, who was only nine then, ever after took her politics seriously. So she taught her son: "Anyone who could live on the west line of Missouri in those days and not be a Democrat was a fool for lack of brains."

Even worse than the raid, though, was a Union general's reprisal for some like activity on the part of a band of hot Missouri Secessionists. He ordered all suspicious families in four counties to be rounded up where his bluecoats could keep an eye on them. Half a century later, when Martha saw Harry in his blue National Guard uniform, she shooed him out of the house.

But it did work out that the Youngs' exile had some advantages. Being prosperous, Solomon could manage to have his family spend the three bad years comfortably in what was to become the metropolis of Kansas City, instead of herded into a settlement akin to a concentration camp. Like her older brothers and sisters, Mat got some better schooling then than a one-teacher country school could provide. This prepared her, after the fighting ceased, to aim for the kind of higher education so many other eventual Presidential mothers also secured one way or another. Her father sent her to the Baptist Female College in Lexington, Missouri.

Nor did she have the dreary, chore-laden time at home that was the lot of so many farm daughters. She helped her mother supervise the feeding of up to twenty hired hands, but there were Negro servants for routine kitchen and pantry drudgery. So Mat could take her pick of her father's horses and ride off to pay visits, side-saddle to be sure; in her later years, she would sniff that girls wearing pants looked like the Jack of Clubs. But she had nothing against dancing, no matter that some among the Baptists took a stricter view. "I was what you might call a light-foot Baptist," she liked to say, by which she meant that as often as three times a week she had kicked up her heels to the scratch of fiddle music in some neighboring barn.

Why she waited till she was twenty-nine to marry was nobody's business but her own. Trim and tiny-waisted, she looked girlish enough even then to avoid the spinster label among menfolk at least, and her face had the attraction of a pair of blue gray eyes so full of whatever was on her mind that they kept their sparkle nigh onto a century. Conceivably, she just felt no particular interest in giving up the chance to read a whole morning away if she so chose, or to practice for her own amazement and amusement on a fine piano. After all of her other sisters chose husbands, Mat and her mother got on so companionably that she might have stayed home for good.

But a persistent little fighting cock of a suitor would not let her. John Anderson Truman was a year older than Mat, and two inches shorter; throughout his life, he had to answer to the nick-name of Peanuts. Actually he and Mat had known each other since early childhood because his parents had come out of the same Shelby county in Kentucky that had bred her parents, and the Trumans had also settled in the same part of Missouri. Not nearly as well off as the Youngs, they were nevertheless respectable farm neighbors. Solomon Young had given a piece of his land for the Blue Ridge Baptist Church, which John Truman's father served as a deacon, and it was probably in their Sunday best outside its portals that the future parents of the thirty-third President became acquainted.

John was helping his widowed father run the Truman farm when he convinced Mat to marry him, but it seems she did not care to assume the burdens of farmwifery, nor did John expect her to do so. In after years, their daughter Mary Jane provided one pithy explanation. "I never did milk cows," she said. "Papa told me if I didn't learn how I'd never have to do it." Furthermore, John had more ambitious plans for himself as well as his family. Doubtless inspired by his father-in-law's success, he aimed to make his own mark as a livestock trader.

So right after he stood up with Mat before the preacher in the Youngs' parlor on December 28, 1881—he sat down, though, for the wedding picture, as he always would when they posed together, to keep the disparity in their height from showing—he borrowed the Youngs' carriage to take his bride and his own elderly father down to the little town of Lamar, which he had chosen for his base of operations.

Had he stayed in the Kansas City area instead of going a hundred miles south of it, the Truman story might have been somewhat different. For that river port was starting to explode into a city in fact as well as name, and the cattle industry would be one of its biggest. But John Truman decided to deal in mules instead of steer, and he selected a sleepy Southern sort of village instead of a metropolis as his headquarters. Although he had much of the natural equipment required to be a big-time speculator, he lacked one basic ingredient; call it luck or call it horse sense, he never would be in the right place at the right time to make a real killing.

His choice of Lamar had only one lasting result. Two years after settling in a tiny cottage there with a bedroom just six and a half feet wide, Mat gave birth to a stillborn baby, which reduced her spirits to the lowest ebb of her long life. But soon she was pregnant again, and on May 8, 1884, she produced a healthy, satisfactorily noisy son.

She wanted to name the boy for her favorite brother, who came visiting often because he was a bachelor. From the depths of his own experience, he warned: "Don't call him Harrison—they'll call him Harry anyway." So Harry it was, with a judicious S for a middle initial; if one grandfather wanted to conclude Solomon was intended, and the other that Shippe, a Truman family name, was really the source of the S, nobody could challenge either claim.

Such a sensible solution must have been Mat's idea, for her husband would never stand away from a possible scrap. He took his politics seriously, too, and toward election time he would come

home bruised but unbowed if he ever heard any Republican talk;
despite his size, he would try to pummel any black-hearted Republican he happened to encounter. This pugnacity was modified but
by no means missing in his first son's character—and nothing set
the sparks to flying right through Harry Truman's eyeglasses faster
than a remark intimating that his father had been a failure.

Yet John Truman was down a lot more often than most men
are, and the mere record of how many times he moved his family
from place to place for a fresh start suggests an even less charitable
view of his career. Two years after Harry's arrival, when Mat had
her second baby—a boy they named Vivian—they had already
moved to another county, but once again the mule trade proved
slow. By the time the third and last of her children—Mary Jane—
was born a few years later, the Trumans were back on the Solomon
Young farm; Grandpa Truman was still with them. What Martha
thought about all of this is a mystery because on personal matters
the Trumans have preserved a reticence rare in Presidential families. Later she would be outspoken enough to keep a small army
of reporters constantly reaching for their pencils, but concerning
these earlier days only the bare facts can be pieced together.

It seems that her own father by this time was too old to be as
active as necessary for the running of a large place like his, and
ostensibly John Truman brought his family back to the farm so
he could take charge himself. He certainly did a brisk job of
planting and plowing—he never was afraid of hard work, nor, by
then, was Mat either. Although her mother still kept kitchen help,
three active youngsters guaranteed enough commotion to prevent
much leisurely reading of Tennyson.

It was Harry who engaged the largest share of Martha Truman's
attention. Right from the start, he and she had a special closeness
that made everybody accept him as Mama's boy in the same way
Vivian was Papa's. Not even Mary Jane minded this arrangement
because Harry was more than just a good brother to her; helping
his Mama out, he spent hours rocking her cradle, and when the
time came he braided her hair every bit as neatly as their mother
did.

Around then, a circumstance that bound Harry irrevocably to
his female parent attracted notice. She had taught him his letters

early, and by the age of five he could read aloud from the large print of the big family Bible. But when it came to the smaller type in newspapers, he seemed lost. One Fourth of July, Mat watched him as a glorious array of fireworks went off, and then she understood. Although the sound of each popping rocket made him jump, the sight of the star clusters up in the sky interested him not at all; she realized then that he could not even see them.

Hitching up a buggy, she took him into Kansas City the next day where an eye doctor confirmed her fear. The boy's eyeballs were so unnaturally flat that without thick corrective lenses he would never be able to see much of anything. So at eight, Harry started wearing an awesome pair of spectacles for a small boy—a child with any kind of glasses was a curiosity in those days, but his made him look like a little old man. Till then, his hazy view of the universe had doubtless contributed to keeping him close to his mother; after he got his glasses, which he had to wear every waking minute—"I was blind as a mole without them," he admitted later—there was no possibility of his playing ball, for instance. Breaking such a lot of glass would be no light matter.

So he became a bookworm. About this time, John Truman's old father died, leaving his son a few thousand dollars, and John used it to set himself up in business again. For his third try, he chose the lively town of Independence, not above twenty miles from either Kansas City or the Solomon Young farm near the village of Grandview. Independence made a fine setting for the school years of a bookish boy fascinated by history.

Like Abilene, where the Eisenhowers would be settling down just a year later, Independence in 1890 had a past to be proud of. Both the Oregon Trail and the Santa Fe Trail had started there; the Mormons had tried to establish their new Jerusalem there; and between robberies, the Jesse James gang had holed up there. It made quite a lot for a boy to mull over, but his mother set his mind on a track she preferred by buying him four big red books that he would cherish all the rest of his life—a set of inspirational biographies entitled *Great Men and Famous Women*. These and the resources of the Independence Public Library occupied him on the kitchen floor while other boys his age were out fishing.

Furthermore, not long after they took up town living, Harry

and Vivian both came down with severe diphtheria. Although Vivian recovered with no bad effects, and was soon out helping his father keep five hundred goats fenced in, Harry got better—only to get worse again. Paralysis afflicted his arms and legs to the extent that at the age of nine he had to be wheeled around town in a baby buggy. Years later, when Vivian was asked whether his mother had not dreaded Harry's being permanently disabled, he grinned and said: "She didn't scare easy." But even when Harry recovered the use of his muscles, he remained notably accident prone for many months. Once when he was combing his hair, he fell out of a chair and broke his collarbone. Another time he slammed the cellar door on his big toe, slicing off a piece of it; but somehow the family doctor, who had become used to frantic calls from Martha Truman, got the pieces pressed together again. She had no time to send for the doctor when Harry choked on a peach pit. By forcing it down his throat with her own fingers, she saved his life.

If Harry baffled his father, they still had some common ground. John joked a lot, which Harry and his mother both enjoyed, even such stunts as knocking people's hats off when they were not looking. However, the real bond between this perpetual adolescent of a father and his little old man of a son was politics; that fascinated them both. When Grover Cleveland, after four years out of office, got back into the White House—thereby forever confusing the issue of exactly how many Presidents the United States has had—John Truman was so excited that he scurried up onto the roof to raise a flag from the weather vane. Harry trudged by his side in the ensuing torchlight parade.

Some who knew Harry Truman well many years later thought he admired his belligerent father so much because he himself had never had a single fist fight as a boy. Be that as it may, he did not turn out unmanly after all, which is supposed to be the fate of a noncombatant Mama's boy. Perhaps the total picture presented by John Truman—a scrapper of few notable achievements—gave Harry the balance to make good masculine use of his mother's better sense. But first he had to discover the hard way that he was not cut out to be a concert pianist.

Whether Martha Truman really wanted her boy to make a

career of music has never been recorded, but she certainly acted as if she did. She tried to drive all three of her children to the keyboard, failing completely with Vivian—"Mama couldn't get a lasso big enough," he said complacently. But between the ages of ten and fifteen, Harry was caught; he got up every morning at five to practice two hours before breakfast and school. From local lessons, he progressed to becoming the pupil of a good teacher in Kansas City who brought him up to Bach fugues. Although he had much more of a gift than most Republicans would ever allow, he still lacked the virtuoso touch. Deciding this himself at fifteen, he suddenly quit lessons; but he never held those hours of practice against his mother, or music. In after years, he and his sister Mary happily sat down to play duets every time they got together.

Even if Harry had not chucked music right then, he probably would have soon afterwards because serious financial trouble struck the family. For awhile, John Truman had been riding higher than ever before—he made about thirty thousand dollars by speculating in grain, which was not a small sum then. But when he went ahead and guessed wrong on several occasions, he not only lost it all; he also lost their house in Independence, plus the one-hundred-and-sixty-acre farm Martha had inherited on the death of old Solomon Young. What saddened her most, though, was the plain truth that now Harry could not possibly go to college.

Like Dwight Eisenhower, Harry Truman got the idea of trying for a free education at West Point—but the chances are that he might not have been able to accept an appointment, no matter if his eyes had not disqualified him. For moving into a little house in Kansas City had not arrested his father's fall; at fifty-one, John was reduced to working as a night watchman at a factory. Harry, and within a short time Vivian, too, had to help out as best they could by finding jobs as bank clerks.

The way the family liked to remember this era, Uncle Harrison Young came by one day and asked his sister if the Trumans would not return to the home place for the sake of Grandma Young, who was getting well on in years and needed them. No matter who needed whom more, the move back to the farm helped everybody. "It was on the farm that Harry got his common sense," his mother pronounced. "He didn't get it in town."

Thereafter, almost to the end of her days, Martha Truman stayed on the Grandview farm. But although the grove of maples old Solomon had planted back in 1867 between the house and the road continued to cast the same welcome shade, virtually everything else changed while she and the trees stayed put.

First, Grandma Young quietly died in her sleep at the age of ninety-one. Never having turned childish or fretful, she had remained a good companion to her daughter, and all of the Trumans missed her. But even more than the loss of her presence, her passing meant trouble aplenty for them. All of the seven surviving Young children had received one hundred and sixty acres apiece from Solomon's will, and his widow got the six-hundred-acre home place for herself. She, in turn, reasoning that the others had all scattered, chose to cut them off with five dollars apiece—meanwhile giving Harrison and Martha Ellen equal shares in a farm worth about $150,000. As happens in the best of families, a long, tedious, and embittering series of lawsuits ensued. By a complex arrangement of quitclaims, the dispute finally was settled to nobody's particular satisfaction, the process having taken the better part of a decade. Martha ended up owning the farm and an unhealthy sum in mortgages, which had been taken out to raise cash in order to pay off other claimants.

Meanwhile, Harry managed the farm pretty well by himself. Eyeglasses and all, he did such a conscientious job of it that his father took to devoting most of his time to local politics; and Vivian, who was much more a natural farmer, settled down to running his own place nearby. John Truman's death and then the First World War ended this period.

In his sixty-third year, John had a small political niche; for past services to the Democratic faction then in power, he had been appointed one of the thirty-six road overseers in Jackson County. Characteristically, he took the post seriously enough to grapple with a boulder he discovered blocking a local road one summer day in 1914. The internal injuries that resulted required surgery, but although he seemed to be getting better he died a few weeks later of complications brought on by the incident. Then Harry became in fact the man of the family. But less than three years later, the National Guard unit he had trained with went to war, and although he could have avoided active duty, he did not. "It was quite a blow to my mother and sister," he conceded later.

Mary, who was twenty-eight and as good a companion to her mother as Martha herself had been to Grandma Young, supervised the field hands for the rest of the war. Except for this latter detail, the basic pattern for the next quarter of a century became established during Harry's absence overseas. For no sooner was he mustered out—as a major who could be tough and make his men like it—than he announced that he planned to marry and make his home with his wife's family in Independence.

Martha Truman could not have been surprised. Perhaps she had not realized how strongly her young Harry had been struck by the yellow curls of a girl in his Sunday School class back in the family's Independence period. But Harry and Bess Wallace had studied Latin together during high school, he had taken countless buggy rides and train rides over to Independence to see her since the Trumans had moved away. There had been talk, of course, that Bess would never say Yes to Harry because she had been brought up to have plenty, and he was a good cut below her; yet this kind of talk could not impress Harry's mother. She had been brought up to have plenty, too. The only question she could see the sense of was, Why had Harry and Bess delayed so long, till they were both pushing thirty-five? It could have been from the depths of her own experience resisting John Truman's suit that Martha once dredged up the answer that maybe Bess would not have him till then.

Even if the marriage meant renting out most of the acreage because Mary could not run such a big place indefinitely, Martha had no real objection. Right after the wedding ceremony, one of her son's soldier friends said: "Well now, Mrs. Truman, you've lost Harry." Instantly, her eyes flashed. "Indeed I haven't," she said.

Nor had she. Virtually every Sunday, year after year, Harry drove over from Independence to spend the afternoon. No matter how harassed he was when his haberdashery store failed, no matter how busy he was when he began running for county office, Sunday after Sunday Mama made fried chicken for Harry and Bess and, in time, their bright little Mary Margaret, too. Mama also sat with Harry on platforms, and nudged him to let him know which of the other speakers were really for him, which were fakers. That trace of spice in her personality kept them all interested. Once when Harry's being an office holder made it politic not to press for payment after a road was cut through her land, she grumbled to a reporter: "I'd have gotten eleven thousand dollars if my boy wasn't a county judge."

After Harry won a seat in the Senate and went to Washington, the visits could not be as regular but she kept tabs on him anyway. She had him send her the *Congressional Record*, which she read daily till she was far up in her eighties; and then it was failing eyesight rather than any lack of interest that changed the routine. Thenceforth, her daughter Mary read the salient sections aloud to her while she sat with a lavender shawl over her shoulders, drumming with her fingers on the arm of her rocking chair every time a Republican provoked her.

When Harry ran for reelection to the Senate in 1940—without the support of the Prendergast machine this time—internal warfare within Missouri's Democratic Party caused her even more upset. Some who were less than friendly to Harry's cause took advantage of her delay in making various payments, and foreclosed on her farm. At the age of eighty-eight, she and her belongings were all but dumped on the street in a maneuver clearly designed to embarrass her son. It was true that thirty-five thousand dollars were owed, but the farm was worth much more than that sum; and Harry always would be positive the foreclosure could have been staved off, had he received any warning in advance.

As it was, his mother and Mary moved into a little yellow bungalow in Grandview, where reporters sought them out when rumors arose that F.D.R. wanted Harry Truman for his next Vice President. Harry ought to stay put where he was as head of the Senate's war investigating committee, she said tartly. "He can do more good there." But, of course, he was not destined to remain long in the obscurity of the Vice Presidency. Only a few months later, the reporters were back to find out what Mother Truman thought of her son's sudden elevation to the nation's highest office.

"I can't really be glad he's President because I'm sorry that President Roosevelt is dead," she said. "If he'd have been voted in,

I'd be out waving a flag, but it doesn't seem right to be very happy or wave any flags now."

Amid all his new cares, Harry Truman still phoned Grandview once or twice a week, besides writing to Mama and Mary at least that often. Within his first few days in the White House, he wrote to tell her: "Well, *The Washington Post* had your pictures yesterday morning and the finest kind of statements. . . . My Press Staff said that the smartest press agent in the world could not have written any better ones. I told them that my family all told the truth all the time and that they did not need a press agent. . . ."

That was certainly the last thing Mother Truman needed. No, she would not have any tall, strong fence around her yard, she insisted to the Secret Service—"It isn't neighborly." As for offering advice to Harry, she modified her favorite precept to fit the new occasion. "Just belong to the key of B-natural," was what she used to tell her children. Now she suggested: "Be good and be game, too." Then when Harry could not come to see her as usual on Mother's Day, she blithely took the first airplane trip of her ninety-two years.

She enjoyed the flight and even all the fuss and feathers in Washington. She and Mary returned to Missouri by train, though— "I'd rather stay on the ground. I can see more." Then back in her comfortable rocker, she kept right in touch with all that was going on via the radio and her own private source of news. Thirty minutes after Harry Truman announced the surrender of Japan from the White House, he was on the phone speaking to his mother, and as soon as she hung up, she told the reporters who were standing by: "I'm glad Harry decided to end the war." Partial though she was, she had a point. The fateful decision to use the atom bomb was her boy's, and no matter that many thought he was wrong, nobody ever could accuse him of ducking responsibility, not Mother Truman's boy.

On her ninety-third birthday, she proclaimed her intention to live till one hundred, which glad tidings the Associated Press dispatched throughout the land. But in February of 1947, when she was only ninety-four, she slipped and fell in her bedroom, fracturing a hip. The accident itself was not nearly as serious as the complications to be feared in a patient of her age, so the President brought his White House physician to Grandview when he flew in the next day. Although the medical communiqués were hopeful at first, encouraging the President to fly back to Washington, some weeks later the dangerous complication of pneumonia did set in.

Then the state of Mother Truman's health engaged the attention of the nation compellingly. Every day *The New York Times* described her progress in detail, often on its front page; when she felt well enough to ask for pork chops for dinner, that fact was solemnly noted. Only afterward did members of the White House staff disclose that the patient had also had the stamina to demand: Was the Senator Taft she disliked so much really going to get the Republican nomination to run against Harry?

For twelve days, President Truman stayed in Missouri, conducting official business in between visits to his mother's bedside; a temporary White House was established at a nearby Kansas City hotel. "She sat up with me many times when I needed her," he soberly told reporters. But he returned to Washington at the end of May when it appeared that she had passed the crisis and could spare him. Nearly two months later, Mary telephoned him to say he had better return, and he was in the air over Ohio when his plane's radio picked up a message letting the President know he would be too late. Toward noon on July 26, 1947, Martha Young Truman died at the age of ninety-four.

In the White House, Harry Truman had a portrait of his mother painted from life a year or two before her last illness. "She's wonderful!" he often told visitors. "They don't make them like that any more." Never at a loss for words, the subject of the portrait could have quoted her favorite verse from Scripture if she ever heard her son say this. It was Matthew 7:1—"Judge not, that ye be not judged . . ."

QUEEN MARY ON THE HUDSON

Sara Delano Roosevelt

ONCE UPON A TIME in a lovely park overlooking a wide river there lived a little girl who had a great many brothers and sisters. These children never quarreled with each other. If the slightest sign of any altercation ever did arise, their father stopped it instantly by speaking just three words. "Tut, tut, now!" he would say, and the unseemly behavior ceased—or at least that was the way Sara Delano Roosevelt liked to remember her childhood.

The castle in which she spent most of this happy period was called Algonac. Here she was taught to walk well and to modulate her voice, along with various more commonplace lessons conveyed by a series of governesses; when the morning room became a schoolroom, only straight-backed chairs were used to make certain that no Delano child slumped. Had Mr. Warren Delano foreseen the future in store for his daughter Sallie, he could scarcely have provided better training. He gave her an ideal preparation for becoming the first dowager queen of the United States.

While the title may have lacked official sanction, it was indisputably hers for almost a decade—and a good thing, too. Without her splendid adherence to the code of her past, the portion of the population agitated by her son's New Deal would have suffered much more than it did during the 1930's; and even that man's friends found reassurance in the stately Mrs. Roosevelt senior. When F.D.R. overplayed the role of Dutch patroon, holding forth on the theme that his family's Hudson River estate had originally been known as Krum Elbow, only his mother could put him down a peg. The estate at Hyde Park did have a name, she told reporters, which was and always had been Springwood. "Franklin doesn't know everything," she added.

Her own roots had sprung from similar ground, Algonac having been located across the Hudson on its west bank and about twenty miles south of Hyde Park. But before her time, the Delanos had belonged in Massachusetts, although her ancestry did have a Dutch tinge by virtue of one Philippe de la Noye, who had been born to an exiled French Huguenot family temporarily settled in Holland; he landed at Plymouth in 1621. Then his progeny married so prudently that the mother of the thirty-first President could also claim some degree of kinship with seven passengers on the *Mayflower*.

The sea had a powerful attraction for this family. Sara's grandfather had captained his own ships plying the China trade, and her father had profited handsomely from the same commerce. By the age of thirty-three, he had accumulated sufficient capital in Hong Kong to begin investing in New York City waterfront property. He also married the daughter of a Massachusetts judge, then took a house close to Wall Street—on Lafayette Place, opposite the son of John Jacob Astor. But soon after his sweet, submissive young wife started presenting him with a steady increment of offspring, he determined on moving them to a safe distance from the vulgarity of the city. That he had an eye for beauty was proved by his selection of a site jaded travelers described as the equal of anything in Europe; it was sixty acres of woods and orchards sloping down to a bend in the majestic Hudson, affording magnificent vistas of blue water and green hills. A brick and stucco mansion already sat surveying the scene, yet it was wanting in elegance —so extensive remodeling was ordered for both building and gardens, based on plans by the same landscape designer who laid

Sara Delano Roosevelt

out the grounds for the Capitol and the White House in Washington. At the newly aristocratic Algonac, on September 21, 1854,
Sara Delano was born.

They called her Sallie to distinguish her from the aunt after
whom she had been named; there was no taint of frivolity intended.
For this Sallie obediently wore her flannel petticoats till late in the
spring when Mama decreed the weather warm enough to leave
them off, and she never demurred when asked to help arrange the
flowers for the drawing room vases Papa had brought home from
China. Still it must not be supposed that her days were filled only
by duties. Time was also regularly allotted to such healthful activity as pony riding, and there were jolly sledding parties in season;
for rainy days, a two-room playhouse beyond the formal aura of
the main house had been thoughtfully provided. Here troops of
cousins and friends often joined the Delano brood, which reached
an eventual total of eleven, including the two who died in early
childhood.

Sallie grew up exactly in the middle, with three sisters and one
brother older than she and the same grouping her junior. Being
so surrounded may have encouraged her to seek distinction by
good works; the whole family marveled when she managed to
complete every stitch of a shirt for one of President Lincoln's
soldiers all by herself, and it was sent off labeled: "Made by a little
girl seven years old." But if the Civil War could not quite be kept
from her ken, she was carefully protected against most kinds of
unpleasantness nearer at hand. In a family diary—the Delanos
being tireless diarists—Sallie's father related one such episode:

> . . . Catherine Morrissey, engaged as cook at $14 a month, arrived.
> [A few months elapse]
> . . . James McGinn absconded from the stables early this morn-
> ing . . . [Three more weeks elapse]
> . . . Catherine Morrissey went to New York by barge to attend to a
> matter of some importance in which she is to have the assistance of
> Rev. Father Cloury of St. Gabriel's Church, 308 E. 37th Street.

Apparently, the priest was unable to convince the coachman to
marry the cook, after all, for in an entry closing the subject a few
days later, Mr. Delano righteously wrote:

. . . Our slut of a cook, Catherine Morrissey, left our services and returned to New York, having lived with us six months and having been treated with every possible kindness, even in trouble, for which she returned impudence, waste, dirt and discontent.

Although Sallie could mercifully be spared knowing the cause of poor Kate's downfall, there were some trials from which even her father could not shield her. Visiting her grandparents near New Bedford, she developed whooping cough; then another visitor in the house, Dr. Oliver Wendell Holmes, had to be called on to relieve her. But Sallie was a tall, strong girl who survived childhood ailments hardily, and in time she would boast that she had not known a sick day in seventy years. Her placid course was more seriously changed by crass money woes—although, of course, she and the other children received no hint about why the family suddenly moved all the way to China.

In truth, Warren Delano's fortune evaporated in the aftermath of the Panic of 1857, and even though he seemed for some years to have staved off disaster at last he had to admit—to adults—that he was ruined. He put Algonac on the market, but instead of tamely retreating into genteel poverty he went back to Hong Kong when he was fifty, set on making himself a second fortune; soon he sent for his family to join him. Sallie was eight then, and she adored the trip.

She did because she was more than just a stiffly proper little girl —or old lady, either, when that period arrived. The fashioning of an acceptable self-image is no new pastime, and she had few peers in this department; it suited her to keep up a perfectly starched appearance. But beneath the outer layers of unnatural sobriety there certainly did beat a joyous heart which delighted in adventure. This zest and the sense of humor she allowed only those closest to her to suspect were two of the major gifts she gave her son; the third, of course, was willpower. That his chin had the same jut to it as hers could hardly escape notice, but not many of F.D.R.'s admirers knew his jaunty air came from her, too. They never heard her rendition, when she was over eighty, of the sea chanty she had learned aboard the clipper *Surprise* three quarters of a century earlier: ". . . Blow, my bully boys, blow!"

In Hong Kong during that distant era when the white man's burden could be carried off lightly, Sallie's father rescued Algonac, after all, and although he could no longer dream of rivaling Commodore Vanderbilt, he would leave his daughter about one million dollars—compared with the approximately three hundred thousand dollars comprising the assets of the gentleman she married. But this event was still far in the future when Sallie returned to America, by way of Europe where two years were devoted to various educational excursions.

Back at Algonac, life resumed its former pattern with fewer changes than may seem believable a century later. As the children grew older and began making suitable marriages, amateur theatricals replaced sleigh rides, but the more things changed, the more they stayed the same. Of course, at Algonac the phrase would have been spoken *en français,* for annual expeditions abroad had become *comme il faut;* and so was lacing one's conversation with appropriate Gallicisms. Following all of the rules, Sallie grew into a haughty young lady.

The Delano sisters as a group were often spoken of as beauties, yet in her case the right word would seem to be handsome. Just as she excelled the others in moral purpose, she stood above them in actual stature; she was a full five feet and ten inches tall, and she carried the height imposingly. With her brown hair coiled into a dignified chignon, she looked rather regal already. Yet she was no mere daguerreotype, for she had a good mind and she read incessantly. She also took pleasure from musical performances of any merit. But despite her possessing so many of the social graces, she had some difficulty in finding a husband she and her father both could approve.

Of female friends who were similarly situated she had a good number because in her comfortable circle there was no harsh necessity forcing girls to marry early. There were disadvantages to spinsterhood, but there were advantages, too—Miss Sara Delano's education would not have failed to make this point clear. Among her warmest friends was an effusively capable contemporary down in New York City keeping house for a widowed mother and devoting vast effort to furthering the career of her own younger brother. His name was Theodore Roosevelt, and he had just begun attracting incredulous comment from the ranks of Republican politicians. Fortunately, his sister was not so absorbed in advancing the interests of this future President that she forgot to invite Sallie Delano for a visit during the spring of 1880.

Approaching her twenty-sixth birthday, Sallie was wasting no energy repining on her single state. Whenever she wished to vary the rural charm of Algonac, she went abroad with a married sister, or spent a few weeks enjoying New York City's music and theatre. She accepted the invitation of Theodore Roosevelt's sister with no special sense of anticipation. But it happened that during her stay a distant cousin of these Roosevelts came to dinner—a whiskered widower twice Sallie's age. He and she suited each other superbly.

He was James Roosevelt, a man rather remarkably like her own father. Indeed these two had sat together on various boards, both financial and philanthropic, although their acquaintance had never ripened into intimacy. No doubt Warren Delano was mildly baffled when Sallie told him soon after returning from the city that she had been bidden, along with Theodore Roosevelt's mother and sister, to stay for a week at Hyde Park. One may guess, though, that Sallie already suspected what she put into words more than fifty years later in a letter to her son: ". . . If I had not come then, I should now be 'old Miss Delano,' after a rather sad life!"

Her suspicion concerning James Roosevelt's intentions was amply confirmed one morning toward the end of the sedate visit—Mr. Roosevelt asked Miss Delano if she would care to arrange the flowers for the luncheon table. In that decorous society, he could hardly have spoken more plainly. Now they both knew the next step was for him to pay several polite calls at Algonac, which he did in the ensuing weeks. Then it became possible to mention the subject of marriage. When this occurred, Sallie's father was dumbfounded—he had thought that Mr. Roosevelt was coming so often for the pleasure of his own company.

Yet Mr. Delano had only limited grounds on which to object to the match. Mr. Roosevelt could trace his lineage back to the New Netherlands of the 1640's, via a direct line of reputable merchants who were also devout and patriotic citizens. His own character was unblemished, except for a political flaw—he chose to vote Democratic—but even this aberration could be overlooked. "James Roosevelt is the first person who made me realize that a Democrat can be a gentleman," Mr. Delano is supposed to have remarked. The one serious impediment that could not be blinked away was the age of Sallie's suitor. Before she was born, he had already become a bridegroom, and his first wife had given him one son as old as she; such a disparity was entirely unsuitable, Mr. Delano fumed. Displaying the full strength of her will for the first time, his daughter changed his mind. At Algonac, on October 7, 1880, Miss Sara Delano married James Roosevelt; she was twenty-six then, and he was fifty-two.

Their marriage proved wonderfully happy. It had already become second nature to her to cater to her father, and now she simply transferred her allegiance to her husband. Indeed her unquestioning acceptance of the principle that the young owed the old whole-hearted fealty would cause constant friction when she herself became old; but one can scarcely blame for her expecting what she had given so willingly during her own younger days. Not that her James was quite such an antiquity as to require constant care. He had more than a few good years remaining to him.

He struck most people as a decent and generous sort, with a large fund of entertaining anecdote at his disposal; and when he told a joke, he would throw back his head and laugh so heartily that his whiskers shook. His main occupation ostensibly was attending to his railway and other business interests, but he spent as much time as he possibly could riding out to inspect his farm. In keeping with this adherence to the British style of country squiredom, he also sat patiently on local school and hospital committees. Said a caustic relative: "He tried to pattern himself on Lord Lansdowne, sideburns and all, but what he really looked like was Lansdowne's coachman." His Sallie would not have been amused.

For she idolized him more with each passing year, but, of course, he was not her only interest. From the date of her marriage, she had begun keeping a diary just as her parents did, and after two years of entries relating the highlights of her European honeymoon, then the placid routine at Hyde Park, there was a gap of several weeks. The next entry, in James Roosevelt's handwriting, was dated January 30, 1882: "At quarter to nine my Sallie had a splendid large baby boy. He weighs 10 lbs., without clothes."

Sallie planned to call the boy Warren Delano Roosevelt, but one of her brothers objected. A child of his bearing this name had only recently died and he thought another such christening so soon would cause his wife unbearably painful emotion. Bowing to her brother's wishes, Sallie substituted the name of an uncle, thus saving the world from having to cope with an awkward trio of initials. But she did not even remotely visualize the future in store for this infant—and she would exert enormous effort to prevent her son from going beyond the path taken by his father. In fact, her supreme contribution was serendipitous. By trying to order her son's life in minute detail over six decades, Sara Delano Roosevelt inadvertently gave him matchless practice in overcoming obstacles.

Toward her husband, she continued to behave as subordinately as she thought she should, but Franklin gave her the scope her strong will needed. He was to be her only child, and she focused her extraordinary drive for perfection directly on him. What saved them both, however, was the sense of humor they shared; quite early in the game, Franklin discovered that he could circumvent her more easily by lighthearted teasing than by any other tactic. Before he was five, he had the effrontery to address her in a letter as "Dear Sallie"—and she saved this, along with every other scrap of paper pertaining to his early years.

Yet the quantity of her treasure was limited, owing to the circumstance that she and her son hardly ever left each other's company for more than a few hours at a time until he was fourteen. Although she spent substantial portions of almost every year traveling with James—most particularly to European health spas as James's strength began ebbing—usually Franklin came along, too. He had been put down for the select new school of Groton shortly after his birth, but his mother found it too difficult to part with him when he reached the customary entrance age of twelve and she kept him at her side for two more years.

After being so much with adults and so little with boys of his own age, excepting the sons of a Standard Oil captain who lived just down the road at Hyde Park, Franklin faced quite a number of problems when he finally arrived at Groton. While classwork posed no exceptional difficulties, for he had been tutored well at home, he had to learn overnight, as it were, how to win friends; having long since mastered the art of enthralling adults with his Little Lord Fauntleroy manners, he was accustomed to approval, but all the rest of his life he would never cease seeking still wider popularity. At Groton he also had to contend with an onslaught of childhood ailments which he had previously escaped, owing to his virtual isolation from other children. Naturally, his mother came hurrying to the school whenever he was sent to the infirmary— once she even circumvented his being quarantined for scarlet fever by procuring a ladder, on which she stood outside his window to inspect him daily.

Yet it was not till Franklin entered Harvard that her devotion to him became utterly single-minded. That happened after her beloved husband, who had been growing ever more frail, died of heart disease at the age of seventy-two. In his will, he had written: "I do hereby appoint my wife sole guardian of my son Franklin Delano Roosevelt, and I wish him to be under the influence of his mother." One wonders, though, whether even James expected his wife's influence to be as lasting and as pervasive as it proved to be.

The influence that James Roosevelt himself had had on this son is hard to estimate. The son of his first marriage—James Roosevelt Roosevelt was the strange compromise adopted to prevent his being called Junior, and so he was generally called Rosy—had turned out very much like his father. He was an accomplished horseman and clubman who had pulled off the notable coup of marrying *the* Mrs. Astor's daughter. But Franklin had enjoyed the advantages of riding and sailing and going ice boating with his father only for comparatively few years before James had to curtail such strenuous activities. The boy and his father remained good companions, and yet it was his mother who directed him at every step. Possibly James had merely recognized a long-standing state of affairs by the terminology he used in his will.

Certainly his widow would never, for as long as she herself lived, refrain from striving to influence Franklin. Because Hyde

Park during those first months seemed so terribly lonely, she even took a house up in Boston so that Franklin could spend his every weekend with her. She constructed a soothing future in her mind, wherein she and Franklin would live at Hyde Park, of course, although they would spend a few months every year down in New York City or traveling; if his active mind required further stimulation, surely a gentlemanly law practice would answer. But Sara very soon discovered that she had spawned a will as strong as her own.

Ironically, it had been she who suggested to Franklin that he include his fifth cousin in some of his plans. "His mother was sorry for me, I think," Eleanor Roosevelt wrote much later, with characteristic self-depreciation. Perhaps her mother-in-law truly had pitied the shy daughter of Cousin Theodore's younger brother —Elliott Roosevelt, who had charmed Sara into inviting him to become one of Franklin's godparents. But Sara surely had no plan, at the moment, for making the deceased Elliott the posthumous father-in-law of his own godson. Franklin himself thought up this idea at the beginning of his senior year at Harvard.

Eleanor Roosevelt described herself as an ugly duckling of a girl so feelingly when she wrote her memoirs that many people assume Franklin chose her out of some odd do-good instinct. But the rare grace she was to show the whole world already was apparent to the discerning eye even before she was twenty, and Franklin saw it; he fell authentically in love. He told his mother so during Thanksgiving recess of his final year at college, then shortly after returning to Cambridge he wrote to her:

THE HARVARD CRIMSON
Dec. 4, 1903

Dearest Mama—

I have been absolutely rushed to death since I came back . . .

Dearest Mama—I know what pain I must have caused you and you know I wouldn't do it if I really could have helped it—mais tu sais, me voilà! Thats all that could be said—I know my mind, have known it for a long time, and know that I could never think otherwise: Result: I am the happiest man just now in the world; likewise the luckiest—And for you, dear Mummy, you know that nothing can ever change what we have been & always will be to each other—

only now you have two children to love & to love you—and Eleanor
as you know will always be a daughter to you in every true way—
I shall be here over Sunday working all the time . . .

Your ever loving
F.D.R.

That summer, Sara tried a North Cape cruise, just she and her
son together; then when Franklin refused to be diverted, she held
out for a year's delay in announcing the engagement. Already an
inveterate compromiser, Franklin agreed. The marriage took place
on March 17, 1905—St. Patrick's Day—because Eleanor's closest
male relative was presently occupying the White House, and his
opportunities for coming up to New York were limited. On St.
Patrick's Day, her Uncle Theodore could conveniently review the
parade before giving his niece away. It was a fitting beginning to
one of the most exceptional marriages in all of history.

Much has been written of Sara Roosevelt's despotic rule over
her daughter-in-law, at least during the first two decades of
Eleanor's marriage to Franklin. It was not easy, of course, to be
showered with houses and servants and advice so freely—and to
have one's husband gratefully accept so much of this largess from
his mother. But Eleanor must have understood that Franklin drew
his own line, although doing so was never a simple matter.

When in 1910 he was becoming bored with gentlemanly law
practice, and was visited in Hyde Park by certain Democrats
dangling public office before his eye—an offer his own father had
sternly rebuffed on more than one occasion—Franklin told the
visiting delegation: "I'd like to talk with my mother about it
first." Said the Democratic spokesman for Dutchess County:
"Frank, there are men in Poughkeepsie waiting for your answer.
They won't like to hear you had to ask your mother." Franklin
then and there said he would run that fall for the New York State
Senate—and he won handily.

That, of course, was only the beginning. Sara told him time and
again that to see one's own name in the newspapers must pain any
gentleman, but Franklin publicly supported Woodrow Wilson so
effectively that he was rewarded by an appointment as Wilson's
Assistant Secretary of the Navy. So he and Eleanor and their grow-

ing family of rambunctious children moved to Washington. Sara wrote to them almost daily, frequently enclosing cheques.

Then came a reward Franklin would have preferred doing without—the nomination for the Vice Presidency in 1920. His mother had not mastered political etiquette to the extent of understanding that here was a case of *noblesse oblige* in the realm of politics, that even though the Democratic ticket stood hardly a chance it was necessary for Franklin to make the race anyway to keep in good standing with his party. But Sara displayed her own brand of obliging nobility. She allowed her lawn at Hyde Park to be trampled by five thousand strangers bent on congratulating her son on his nomination. Her experience with political entertaining was only just starting.

But first came the ordeal of Franklin's polio. Sara was spending the summer of 1921 in Europe, and she did not know anything untoward had occurred till one of her brothers met her at the pier in New York. He told her then that Franklin had fallen ill, but only when she arrived up at Campobello, the family's vacation retreat off the coast of Maine, did the full enormity of the blow strike her. Franklin had been attacked by still another childhood disease, and at the age of thirty-nine his legs were utterly useless.

Neither mother, nor son, nor daughter-in-law faltered. They all played the role fate had assigned them magnificently. In a letter to her brother down in New York, Sara wrote:

> I got here yesterday at 1:30, and at once . . . came up to a brave, smiling and beautiful son, who said: "Well, I'm glad you are back Mummy and I got up this party for you!" He had shaved himself and seems very bright and *keen*. Below his waist he cannot move at all. His legs (that I have always been proud of) have to be moved often as they ache when long in one position. He and Eleanor decided at once to be cheerful and the atmosphere of the house is all happiness so I have fallen in and follow their glorious example . . .

At this moment of crisis, Sara did indeed follow their lead, allowing herself only one small barb. Writing that the doctor had just arrived and he and Eleanor were with the patient, all of them laughing cheerfully behind the closed door, she could not forbear mentioning that Eleanor's laughter was the loudest. But after the first awful days, Sara inevitably tried to assume control again.

Her ambition all along for Franklin had been precise. She wanted him to follow the exact pattern set by his father, and to restrict his entirely commendable zeal for improving the lot of his fellow men to those of his fellows who happened to live in the Hyde Park area. Even as an invalid, he still could serve on the local hospital committee . . . and putter with his stamps . . . and collect ship models.

For he must accept invalidism as his lot, she insisted. Doubtless she truly felt that any other course would dangerously sap his strength, but her concern was surely not wholly selfless. She brushed aside any medical opinion that conflicted with her own views, she fought desperately to win her son's entire loyalty, she strode the rooms of the New York City house where Franklin was recuperating, countermanding orders exactly as she saw fit. It was a dreadful winter.

But if Eleanor had once wept when her mother-in-law bullied her, now she fought back—and Franklin did, too. Conceivably the effort involved in triumphing over Mama tested these two in such a way as to bring forth unsuspected reserves of resolution; the question of what it is that causes some individuals to live up to their potential can never be answered. But the record shows that in 1924 Franklin Delano Roosevelt appeared on the platform at the Democratic National Convention, wearing painful leg braces to make it possible for him to stand erect, and with a smile that lifted millions of hearts he nominated Al Smith for the Presidency. Four years later, he himself was running for the governorship of New York.

This was a very close race. Almost everybody had left Democratic headquarters in the early hours of the morning after the election, when it seemed that Franklin Roosevelt must be defeated by just the barest majority. But one stiff-backed old lady still sat by the radio alone. If her son was so set on politics, she had to help him in any way she could; that she willed him to win may or may not have been the reason he squeaked through after all.

"Hello, you old potato!" was one of the milder greetings customarily affected by Al Smith, the retiring governor. At the ceremony in Albany inaugurating his successor, he turned more sentimental when he saw Mrs. Sara Roosevelt. He well knew how his cigars irked her, as did his slum vocabulary, but now he reached across the gulf between them to congratulate her and tell her how his own mother had rejoiced on the occasion of his oath taking; and Mrs. Roosevelt did not rebuff him. She rose to this new challenge of letting a chink appear in her dignity, and the newspapers reported the next day that her eyes had been wet as she thanked him.

Probably she even enjoyed having Franklin run for President. She certainly demonstrated a grand aptitude for the sort of duty that devolved upon her during the campaigning, and actually cooperated, in her grandiloquent way, with the Associated Press. In her own handwriting, she prepared a statement on her son's victory. "I shall be glad," she said, "if every mother will pray God to help and preserve him."

Her instinctive grasp of what was called for, as well as her startling resemblance to Britain's venerable Queen Mary, made the senior Mrs. Roosevelt a public figure in her own right. She received an astonishing quantity of mail after her son entered the White House, much of it original poetry which she herself had inspired. She saved it all, including an ode by Rose Sverdlik of the Bronx starting:

> *To you we are grateful, for you are the one*
> *To give our country such a noble son . . .*

Mrs. Roosevelt's emotions on reading such effusions can only be imagined, but her feelings on various other occasions were no secret. When Huey Long unavoidably had to be invited to lunch at Hyde Park, she bore with his rantings until a quiet moment, then whispered—and she could whisper louder than anyone else in the world if she so chose—"Who is that dreadful person sitting next to my son?" More to her taste, she became the first American hostess ever to entertain the reigning King and Queen of England in a private home, although surely if left to her own devices she would have fed them something besides hot dogs, which Eleanor had arranged.

The tensions between these two Mrs. Roosevelts never did en-

tirely subside. Much of the difficulty, as might be expected, re-
volved around Sara's five grandchildren, whom she persisted in
spoiling outrageously. She even gave them cars for their birthdays
after their parents had forbidden them to drive following some
infraction of the traffic rules, yet she was not uncritical of them.
She spent many fruitless hours trying to teach them her own fine
distinctions in the use of language; while hands might become
"soiled," she would point out patiently, they could not be called
"dirty."

When she was past eighty-five, she still retained her full sense of
the fitness of things. On being taken out to a restaurant in the
Hyde Park area, she was pleased to note the sign on the door of
the establishment, to the effect that gentlemen in shorts or without
jackets would not be admitted. Her lips puckered in a satisfied
smile, and her companions understood that the evening would be
a success.

But, of course, at eighty-six she was no easier to get along with
than she ever had been. Eleanor Roosevelt told a friend then that
although Franklin would be very much affected by his mother's
death, they still could not stay in the same room half an hour
without an argument starting. There were many who could testify
to this talent of the President's mother, including an officious
young Democratic appointee who made the mistake of trying to
shield her from a newspaper interviewer. Sara Delano Roosevelt
rarely spoke anything except platitudes in public, but she preferred to do her own speaking. "Young man," she said chillingly,
"I talked to newspapermen before you were born."

But finally on September 7, 1941, the vicissitudes of old age
caught up with her. Suffering no particular ailment except a general enfeeblement, she died that morning at Hyde Park, three
weeks short of her eighty-seventh birthday. Four large boxes of
clippings have been preserved in the Roosevelt Library to record
her passing, yet no newspaper printed any epitaph that did her
justice. Perhaps only she could have provided the right touch, as
she did in the royal letter she wrote when her son was planning to
break with American tradition by running for a third term in the
White House. She wrote the note to that intensely political Irishman, James A. Farley, who had managed F.D.R.'s first two cam-

paigns, but was bridling at supporting him again; he thought his own turn had come. Mrs. Roosevelt wrote:

Dear Mr. Farley:

I think I wrote to you to thank you for your kind letter after my sister died.

Now I want to tell you that *I do hope* you will manage my son's campaign. I have such confidence in you!

Ever sincerely,
Sara Roosevelt

Jessie Woodrow Wilson

JOCASTA IN
VIRGINIA
Jessie Woodrow Wilson

Even a well-educated girl like Jessie Woodrow would not have studied much about Jocasta of ancient Thebes. Presbyterian female seminaries were hardly likely to dwell on incest, no matter that the mythology of pagan Greece and Rome lent a classical tone to most curricula during Jessie's schooldays. Obviously, the fearsome sin of Jocasta and her son Oedipus could not be considered a fit subject for feminine minds; there were sufficient other sins more suitable for young ladies to be warned against. It is one of the finer ironies of our new enlightenment that poor Jessie has come to be celebrated as the central figure in the great American version of the Oedipus tragedy.

No less an authority than Dr. Sigmund Freud himself has so proclaimed—belatedly and posthumously. As recently as 1966, the Jocastrian crown was placed on the brow of the frail Jessie, whose horror at the honor can only be imagined. The probabilities are that Freud's own part in literarily certifying the guilt of Woodrow Wilson's mother was subordinate to his collaborator on this occasion, but Freud's name still carries such weight that his possibly inadvertent sentencing has been taken seriously. But not everywhere. At Princeton, the repository for every shred of paper relating to Wilson's life and career, the reaction to the Freud exposé had a casual ring. Said one pipe-smoking gentleman to another: "Have you heard the tale from the Vienna woods?"

Not that Jessie Woodrow Wilson stands condemned for a literal duplication of Jocasta's crime. In the more sophisticated culture of our own day, intent has become the decisive factor—Jessie is alleged to have played the role of Jocasta, and that, in the new dogma, is enough. But is it really? A more charitable verdict can be arrived at by looking at the full record.

Jessie Woodrow was a slender, wispy-haired girl born in Carlisle, England, on December 20, 1830. Yet that fact in itself gives the wrong impression, for she was Scottish to the core—intelligent, intensely Presbyterian, dour on the outside but mild as milk within the bosom of her family. If she had any passionate convictions beyond the realm of religion, they had to do with education, and she accepted her father's dicta on both matters unquestioningly.

He was a scholarly pastor who could uphold the Bible in Hebrew, Greek, and Latin; he put such undivided attention on what he was saying that his spectacles were forever slipping down to the edge of his nose. Still he found the time to beget so many bairns that migration from the depressed homeland became imperative. He was said to have been the first Wodrow, as the name was then spelled, to leave Scotland in five hundred years.

Jessie, the fifth of his eight children, arrived during the family's temporary sojourn in England. It proved to be only temporary because Dr. Thomas Woodrow soon discovered that his University of Glasgow erudition commanded respect but not enough money; he was able to afford a cottage backing up on a castle, against the wall of which his boys played handball, yet he could not see his way to educating them as he wished. So he moved on to America.

Jessie was not quite five when they sailed from Liverpool in the autumn of 1835, but she would always remember their miserable voyage and hate the sea. Years later, both of her sons liked playing admiral, which she did her best to discourage. She maintained—

and her older brother supported her—that their packet ship met a storm of such ferocity after sighting the coast of Newfoundland as to blow it clear back to Ireland, and they did not dock at New York till more than two months had elapsed. Only a few weeks later, Jessie's mother succumbed to the rigorous adventure, leaving Dr. Woodrow with eight children on his hands. He solved his problem promptly by marrying one of his wife's sisters.

Jesise's father had thought to raise a congregation in Canada, but the harshness of the Ontario climate along with various other difficulties changed his mind. He went south then to Chillicothe, Ohio, where he and his second wife brought up his sons to emulate his own scholarly Presbyterianism, and his daughters to marry religiously. Jessie at nineteen had an ethereal quality that substituted quite effectively for mere earthly beauty, for she attracted a promising young theologian. He was also exceptionally handsome.

The first impression Joseph Ruggles Wilson presented was almost theatrical in its virile strength. He looked like the motion picture actor John Wayne would have looked, had he been cast some years ago as a pre-Civil War preacher; but Joseph at twenty-seven had a weakness Hollywood would not have tolerated. When Jessie first laid eyes on him, he was raking leaves in the yard of his family's house—wearing kid gloves to protect his hands.

She was a boarding student then, attending a female seminary of some repute in Steubenville, Ohio. He was taking respite from his teaching duties at the town's male academy, where he was testing the academic life—he thought he might like to combine teaching with preaching. To the critical eye, Joseph would always seem vain and vacillating, but Jessie could not see him in this light; to her, he appeared godlike, nor was she utterly bemused. He did have more than the normal human quota of talents.

Joseph was the youngest son of a brisk North of Ireland man who had made a mark in the New World by working up from printer to small-town newspaper proprietor, along the way putting enough energy into Democratic politicking to win several terms in Ohio's legislature. All of the Wilsons conceded that Joseph was the intellect of the family, though, after he graduated first in his class at a small Pennsylvania college—and his valedictory address must have been stirring; he was an impressive orator. When he acquired the additionally imposing credential of a divinity degree from Princeton, his future eminence seemed assured. He had no doubts on this score himself, and Jessie surely had none. She supplied exactly the uncritical adulation he craved. They were married by her father on June 7, 1849.

Then Jessie took up housekeeping in a manse of her own in a nearby Pennsylvania town. Her first child, a daughter she named Marion after her own mother, was born there in the autumn of 1851, shortly before Joseph came to a major decision—he accepted a post on the faculty of Hampden-Sydney College in Virginia. Although he was destined to keep moving every few years, no other step along his nomadic path would have the significance of this first one; it made him a Southerner.

As in religion, the zeal of such a convert is dauntless, but Jessie was developing a mind of her own. "After all," she wrote to her first son some years later, "there is a great deal about the Southern people that I don't like—only I like them decidedly better than I do the Northern." Here, alas, was the key to her character. She never could and never did get on well with people outside her immediate family; in the current parlance, she related badly.

But safely close to her own hearth, Jessie radiated devoted warmth, or at least one has every reason to suppose this was so from her letters. They are available to any interested reader because, after producing another daughter and moving again—to the pleasant town of Staunton, in Virginia's Shenandoah Valley—she gave birth on December 28, 1856, to a boy she named after his maternal grandfather.

Of course Thomas Woodrow Wilson adored his mother. He was a Mama's boy, *par excellence,* and he knew it. "I remember," he once wrote to his wife, "how I clung to her (a laughed-at 'mama's boy') till I was a great big fellow: but love of the best in womanhood came to me and entered my heart through those apron strings . . ." It is sad that the world is no longer willing to accept such professions without assuming the professor really wanted to slay his father and sleep with his mother.

But even if this is the awful truth, surely it is only part of the truth about little Tommy Wilson and his parents. Psychiatry itself teaches that above all else, love provides the security a child needs

—that a child who is cherished learns the most important lesson in life effortlessly. Within the various parsonages where the Wilsons lived, a bounteous portion of love was always available.

Each member of the household, down to Josie—Joseph Ruggles Wilson, Jr., who was born when Tommy was almost nine—seems to have shared in this private feast. "My precious son," both parents wrote to or about both boys. "My darling brother," the girls wrote. The effusiveness of hundreds of letters, written over a period of several decades, does not support any claim that Tommy and his father exchanged embarrassingly loverlike missives; the whole family joined in the strange exercise, which may strike modern sensitivities as unnatural and yet was not so rare in that more repressed era.

Although standards of deportment in public were so much stricter, people appear to have been less self-conscious about expressing their feelings to their close relatives. Certainly the Wilsons of most interest to the world at large had reason to need reassurance from each other: Jessie lacked the grace to make any real contact with the ladies who came calling on the pastor's wife; Joseph rose neither as fast nor as far as he had hoped, and perhaps deserved, so he fell victim to frequent blue moods; and Tommy was a delicate, uncertain sort of boy.

He did not even learn to read till he was nine—possibly by no coincidence, his difficulty involving seeing words backwards cured itself shortly after his mother had a new baby and could no longer read aloud to him so patiently. But Tommy still was not deemed sturdy enough to go to school for another few years. During this time, he seems to have applied himself to surprisingly intricate solitary games like constructing toy armadas which he could boldly captain; he took it for granted that his parents were absolutely right when they told him he had the ability to be a great man.

And despite any amount of delving into his psyche to investigate how he disposed of the hostile feelings he had to hide, it happens that Jessie and her husband were quite right about this son. He did have extraordinary ability. While watching Jessie fret over him and cater to him until he finally married, that fact must not be forgotten. The number of other earnest mothers and fathers who similarly urged on a son—in vain—must also be remembered. Tommy Wilson had at least a touch of genius, although hardly anyone outside his family would have believed it during the years he was growing up.

Strangely enough, the Civil War does not seem to have impinged in any important way on his consciousness. The family was living then in Augusta, Georgia, a major Confederate supply center around which the tide of battle swirled; and his father was such a fervent Confederacy man that he turned his church into an emergency hospital, but Tommy's horizon still was bounded by the magnolias shading the parsonage. Not till he was eighteen and departed for Davidson College, a strictly Presbyterian institution in the North Carolina hills, did he begin to untie those apron strings. Doing so was not easy, when he constantly received letters such as the following from his mother:

My darling Boy,
    I am so anxious about that cold of yours. How did you take it? Surely you have not laid aside your winter clothing? Another danger is in sitting without fire these cool nights . . .

Yet he did play second base on the freshman baseball nine; perhaps the Freudian assumption that he never once had a fist fight is not even accurate. But the year he spent at Davidson had far wider repercussions—it gave him the freedom to decide irrevocably against becoming a clergyman like his father. Beyond question, the Reverend Dr. Wilson had a great influence on this son, and that disappointed gentleman did focus the full strength of his thwarted pedagogical instinct on teaching Tommy the elements of effective public speaking, among many other things. Nevertheless, when it came to choosing a life's work Tommy was influenced more decisively, if indirectly, by his mother.

It is possible to say so because Jessie's English origin deeply stirred her son's imagination. When he had played sailor, the navy he built was the British Navy; and when he picked an idol on whom to model his own future, he chose a British statesman. He had a portrait of Mr. Gladstone, the British Prime Minister, tucked up on his wall when he made up his mind to avoid the pulpit—as such—and to pursue an evangelically political career. He came to this decision at Davidson, where he also improved his marks sufficiently to qualify for a more wide-ranging education; in September of 1874 he departed for Princeton.

Even then, though, mother and son preserved a special closeness. On scholastic matters, Jessie deferred to her husband, who sent off long and thoughtful essays criticizing Tommy's theses; she contented herself with assuring her son time and time again that she was certain he would do well at whatever he attempted. But he and she were allied by bonds of more than sympathy—in physique, Tommy was much more a Woodrow than a Wilson. He had his mother's sallow complexion and susceptibility to illness, he lacked his father's manly beauty. Almost as if in recognition of this state of affairs, he assented to a change in his name soon after he graduated from Princeton. He began signing himself "T. Woodrow Wilson," and when he did so at the close of a letter to a college friend, he added: "P.S. Don't think my signature affected. I sign myself thus at mother's special request, because this signature embodies *all* my family name." Jessie gloried in the change, of course. "Tommy is certainly an unsuitable name for a grown man," she told him, and promised to make "a desperate effort to remember to *call* [him] Woodrow from this time on."

Although it doubtless pleased them both to think of him as a grown man, one may suspect that neither of them had yet made the distinction emotionally. The malarial fevers that caused summer to be dreaded in many Southern cities afflicted Jessie so severely that Woodrow went to the market every morning for her when he was home, and did all manner of other household chores; after a new wing was added to their house, he laid the carpet and arranged the furniture while his father was off attending one of his incessant churchly meetings. Woodrow's domestic activity was increased by the marriage of his two sisters during this period—one to a clergyman, the other to a doctor—and, perhaps, also by his consciousness that any such independence was still impractical in his own case. For after Princeton, he enrolled in law school at the University of Virginia; when he was twenty-three, he could not yet see the time when he would earn his own keep, let alone a wife's.

Furthermore, his health was not to be taken for granted. "You tell us nothing about one thing," Jessie wrote to him at law school.

"What sort of *eating* have you?" More than ordinary maternal solicitude prompted the question because at Charlottesville he began suffering a series of torturing stomach upsets; his digestive troubles became so disturbing that in the middle of his second year he quit to come home and be nursed by his mother. From the letters they wrote to each other, one can deduce that they both tried to minimize their respective ailments when Woodrow's father was present, and to confide symptoms only to each other as much as possible.

If Jessie grew progressively more feeble, Woodrow happily improved sufficiently to prepare himself to enter into practice of the law. (At the same time his brother was entering college, preparatory to a respectable if undistinguished newspaper career.) Atlanta was the site Woodrow chose for putting out his shingle, but even in that city so busily snapping back from Sherman's ravages, clients failed to appreciate the opportunity to hire a future President. In addition, the petty detail of legal routine irritated him, and he was soon contemplating a drastic switch in his plans; instead of using the law as an avenue toward political office, he would settle for a lesser fame—he would devote himself to teaching others about the science of government. But before he abandoned the law, he took a case that in the long run changed his life more momentously than the change in profession did. With a neat aptness, his mother was the chief client involved.

In order to clear up various issues arising from the disputed will of one of her brothers, Woodrow went on a trip during the summer when he was approaching his twenty-seventh birthday. His destination was Rome, Georgia; while there, he naturally went to church on Sunday with his local relatives. Sitting in their pew awaiting the start of the service, his mood was not too reverent for him to notice the arrival of the minister's daughter. "I remember thinking," he wrote later, "what a bright, pretty face; what splendid, mischievous, laughing eyes!" They belonged to Ellen Louise Axson—the Miss Ellie Lou whom he married almost two years later, after he had completed the graduate study at Johns Hopkins that qualified him to become a college professor.

Jessie was pleased by the match—"From all I have ever heard of Ellie Lou," she wrote to Woodrow right after he had confided his hopes, "I feel assured that there does not live a sweeter or purer girl than she. So that if you succeed in winning her, some day, no one will be gladder than I . . ." And Jessie proved that she did mean it, welcoming Ellie Lou with the warmth she reserved for her nearest and dearest. Yet her course should occasion no surprise; as in so many other instances, a son had, all on his own, chosen exactly the girl his mother would have selected for him.

In fact, Ellen Axson offered just the protecting warmth Jessie herself had provided for her boy up until this point—leavened, it must be added, by a refreshing gaiety Jessie could appreciate if not duplicate. That Woodrow was able to transfer his allegiance so successfully when the appropriate time finally did come must also be credited to his mother; thanks to her, the apron strings came untied, after all. Three years later, Jessie faced her own fatal illness with the equanimity that arose from the sure knowledge that Woodrow would be taken care of as she would have wished; Jessie died on April 15, 1888, in Clarksville, Tennessee, where her husband was then teaching theology. She was fifty-seven years old.

If this record justifies an Oedipean diagnosis, so be it—but more remains to be said. No matter that little Tommy Wilson showed the classic symptoms of an Oedipus complex, the grown man Woodrow Wilson still rose astonishingly far above the general run of neurotic. Without benefit of therapy, he managed to convince a generation of Princeton students that he was the best teacher they ever had encountered. He entered the political arena in middle age and then convinced millions of his fellow citizens to choose him as their President. He also had two unusually successful marriages despite the basic Freudian tenet that such normalcy precludes neurosis. Curiously, this was not discussed in the study of Wilson published under Freud's name. Instead, the President of the United States who idealistically and doggedly and perhaps naïvely tried to make the world safe for democracy was dismissed as a desperately disturbed man who thought he was Jesus Christ; but it does seem unfair to belabor him and his parents because he did not turn out, after all, to be mankind's new Savior.

Louisa Torrey Taft

ALPHONSO'S LADY
Louisa Torrey Taft

AT THE AGE OF FORTY-TWO, Mr. Samuel Davenport Torrey of Boston conceived the idea that his lungs were unsound and determined to retire from business. Having already acquired a reasonable competency in the West India trade, he removed with his wife and daughters in the year of 1831 to Millbury, Massachusetts, where he continued expounding positive opinions on a great variety of subjects until he died of apoplexy when he was eighty-eight.

What a pity that Miss Jane Austen could not have observed the Torrey household at some point during this period, for only she could have done it justice. Having already accomplished something of the sort in her *Pride and Prejudice,* she surely would have enjoyed showing how closely nature on the far side of the Atlantic tended to imitate her own art. For Mr. Torrey had four daughters, at least two of whom deserved Miss Austen's interest—Delia, who never married; and Louisa Maria, who married Mr. Alphonso Taft.

This is not to say Mr. Taft was quite the match of Mr. Darcy, but transmute that latter gentleman from a supercilious aristocrat into a righteous Republican and the result is equally arresting. Of course, Mr. Darcy did not, at least as far as one knows, manage to found a dynasty. However, both of these heroes—Alphonso and his fictional counterpart—suffered from the similar defect of failing to be convincingly heroic except when seen through the eyes of the delightful young women they married. To say Louise Torrey rivaled Elizabeth Bennet is saying a lot, but certainly Louise plus Delia did—and that, in a totally respectable sense, was what Alphonso got.

Where fact parts company with fiction, the Torrey girls did not have a silly mother. She was eccentric, certainly—splendidly so; her enthusiasms ranged from astronomy to slashing down walls with an ax when the urge to remodel her Grecian-pillared mansion came upon her. Yet she was intensely sensible, even in her assessment of her own character. As a willful and intellectual young teacher, she had told Mr. Torrey she doubted whether two such definite creatures as he and she should attempt marriage, and she was absolutely correct. Nevertheless, she also saw that logic could be cold company in comparison with the feelings Mr. Torrey aroused, which prevailed. Their life together may not have been serene, but the rewards were worth the turmoil.

It is possible to tell all this because the Torreys wrote letters with stupendous zeal—a habit the Tafts also acquired. If other families of their era produced as much correspondence, they did not produce, in addition, a President of the United States; and thus their papers have escaped tabulation. With the exception of the remarkable Adamses who gave the nation two Presidents, the Taft collection in the Library of Congress is the largest known assemblage of this kind of documentation.

To the cool eye of history, William Howard Taft stands out (apart from his bulk—he was incontrovertibly the heaviest President) only because he was the sole President who also served as Chief Justice of the United States. But he was, besides, enormously likable, and so were his maternal grandparents. Their letters illuminate the past with a natural light that casts some doubt on the grim Puritanic legend taught in every grade school.

Of course, the orthodoxy of Jacksonian New England was as nothing to the colonial variety, but to be a Unitarian was still scandalous, as Susan Waters Torrey well understood when she undertook a return to her home ground after a liberating sojourn in Boston. Susan, the occasional ax-wielder who became Will Taft's maternal grandmother, cared enough for appearances to reembrace Congregationalism, yet she did her share to make life in Millbury diverting; and she could do so with impunity.

Susan's connections in the prosperous little town forty odd miles west of Faneuil Hall explained Mr. Torrey's choice of a retirement site. Her connections in Millbury were impeccable, which was a little more than could be said of his own a trifle to the north of Boston. Having been born a Waters, Susan was related to everybody in Millbury who mattered; her brother was the Colonel Asa Waters whose operation of the largest local industry—a firearms manufactory which received lucrative contracts from the United States Army—entitled him to a generous leeway. He played the flute every Sunday at the First Congregational Church to accompany the hymn singing, and he opened his capacious parlors to *dancing*.

Between their own parents and Uncle Asa right across the street, the Torrey girls received a liberal education. Besides Louisa Maria —born in Boston on September 11, 1827—and Delia—two years her senior—there was a younger pair, Susie and Anna, who were practically another generation because almost a decade elapsed before their appearance. By the time they were being waked up to see eclipses or kept up to listen to Dr. Holmes at the supper table— their mother made a point of securing every visiting Lyceum lecturer for a meal with her family—the two older girls had already departed on the outside seats of a stage, the better to observe the countryside, bound for Miss Mary Lyon's new Mount Holyoke Female Seminary. Delia was eighteen then and her sister, almost always called Louise, sixteen.

". . . There is something very delightful to me in the novelty of a first introduction to a school like this," Louise wrote home on their arrival, but subsequent discoveries soon altered her tone. For it was part of Miss Lyon's original plan to promote the health of her young ladies and instill in them regular habits of domestic management by requiring each to perform specified housekeeping tasks; and such a scheme also freed the institution from the necessity of depending on servants. Louise assured her mother she did not object to spending an hour and a quarter a day molding loaves of bread, feeling herself fortunate that she had not been chosen to mop floors or wash tablecloths. Yet the schedule of recitations and prayer meetings and systematic study required, in addition, of each pupil altogether took prodigious effort. After six months, Louise wrote home:

> . . . I have always thought that one of the pleasantest things about a boarding school would be that we should have so much intercourse with each other. But we are so restricted by rule that we have no chance for it here. Miss Lyon keeps making new rules cutting off our privileges one after another. Oh I shall be so glad to get home where I can speak above a whisper and not have to move by a line and plummet . . .

Although she was the older, and perhaps even more quick mentally than Louise, Delia gave up; she suffered a series of bilious colic attacks and left Mount Holyoke for good in April of her first year there. Louise stayed out the term and bravely professed herself willing to return the following fall. By this resolve, she was seeking more to please her father than her mother; for although Mr. Torrey's financial position continued as sound as his lungs, like many another male parent of numerous daughters he felt some alarm at the possibility of having to feed—and, much worse, clothe—them all indefinitely. If Louise completed the course of study, which at that time could be accomplished in two years, she would receive a diploma admirably qualifying her for earning her own keep as a teacher. "I think, however," she wrote to her mother, who was forever after her to polish her literary style, "if I am thrown upon my own resources I shall not be obliged to teach as I can support myself very comfortably with my pen. Why do you smile?"

Put upon though he sometimes acted, Mr. Torrey indulged his daughters with a freedom that made a sham of his craggy scowling. Thus there was no objection from him when Louise allowed that she would rather forego another year with Miss Lyon, after all. Again like other fathers similarly blessed, he doubtless enjoyed being surrounded. And even if his young ladies took incomprehensible pleasure from adding to their wardrobes, they were no more foolish than their mother, which meant that better company could scarcely be expected in this imperfect world. Nevertheless,

Mr. Torrey assented when his wife proposed an alternate plan for finishing off Delia and Louise.

Indeed he must have congratulated himself. For the scheme was simply to send them to Mrs. Torrey's sister in New Haven, whose husband had a sister in the schoolmarm line; therefore the girls could board with their aunt, and attend classes at the establishment kept by their uncle's maiden relative. It would not have escaped Mr. Torrey's attention that Yale was also in New Haven.

Louise and Delia both could be counted on to make their presence felt among the young gentlemen studying there—in this department, Louise had the advantage over her sister. "This is owing," Aunt Harriet Dutton wrote to Mrs. Torrey, after having some opportunity to observe the girls, "partly to her confidence in herself and partly to her musical gifts and also to her fine figure and manners." Such social assets were certainly helpful, but the pupils accepted by Miss Mary Dutton all shared another even more valuable benefit. To acquaint them with natural science and philosophy—not to mention young men—they were privileged to appear daily in various Yale lecture rooms.

Delia and Louise both profited by their New Haven experience, although not precisely in the way their father had intended. Being tart-tongued, and if the truth be told rather scornful of men, Delia made no conquests; but she saw enough of their society to decide that she could do worse than teach and travel very happily thereafter without the impediment of a husband. Louise was taller and handsomer—her glossy dark hair, parted in the middle and drawn back into a quite elegant chignon, secured her the respectful attention of widowers in particular. Flirting with them amused her, but the prospect of marrying any one of them did not. "Don't you know that I am rather given to having hobbies?" she wrote home flippantly. "My present passion is a great desire to learn to play upon the guitar." At nineteen, she thought she agreed with Delia on the superiority of the single state; not till she was twenty-six did she discover her mistake.

During those years, Louise and Delia created a satisfying pattern for young spinsterhood. Teaching—in moderation—appealed to them, so they taught for a few semesters, and then took time off to travel. They saw Niagara Falls, Quebec, New York City, suitably chaperoned on some occasions but entirely on their own just as often; their mother—oh, how she admired Miss Lucy Stone!— raised no objections. Nor did Mr. Torrey, who presumably had suffered a great deal when his church debated the propriety of allowing women to speak in meeting, and the majority resolved "that the whole subject be indefinitely postponed." Having no majority to count on at home, he bore his daughters' wanderings uncomplainingly for the most part.

Since the salary young women received for teaching at small private academies could not provide more than a portion of the pleasures Delia and Louise appreciated, they did have to ask their father's help from time to time. Once when Louise went off by herself to visit Aunt Harriet Dutton in New Haven, she found herself obliged to write home for funds for a new French straw hat; and she wryly remarked in a separate note to Delia: "If Father finds us too expensive I'm afraid we shall have to get married. That would be a disagreeable expedient. I had rather economize." But on a subsequent visit to Aunt Harriet, Louise revised her opinion.

When nearing her twenty-sixth birthday, she went once more to New Haven, and while she was staying at the home of Aunt Harriet and Uncle Samuel, a gentleman came to call. A former Yale classmate of Uncle Samuel's, he had just arrived from distant Cincinnati. Mr. Alphonso Taft was above six feet in height and neither stooped nor seemed anything but comfortable with his imposing size; there was no fault to be found concerning his appearance. Yet quite unintentionally he struck Louise as comical.

For Mr. Taft was a recent widower, unhappily left with two young sons. This sad fact could, of course, elicit only sympathy, but the gentleman's present conduct was another matter. Of sober New England stock, Mr. Taft had chosen the law as his profession and then he had gone out to Cincinnati to set up in practice rather than stay in the East. From the drift of the inquiries he directed to her, Louise quickly discerned that he had made this summer trip back to Connecticut for the express purpose of finding a second wife—and she could not help teasing him.

But her pert answers to his leading questions failed to put him off. Unlike Mr. Darcy, Mr. Taft was immediately aware of the good fortune that had come his way, and extremely anxious to be captured; but the effect still was intriguing. Not long after she returned to Millbury, Louise received a hasty letter from Aunt Harriet, informing her that Mr. Taft had written to ask, were her affections already directed elsewhere? Aunt Harriet continued:

> The second difficulty is respecting your character and this arises from the energetic manner in which you decried yourself to him, and he wishes to know of Mr. D or rather of me if all you say is true. In substance, if you are as profuse and extravagant, as romantic, as undomestic, as willful as you represent yourself? He wants to know if you have been badly crossed in love matters! Isn't it funny?

Assuredly it was, but Louise must have already suspected herself of harboring other reactions toward Mr. Taft besides mere amusement. So did Aunt Harriet, who wrote further:

> In conclusion he says "I need not be told that Louise is a splendid woman—one of whom a man might be proud. I sincerely hope that it will turn out that she is just the companion I want and I hope it would be a fair match. Whether she may think so is more doubtful." But you know he says that "even a splendid woman without domestic qualities makes a sad wife, and though I believe she has them, my knowledge and belief is drawn from very slender observations." So he wants from me a "well-considered opinion" which I am going to give him . . .

In short, Mr. Taft deserved serious attention after all, and Aunt Harriet proposed to do the right thing by her niece. Indeed she ended by cautioning Louise not to let him suspect that his communication to Mr. Dutton had been made known to her, as he would undoubtedly write directly to her after receiving the character reference that would soon arrive in Cincinnati from New Haven.

Thus it happened that Mr. Taft made another journey to the East in the course of the same year, and answered a few questions himself. To Louise's increasing contentment, he proved sufficiently liberal-minded to suit her—he was quite willing to consider a broadening of the legal and political rights of women as a desirable end; and all on his own, he had even come to the Unitarian persuasion religiously. These considerations were important to her, but more than she would have thought possible his mere appearance pleased her. At forty-three, he was surely a fine figure of a man; and she quite forgot that he had no sense of humor.

So Mr. Taft ate Thanksgiving dinner with the Torrey family in Millbury—and the feast also celebrated the announcement by Miss Louisa Maria Torrey that she had just agreed to change her name, soon. For in happy omen of the rapport to come, it struck Louise the instant she made up her mind to marry that long engagements were absurd; and it suited Mr. Taft to stay away from his office in Cincinnati as briefly as possible. Accordingly, the wedding was set for the day after Christmas. There then ensued four weeks of feverish sewing while Mr. Torrey expanded in the comfort of at last having acquired at least one son-in-law. In the parlor of her parents' home, Louise became Mrs. Alphonso Taft on December 26, 1853.

Beyond merely living happily ever after, she embarked on the chief business open to a woman as soon as she arrived in Cincinnati; and not unnaturally, considering the talents she brought to it, she achieved singular success. Before her time, the Tafts in nearly two centuries had risen from carpentry to farming to middle class solidity, contributing first selectmen and justices of the peace along the way, but that was all. Her three sons did rather better— the third founded an outstanding school; the second made a lot of money practicing corporation law in New York City; and the oldest became, as has already been mentioned, President and then Chief Justice of the United States.

Nor does that tell the whole story, because her husband and one of her two stepsons also had careers for which she could take some credit. And as to grandsons, the one who narrowly missed the Presidency certainly made his mark in the Senate. Others bearing the name of Taft have continued to crop up in Ohio and Washington politics, still owing a debt to Louise Taft.

Make the best of your opportunities—her mother had drummed away at this motif, and Louise taught it as well as lived it. Could any dynasty have a sounder motto? Of course, she said it not only with earnest purpose, but also with humor, and a few other Tafts besides Alphonso have lacked this saving grace. But to an astonishing extent they all followed her on that other important matter of making exceptionally fulfilling marriages.

As far as can be learned, Louise never referred to her husband except as Mr. Taft; she surely never went into detail, even to Delia, about matters that concerned only Mr. Taft and herself. But his departed first wife had once, soon after marrying him, written that of all the women alive she was the most fortunate, and soon Louise did confide exactly this same sentiment to her sister. It must therefore be assumed that Mr. Taft had an unusual aptitude for matrimony.

He, in turn, repaid the compliment. Writing to Delia as "Dear Sister," he assured her: ". . . no man was ever more fortunate than I have been in forming this connection." Until she became used to the new state of affairs, it was poor Delia whose emotions remained unsettled. After bravely describing a recent lecture by Horace Greeley, she could not resist adding: "Oh Louise, Louise, how can I live the rest of my life without you? I am but half a pair of scissors." But soon she was planning a summer visit to Cincinnati, and although Massachusetts would always be her home, her heart expanded to take in Ohio, too. No child of Louise's could make any plan—even, in later years, to run for President—without consulting Aunt Delia first.

So Alphonso and his children had the advantage of Delia's tartness, which, predictably, grew more pronounced, along with Louise's blander domesticity. It was Delia who observed: "I suppose we might almost as well ask for a train of cars to go out of its course . . . as to expect Mr. Taft to turn aside from business for the pursuit of pleasure." Louise would never have thought of criticizing him. Not that she ever completely submerged her own personality; she was too much her mother's daughter to disappear under anybody's shadow, even if she relished being Mrs. Alphonso Taft so much that she lost interest in attending woman's rights conventions. What she applied herself to, besides advancing the careers of Mr. Taft plus their sons, was the inspiring of an assortment of civic improvements from kindergartens to Y.W.C.A.'s. "When woman's field widens, Mother, you must become President of a Railroad Company," her son Will wrote to her. "I am sure you would be a success."

But she preferred her own preserve, which did not seem to her at all narrow. In truth, she had Mr. Taft's two older boys, and his

aged parents, and a little girl besides her own three boys to cope
with—all this and Alphonso, too. It was quite a household that she
ran, and how she ran it could be described encyclopedically,
owing to the full chapters she and Alphonso regularly dispatched
to Millbury. On the topic of Louise's maternity, the record is particularly full.

Alphonso to his father-in-law, on February 7, 1855:

> At half-past nine this morning, Louise gave birth to a fine boy,
> weighing nine pounds—after a very short labor, and before the
> arrival of doctor or nurse. She appears to be doing very well. . . . It
> was quite a surprise to us all. Louise calls it a surprise party, and so
> it is. . . . This boy raises high expectations and we hope he will be
> worthy to bear a good name and so we call him Samuel Davenport
> Taft . . .

But Sammie, plump and healthy though he seemed, died of
whooping cough not long after his first birthday; then, thankfully,
she became pregnant again. It was on September 5, 1857, that she
was delivered of another boy they named William Howard Taft.
Louise to Delia:

> I feel as if my hands and feet were tied to this baby. I suppose
> Mother would think it poor management but I do not understand
> making him take care of himself . . .

His eyes were "deeply, darkly, beautifully blue," and he was
wonderfully large for his age. Before the process Alphonso euphe-
mistically referred to as the baby's "change of diet" had to be
undertaken, the lusty Willie was thirteen months old and his
mother was pregnant again. Louise to Delia:

> You will perceive that no time has been wasted . . . I am not
> afraid of having too many. I began too late for that . . . I delight
> in large families . . .

On her personal philosophy of childrearing, Louise to her
mother:

> I do not believe we can love our children too much. I think we
> ought to take all the comfort we can in them while they are spared
> to us and if we must give them up we ought to be thankful that we
> were blessed by their angelic presence even for a little while . . .

[but] I am more and more impressed with the responsibility of training children properly. I find that Willie needs constant watching and correcting, and it requires great caution and firmness to do the right thing always. It seems to me there can be no stronger motive for improvement than the thought of the influence on our children. It is what we *are,* not what we do in reference to them, which will make its impress on their lives. They will be sure to find out our weak points whatever professions we make . . .

If her own example was high, so was Alphonso's. With his solemn tenderness, he made a good father but a demanding one, for he and Louise both expected their sons to improve on his own record. Nothing less than becoming Chief Justice of the United States was his ambition, and when it became apparent that he would not achieve it, the goal was simply passed along to Will.

It was not entirely unrealistic for Alphonso to aim so boldly. Being a more than just competent lawyer conscientiously devoted to the new Republican party, he did reach Ohio's Superior Court bench, and had there not been such a plentitude of deserving Ohio Republicans during the ensuing decades he might have received the appointment he coveted. As it was, he eventually gained the dubious distinction of serving in General Grant's cabinet, first as Secretary of War, then Attorney General; and it pleased President Chester Arthur to reward Mr. Taft further by sending him abroad as United States Ambassador to Vienna and then St. Petersburg. Since these posts were almost entirely ceremonial at the time, they were the equivalent of being sent out to pasture.

By this time, Louise Taft's work was almost done, too. She could enjoy the sparkle of society in Washington, then Europe, serene in the knowledge that the five boys she raised all had made outstanding records at Yale. Whether or not it was because he was her first after the painful loss of poor Sammie nobody can say, but Will had her strongest hopes—which somehow the entire family had come to share—and Will was far too amiable to resent the position in which he found himself. From law school to assistant prosecuting attorney to the same judgeship which his father had held twenty years earlier, and then on to Washington, Will rose exactly as his mother had hoped he would.

All but one of the other boys equally justified her faith. Her son Henry Waters Taft became the New York corporation lawyer whose behind-the-scenes influence was of inestimable help to Will; her son Horace Dutton Taft, after implausibly deciding to stop practicing law, reinstated himself more than adequately as a solid citizen by founding the Taft School for Boys in Connecticut; and Charles Phelps Taft, the older of Alphonso's sons by his first wife, became Cincinnati's leading newspaper publisher as well as public benefactor. Only Peter Rawson Taft, Charles's younger brother, could not live up to the family standard; after making a brilliant record at Yale, achieving the highest marks that had yet been scored, he sank into a series of ever deeper depressions till he died in a sanitorium at thirty-three.

That and her loss of Sammie were the only real sorrows Louise Taft endured till her aging but seemingly ageless husband collapsed in St. Petersburg. A combined attack of typhoid and pneumonia, complicated by acute asthma, felled him then, and although he recovered he was never well again. It was necessary for him to resign, and after he had weathered the trip home the urgency of keeping him in a warm climate became utterly apparent. Louise brought him to a cottage in California, high on a hill overlooking San Diego's harbor, and there they spent long months together, waiting for the end. "What a resource is a cultivated mind!" Louise wrote to her son Will. "What can people do when old and sick without intellectual resources? I can always entertain him." On May 2, 1891, Alphonso at last lost his struggle; he was eighty then, and Louise sixty-three. She spent that summer helping Will's wife, Nellie, who was expecting a second child.

But two women dedicated to the advancement of the same man could not easily fit within the same house, and Nellie Herron Taft was nothing if not ambitious; it was undoubtedly she who convinced Will to forget about the Supreme Court for the time being, and aim for the Presidency.

So Louise and the ever-faithful Delia resumed something like the style of living they had followed long ago. They wintered in Boston, getting their fill of music and theatre; or perhaps they tried New York instead, staying in their favorite boardinghouse on Murray Hill. At other seasons, they gallivanted from the Taft School to Cincinnati to California, where Louise's daughter Fanny had settled after a surprise marriage to Alphonso's surgeon. These two old ladies even mellowed sufficiently to visit Mount Holyoke for a Founder's Day celebration, which they enjoyed more than they would have believed, possibly because it enabled Louise to comment that several former classmates looked even more venerable and decrepit than she and her sister did. Yet she did not delude herself; she wrote to Will:

> Old age is still old age. It is the waning, not the crescent moon. But I will not repine. I have had my day. The future looks very much "of a muddle" and I am rather glad I am to have little responsibility about it.

On the other hand, she never stopped interesting herself in the vagaries of this world. When she was seventy-four, President Theodore Roosevelt gave Will a mission of extreme delicacy. Judge Taft had recently returned from the Philippines to confer about the harassing problems posed by trouble-making Spanish friars. Roosevelt wanted him to go to Rome next, to see if something could be done there about controlling the troublesome priests. "You will have the whole Catholic world down on you," Louise warned her son. "They quarrel among themselves, but like the Democratic party, they stand together against outsiders." But Will accepted President Roosevelt's word—not his mother's—and decided to make the trip.

For all his outward stoutness—if his father had seemed imposing at something over two hundred pounds, the son at something over three hundred was monumental—Will had not weathered his recent stints in the tropics easily. Neither his wife nor his mother was satisfied that his health could stand the tension of a diplomatic assignment to the Vatican. Nellie planned to accompany him to watch over his diet, but just before the sailing one of her children came down with scarlet fever and she had to stay home. Learning this up in Millbury, Louise was not sorry to be needed again. Within twenty-four hours, she was packed and greeting Will on a New York pier.

She fell back easily into the role of diplomatic hostess, but that month in Rome was her last taste of the great world. Afterwards, she and Delia stayed mainly in Millbury, in the old Torrey mansion which Delia had inherited; the other two sisters, having emulated Louise by making late marriages to widowers, were settled at some distance from Massachusetts.

In the fine old New England tradition, Louise and Delia busied themselves studying genealogy, both Torrey and Taft—Delia with her ear trumpet, Louise with her white lace cap. Louise also found ample time for serving as the family's "scissors editor," clipping newspaper stories about Will for scrapbooks. Growing almost as tart as Delia now, she peppered him with requests, too. In 1906, when Will was Secretary of War and his mother was almost seventy-nine, she told him to appoint a certain relative of some local acquaintance as master of an Army transport. When Will did so, she was moved to write: "I hope the man is equal to the position. We cannot be responsible for his fitness." That provoked Will to reply:

> I felt certain that such civil service reformers as you and Aunt Delia would never have recommended a man for a place . . . where he will have hundreds of thousands of dollars of the property of the government in charge, unless you knew . . . that he was a competent mariner, navigator and sailor of the seas! However, it is only another instance of how reformers, when they seek to be spoilsmen, lose all their principles . . . so that their friends may be put at the public crib.

After her seventy-ninth birthday, Louise suffered an attack of acute appendicitis and doctors told her an operation was necessary; and they felt constrained to add that at her time of life, it might prove fatal. "When do you want to operate?" she asked. "I'm ready now."

She survived to watch, although with increasing detachment, as Will came ever closer to the prize Nellie craved for him. Early in 1907, Theodore Roosevelt was strenuously striving to decide who to support for the Republican nomination for President the following year; he wanted it for himself, of course, but he had rashly vowed three years earlier that he would not run for another term. Unwilling to go back on his word, he kept trying to choose between Elihu Root and Taft.

There had been repeated Taft family conclaves to consider what

Will's course ought to be. Louise and Delia both took part in several, and held out against his aiming for the Presidency; and Will quite agreed with them that the judicial life would suit him better. But the onrush of events became too much for these three, particularly after Charles and Harry, both now wealthy men of considerable political influence—Charles in Cincinnati and Harry in New York—generously put aside their own concerns to concentrate on getting Will elected. Yet Louise could not but warn Will early in 1907:

> Roosevelt is a good fighter and enjoys it, but the malice of politics would make you miserable. They do not want you as their leader, but cannot find anyone more available.

Now Will could no longer take his mother's advice. Carried on by the momentum of the drive instituted by his brothers, he began to campaign actively for the nomination. No less in public than in private Louise refused to moderate her own views. Five months before her eightieth birthday, she took a trip out to see her daughter in California, and a reporter facetiously asked who her candidate was for the Presidency.

"Elihu Root," she said firmly.

But for her to think otherwise would have been disloyal to Alphonso, besides doing violence to her own good judgment. It is a sobering thought, but perhaps if one could have watched Elizabeth Bennet grow old, one might have seen her develop into something of a Lady Catherine de Bourgh. Not that Louise Taft ever went quite so far as to insist her son must stop trying to be President. After the exertion of her Western trip, she grew steadily weaker until in the autumn Delia thought Will might want to postpone a foreign tour being undertaken at least indirectly for campaigning purposes. Doing Alphonso proud, Louise protested. "No Taft, to my knowledge, has ever yet neglected a public duty for the sake of gratifying a private desire," she said. Then Will sailed as scheduled, and he was at sea when his mother died on December 7, 1907, two months after her eightieth birthday. So she was spared seeing the muddle he made of the Presidency, before he finally reached the safer harbor of the Supreme Court.

Martha Bulloch Roosevelt

8

"DARLING, BELOVED LITTLE MOTHERLING..."

Martha Bulloch Roosevelt

At FIFTEEN, Mittie Bulloch was enchanting. She had every advantage that comes of living in a wonderland, which is the simplest way to describe her family's Georgia plantation—in 1850. Even a high-minded young man from New York who arrived there in that year, armed with a proper letter of introduction, was charmed out of his senses. Visiting the South for the first time, he fell utterly under the spell of Bulloch hospitality and, most particularly, of Mittie herself; but he needs no pity. Before his departure northward, he and she were secretly engaged.

Being only nineteen, Theodore Roosevelt—that worthy young man who with Mittie's cooperation would beget a President—had not the slightest notion of the deeper currents running beneath the surface at Roswell. Apart from the agony storing up wherever there were slaves, this plantation had its own peculiar history. But like the whole legend of Dixie, the Bulloch version did possess an undeniable core of reality; an atmosphere richer in love would be hard to imagine. It is 'not strange that such was the case.

Although James Stephens Bulloch, Mittie's father, had dropped dead of a stroke while teaching Sunday School a few years back, his spirit still pervaded the pillared mansion. Superficially, he had been merely a gentlemanly planter. Descended from good Scottish stock, he had excellent connections. He was, for instance, the grandson of Georgia's first governor, but that is not to say no breath of scandal had ever touched his handsome figure. In fact, he had been virtually exiled from Savannah for the marvelously chivalrous feat of marrying his own mother-in-law.

Yet the episode was more romantic than bizarre, after all. He had actually adored Martha Stewart right from the beginning and her father having been a Revolutionary general, a match between these two could raise no eyebrow. But at the age of sixteen—whether coquetry or some other motive inspired her, nobody could be sure—she had dashed his hopes. Then he rushed into marriage with another girl whose father was the United States Senator from Georgia, John Elliott, a widower. One year later, Martha Stewart married the Senator himself, thus becoming, precisely speaking, her former suitor's stepmother-in-law. But when death took both Senator Elliott and his daughter, and Mrs. Elliott accepted her son-in-law, Savannah society drew a finer line than might seem called for, and froze out the newlyweds.

So they moved, ostensibly looking for a more healthful climate, to an upland plantation just to the west of Atlanta. Supremely happy after the vicissitudes they had already endured, they created an outwardly Elysian new life together at Roswell. Still, the rancors of the past must have pained them sometimes, nor could they pretend to have forgotten what had gone before, since they both brought with them children born of their previous marriages. Martha Stewart Elliott Bulloch was endowed with maternal instinct to spare, however, and she raised the assorted progeny imperturbably. Perhaps she had been genuinely fond of John Elliott—the record is silent on this point, except for her comment in a chatty letter that happened to be saved. "Of all things," she wrote, "I think marriage without love must be most uncomfortable." But her second marriage was decidedly not of this variety, and if she exalted the children it produced above the others, who can blame her? The highest place of all went to an exquisitely dainty little girl born on July 8, 1835.

Named for her mother, the baby was called Missy by most of the population at Roswell and that led to Mittie. No matter what its genesis, the diminutive fit the situation admirably, for Mittie grew into a beautiful, protected, pampered, and altogether bewitching young lady who could not possibly have been a Martha. She had the sort of silky black hair that takes on a russet tinge under the glow of candles, and her skin was the purest white, more moonlight white than cream white, with a coral rather than a rose tint in her cheeks. But for all her delicate bloom, she had the most splendid dash and gusto. She was a magnificent horsewoman—she would throw a cape over her shoulders and gallop over the sandy hills like a creature escaped from the pages of the *Arabian Nights*. Then the next day, she might languish on a hammock, reading Dickens.

Even the death of her father caused no lasting scar, for her mother would not allow pain to linger in their paradise. Every wholesome amusement conceivable tempted Mittie from any unpleasant moments. And she never learned to stamp her little foot when she was displeased; it was totally unnecessary. While this kind of upbringing may not have quite prepared her for growing up, she had no trouble at all with girlhood—as her own words prove. Because one thousand miles separated Georgia and New York, the greater part of her courtship had to be conducted by mail, and the delightful letters she exchanged with her "dearest Thee" have been preserved.

Although Mittie pensively wondered whether "some higher power" might not have ordained their engagement, it took various human agencies many long months to arrange the matter suitably. Not for more than two years after Theodore's first visit to Roswell did the betrothal become official. But Mittie had a half-sister who had married one of Theodore's brothers; that accounted for his having stopped at the Bulloch plantation in the first place. Thus it also came about that when Mittie was seventeen, she was permitted to visit Philadelphia—and Theodore met her there.

She had not yet dared to tell her mother what she had promised —being still of two minds on the subject, one must suspect. She would suffer a terrible wrench leaving Roswell for good, and she could scarcely even think of living without her mother. But Mittie felt other emotions in Philadelphia, which can easily be identified from Theodore's remark in a letter he sent her soon after she had gone home, that "those sofas up at Mary's seem almost sacred." Even before receiving this, Mittie had bravely informed her mother of the engagement.

So in June of 1853, Theodore booked passage on a coastal steamer to come and be inspected again. "I am trying to school myself," he wrote, "to coolly shaking hands with you when we meet—before the family." He succeeded, of course, but it would have been difficult to find any objection to this young man as a prospective husband, excepting the distance he proposed taking Mittie. He was so very worthy and well-intentioned and well-connected—coming of an unbroken line of reputable burghers traceable back to the earliest days of Nieuw Amsterdam—that even a Southern mother could not hesitate to entrust her daughter to him. If such considerations weighed heavily with Mittie's mother, Mittie was certainly pleased, because she could never have married anybody her mother did not approve. But her Thee's diligent knight-errantry pleased her more.

After a breathless round of quadrilles and picnics, he had to return to his desk in his family's glass importing business in New York until November, when they would be married at Roswell. Mittie's first letter following his departure was addressed to Maiden Lane, and folded and refolded to fit into a charmingly absurd little envelope. It started:

Thee, dearest Thee,

I promised to tell you if I cried when you left me. I had determined not to do so if possible, but when the dreadful feeling came over me that you were, indeed, gone, I could not help my tears from springing and had to rush away and be alone with myself. Everything now seems associated with you. Even when I run up the stairs going to my room, I feel as if you were near, and turn involuntarily to kiss my hand to you. I feel, dear Thee, as though you were part of my existence, and that I only live in your being, for now I am

confident of my own deep love. When I went in to lunch today I
felt very sad, for there was no one now to whom to make the request to move "just a quarter of an inch farther away" . . .

For she could not resist teasing him as well as loving him, and
although her formal schooling had been limited to a few years at
a proper academy catering to the daughters of planters she obviously knew how to express herself wonderfully well; even her pen-
manship was a marvel of delicate precision.

Writing eight, ten, twelve pages once or twice every week,
Mittie gave a vivid picture of the life she was daring to leave—and
of her own state of mind at the prospect. As the date for her
wedding approached, her anxiety mounted. She was distracted at
first by a visit to a Georgia spa with her mother, where she had
too gay a time for Thee's comfort, and she tried to reassure him:
"I love you all I am capable of loving *except Mother.*" But almost
petulantly she postponed the wedding from November to December, and she felt obliged to mention she was being disturbed by
"palpitations" so severe that she had arrived at the "candid opinion" that she had "some disease of the heart." On second thought,
she decided all by herself that the symptoms were "entirely ner-
vous," which they surely were. One can almost hear her moan as
she wrote early in December: "I do dread the time before our
wedding, darling—and I wish that it was all up and I had died
game."

Yet she donned white satin valiantly on December 22, 1853,
and before many weeks had passed Mittie Bulloch Roosevelt was
installed as the mistress of a narrow, dark, implacably respectable
brownstone dwelling at 28 East Twentieth Street in New York
City. It was a far, far cry from Roswell's expansive elegance.

Mittie then and thereafter succeeded superbly on one count.
She survived the move with her gift of love and laughter intact,
which cannot be overly emphasized. The warmth that was to
permeate those dim, solemn rooms around the corner from Union
Square owed more to Georgia than most staunch Republicans
would care to admit. But poor Mittie failed in other ways; while
she must not be dismissed as either weak or foolish, she certainly
departs from the general run of Presidential mothers.

For, in effect, she remained suspended in that special limbo reserved for girls who stay eighteen years old all of their lives. Such a condition does not, of course, eliminate the possibility of becoming a good mother. If a few essential factors are present—willing relatives, for instance, and ample funds—the child-woman can make an exceptionally good mother. Mittie Roosevelt did.

But, oh, the vexations she endured during her first months at Twentieth Street. She was naturally expected to assume responsibility for running the household, and she tried gamely at the beginning to do all that Thee thought she ought. Yet she dreadfully missed having capable dark hands to do her every bidding, and she missed having her mother and older sister Anna to lean on even more than she had anticipated. In addition, she was completely unequipped to handle money—it fled through her fingers in quest of lace fichus and silver fans so fast that Theodore was forced to concern himself with domestic matters more than he would have wished.

Although few letters illuminate this period, one can surmise that Theodore or his female relatives took over much of the niggling detail involved in furnishing brown-paneled rooms with appropriate mahogany, and perhaps even the ordering of meals. For Mittie very soon became pregnant, and then she certainly would have required incessant help. Having already begun to fret over her health while at Roswell, she never ceased discovering alarming symptoms. But she had an extraordinary talent for being waited upon—and she could snap back after a sick headache or a bout of dyspepsia with her sense of fun somehow unimpaired. She had no untoward difficulty in producing a bright-eyed baby girl a year after her wedding.

The infant was named Anna, after Mittie's favorite sister, but Bamie was what they called her—taken from the Italian *bambina*, and pronounced to rhyme with Sammy. Bamie gave much heartache as well as joy to both of her parents. Nobody has ever established whether she was dropped by her nurse, or whether she suffered an undiagnosed case of polio, but her spine was so affected that it was feared she would never walk. This sorrow brought the best from Mittie and Theodore. In their separate ways, they showered her with such love and patient attention that the defect

gradually was overcome; Theodore's positive refusal to accept
pessimistic medical advice, and his persistence in making a game of
exercises, would serve as practice for the longer and more celebrated effort called forth by the birth of his first son.

Nearly four years elapsed before Mittie presented her husband
with this baby. In those years of increasing tension between the
North and the South, the opportunities for unrest on Twentieth
Street multiplied, and yet Mittie's marriage stabilized. Although
Theodore harbored the most stalwart Union sentiments and Mittie could not help her passionate loyalty to Georgia, although
Theodore was incurably earnest and Mittie was not, despite the
profusion of possible causes for friction, the love uniting these two
withstood every trial; would that their example had applied more
widely.

A good part of the reason why Mittie managed as well as she
did was the arrival of her mother and Anna from Roswell in 1856.
Having settled all her other children, Mrs. Bulloch sold the plantation and came up to live with her darling in New York then.
Thus she and Anna, who took after her in managerial skill, were
both available to smooth the rigors of Mittie's second pregnancy,
and to do all necessary when the crucial moment arrived on October 27, 1858. Because Mrs. Bulloch felt impelled the next day to
write every detail of such an interesting event to her married
daughter in Philadelphia, the circumstances attending President
Theodore Roosevelt's birth are no mystery:

> . . . When the different servants were flying about for doctors and
> for Susan Newberry, the nurse, I was almost the whole time alone
> with Mittie—Anna had taken Bamie over to Lizzy Ellis'—I sent over
> for her, but she was too unwell to come—I could not bear the idea
> of having no female friend with me, so sent for Mrs. Roosevelt and
> she came over. Mittie continued to get worse and worse until quarter
> to eight in the evening when the birth took place. She had a safe
> but a severe time . . . Mittie says I must tell you she thinks the baby
> hideous. She says it is a cross between a terrapin and Dr. Young . . .

But if Mrs. Bulloch and Anna were of inestimable help to Mittie in caring for little Teedie—as the small Theodore was called
with the family's propensity for odd nomenclature—the senior
Theodore may at times have entertained inhospitable thoughts.

As the crisis in North-South enmity came on, he found himself with something of a rebel beachhead under his own roof. There is a story that Mittie even unfurled a Confederate flag out of a window overlooking Twentieth Street one day. For the most part, though, the ladies confined their Secessionist activities to those times when Theodore senior was away from home.

Mittie had three brothers fighting in the Confederate ranks, and although she knew it would be useless to try to change her Thee's convictions, she told him it would kill her if he took up arms against them. So he did not enlist, but instead devoted long months to the tedious and dangerous work of helping to develop an allotment plan whereby Union soldiers could apportion part of their pay to their dependents at home; no such scheme had as yet been attempted, and putting it into effect meant riding from encampment to encampment in search of signatures. Probably he spent more time in the saddle and under fire than many a soldier, but he always regretted not having played a more glorious role—and his son, who worshiped him, later felt this was his father's sole lapse from perfection.

As a boy, though, Teedie made up an exciting game during Father's absences. Then the three ladies of the house would pack baskets filled with parcels of food, clothing, and money. Hushed and awed little children—Elliott, or Ellie, was born in 1860; and Corinne, called Conie, in 1861—would watch without any real notion of what was going on, except that they would soon be bound for a "picnic" in Central Park. But at a particular bridge, the parcels would be handed over to various agents who seemingly had no problem slipping through Union lines. The game Teedie organized, he being an irresistible organizer right from his nursery days, consisted of much scurrying in the vicinity of that bridge; all this was described as Running the Blockade.

For despite a wearying series of colds, stomach upsets, and—more seriously—asthma attacks, Teedie was a bundle of energy. He looked sickly, even quaintly so with his matchstick legs and large teeth, but he bounced up from each attack ready to climb mountains. Of necessity he became something of a bookworm, specializing in insect and animal lore, yet he had his mother's gusto and his father's dogged earnestness. He was, of course, invincibly priggish, but even more than in the case of Theodore senior it was a priggishness tempered by humor. No matter what effort it cost her, Mittie worked hard over him. Night after night, she sat up with him, cradling his dear funny old man's face on her lap while she soothed away his asthmatic gasping with comic stories about Mom Charlotte and Daddy Luke in the old days at Roswell. If the nursery occupants at Twentieth Street grew up with a minstrel show version of Negro life as gospel, Mittie in the same process convinced all four of her children that she was the loveliest mother imaginable.

Yet selfless as she could behave, she gradually became set in a pattern that approached outright oddity. The venerated doctor from Vienna who had been born just two years earlier than her Teedie would certainly have characterized her as acutely neurotic, for she got so that she simply could not keep appointments. She developed such a fetish for cleanliness that she would always take two baths—one for cleaning and one for rinsing—and she had a sheet spread on the floor each night next to her bed so that she might say her prayers in comfort and not be too conscious of the possibility of dirt when addressing the Lord.

She also had spells of being tormented by indigestion for days at a time, while at night—if she did sleep—she was apt to waken with symptoms she described as "my horror." And her sick headaches, requiring her to retire to her room for several hours with cold compresses on her forehead, came spaced at intervals to suggest even to the non-Freudian that these offered a convenient, acceptable excuse for escaping the strenuous pace of family activity decreed by Theodore senior.

Escape she did, without suffering the slightest lessening in her husband's or her children's enormous regard for her. For the children whole-heartedly accepted their father's lead in treating her as an exquisite object of art to be carefully cherished. They seldom seem to have referred to her as merely their mother; no less than two adulatory adjectives were always prefixed—but the exuberant young Theodore took the prize. "Darling, beloved little Motherling," he began a letter to her.

Over the years, Mittie's taste was catered to in every conceivable matter—no wine, even, was purchased for domestic use without

her first having ceremoniously sampled it. But amid all her vagaries, she managed to keep from sinking into helpless invalidism.
After the Civil War, she participated—enthusiastically—in two
nearly incredible family expeditions to Europe. Theodore senior's
idea of educational travel, before the days of airplanes and stream-
lined luggage, involved an itinerary and an entourage that staggers
the mind. They covered England, Scotland, the Low Countries,
the Rhine Valley, and Switzerland during one trip, which naturally also included extensive forays into France and Italy. The
second tour reviewed much of the same ground, in addition allowing two months for going up and down the Nile aboard the daha-
beah *Aboo Erdan* and three weeks for a saddle-and-tent explora-
tion of Palestine—plus visits by all manner of conveyance to Beirut
and Damascus, Smyrna and Constantinople, then Greece and a
Danube cruise to Vienna and civilization again. Dirt, dyspepsia,
and all, Mittie survived this in fine fettle.

She actually had suggested going abroad in the first place, although she doubtless would have settled for a more limited pilgrimage. With the death of her mother in 1864 and the subsequent
marriage of dear Anna to James K. Gracie, she had a consuming
urge to see her two favorite brothers, both of whom had settled in
Liverpool after the South's defeat. But her Thee was nothing if
not thorough, and the second trip, in 1872, even allowed for im-
mersing his offspring in German schools after the rest of the
sightseeing had been accomplished. Owing to Teedie's asthma—
which did not, however, prevent these orgies of foreign travel
—formal schooling had not yet entered into the experience of any
of the children. Aunt Annie had willingly and warmly tutored
them, along with their father; he was the kind of parent who
brought *The Last of the Mohicans* to read aloud by firelight when
the family camped overnight. But now the time was approaching
when college for Teedie must be thought of, and Theodore senior
decided that Dresden would be the proper locale for testing
whether the boy could stand the confinement of a classroom.

While this experiment was tried, quite satisfactorily, the three
younger children living with a *gemütlich* German family, the elder
Theodore betook himself back to New York to attend to business.
That left the seventeen-year-old Bamie in charge of her mother,

who planned to sample the water at various spas—and do some shopping. Bamie had long since shown herself to be one of the rare females of this earth who can be bossy without being offensive. It was she who managed to keep Teedie's passion for collecting dead animals within some bounds, and ever since turning fourteen she had been in full command of the housekeeping money at Twentieth Street. But when Mittie was let loose in Paris and London with a substantial letter of credit to draw on, even Bamie could not restrain her.

The boxes and crates that went lumbering toward New York defied counting, and their contents were varied, to put it mildly. Just as an example, she sent so many bolts of a claret-colored woolen cloth which had caught her fancy as the most suitable material for her coachman's livery that it probably would have been possible to have outfitted all the footmen in Buckingham Palace. There was some excuse for her shopping binge because Theodore senior had decided to move his family uptown, and a new house at 6 West Fifty-seventh Street was being readied for them. It did not occur to Mittie, however, that certain purchases might be postponed till the expense of moving had tapered off; she even spent the money earmarked for their passage home.

Then when her Thee wrote to her with unwonted severity, she took the only refuge she knew, replying: "I love you and wish to please you more than anyone else in the whole world . . . I think you have been perfectly lovely to me in your care of me always, and so good and indulgent and thoughtful, and I am so proud of you, and honor and respect you so, *don't be too hard on me.*" And she signed herself: "Your own little Mittie." She was at the time thirty-eight years old by the calendar.

But she never would change. Once ensconced in the almost suburban atmosphere of Fifty-seventh Street in the 1870's, Mittie gratefully sank back into her indolent routine. Life was pleasant for her . . . Teedie's terrible asthma had now been all but conquered by the boy's fierce concentration on following his father's prescription for body-building exercises, he was even beginning to look sturdy, he would surely be able to cope with Harvard . . . and Bamie was such a comfort . . . and Conie so sweet . . . and Ellie, the dear boy, would surely discover what it was he wanted to devote his talents to, he was so very personable that he was bound to do well.

That these were restful years for Mittie is a tribute to the efficacy of her own method for escaping turmoil. Not that the family became caught up in any especially notable excitement, but the normal pace set by Theodore senior would have exhausted almost anybody. At Oyster Bay on Long Island, where he had taken a rambling house named—with unconscious humor—Tranquillity, Roosevelt summers were such a boisterous melange of boating, charades, and amateur taxidermy that the strongest non-Roosevelt nerves were bound to quiver. Even in the city, Mittie's husband followed a philanthropic and social schedule, superimposed over his weekday business routine, that was tiring merely to contemplate. Fortunately, Bamie was equal to the rigorous task of providing him with feminine companionship—no mean feat, as her own description of a typical Saturday indicates:

> Generally these Saturdays commenced by a ride on horseback, followed instantly before I had time to fairly get into my clothes, by a visit of inspection to both the Art Museum and the Museum of Natural History, and then to some one of the Children's Aid Society schools. We would get home for lunch very late, and as a rule would find whoever was most interesting of the moment in New York lunching with us. By the time that was over, we either drove in the park or visited a hospital. At all events those wintry days, when five o'clock came, I was a complete wreck. Mother always used to say it was a case of "butchered to make a Roman holiday," that by Saturday evening I was dead, owing to Father's lovely afternoon. Still it was marvelously instructive.

Sundays, it might be added, no matter what else might be on the agenda, there was always a visit to the home for newsboys which Theodore senior had sponsored. And besides his plethora of other activities he also associated himself more and more during these months with reform-minded civic committees, which led to his being nominated by President Rutherford B. Hayes—elected in 1876 on a reform platform—to the post of collector of customs for the port of New York. The choice infuriated old-line spoilsmen, and after a particularly bitter battle the United States Senate refused to confirm Mr. Roosevelt. It seemed to Mittie that the strain of all this caused a frightening change in her adored husband; for the first time in his life, he felt tired. But the trouble went much deeper, and within a few months this strong man was struck down by an inoperable abdominal cancer. He died on February 9, 1878, at the age of forty-six.

With Bamie's support, Mittie survived the blow and even mustered some of her old gaiety after time had begun its healing process. On a spring evening in 1880, she entertained at a small dinner party that forces a matrimonial speculation. Purportedly this was a party for Bamie—at twenty-five, Bamie could still marry, of course, and her mother unselfishly hoped that she would. But the most interesting male guest, a fourth cousin belonging to the Hudson River branch of the Roosevelt family, was a widower of fifty-two, surely a more suitable age for someone else at the table. Approaching her forty-fifth birthday, Mittie still had a girlish manner, enhanced by the embroidered white muslin of her youth, which she continued to prefer above more recent styles. That she remained more appealing than many women much younger must not be doubted, but the face that enthralled James Roosevelt on this occasion belonged to Bamie's dear friend, Miss Sara Delano.

If Mittie could hardly have foreseen that the son of these two would become President, she may have had some inkling of the glory in store for her own Theodore. During this same year, he graduated from Harvard, abandoned his boyish plan to become a naturalist, and married an adorable Mittie-sort of a girl whose name was Alice Lee. "You mustn't feel melancholy, sweet Motherling," he had written from Boston when his Alice accepted him, "I shall only love you all the more." Because the newlyweds moved in with her on Fifty-seventh Street, she heard nothing but politics after he plunged into the New York legislature only a little more than a year later—in almost conscious determination to wreak his revenge on his father's enemies by smashing their political machines.

While it fatigued Mittie to listen to him hold forth on exactly how he proposed winning the post of Speaker of the Assembly, just for a start, she must have suspected he would go further than Albany. Throughout his political career, Theodore Roosevelt would startle even his closest associates by his boyish exuberance.

"You must remember," they warned visitors to the White House on various occasions, "the President is only seven." But if he took after his mother in his eternal juvenility, he also had a sense of purpose so powerful as to approach genius, and she was intelligent enough to recognize this.

About her Elliott she could still be hopeful. It had been his father and not his mother who had been sorely disappointed by this son's early lapses from the pinnacle of high purpose. Mittie was still willing to forgive him, and be charmed by him, even when he began drinking excessively. But then he appeared to have set-tled down, becoming engaged to a lovely girl named Anna Hall, which was enough to convince Mittie that all would be well with him. Perhaps he inherited too much of her nature and too little of his father, for the cure did not prove permanent. Yet Mittie was spared seeing him disintegrate into a hopeless alcoholic who died at thirty-three, leaving a heartbroken little daughter. Her name was Anna Eleanor, and she married the son of James and Sara Delano Roosevelt.

Mittie's own youngest child gave her not the slightest unease. Corinne contentedly became Mrs. Douglas Robinson about the same time that Theodore married, and she brought a capable money adviser into the clan. As for providing tireless emergency duty of every description, Bamie never would fail, even after her astonishing decision at the age of thirty-five to become the wife of an amiable Naval gentleman named Cowles. Before then, the family had endured stark tragedy.

The year of 1884 started more than auspiciously. Theodore was beginning to make quite a splash up in Albany, and his adorable little wife was about to present him with an heir. Under the cir-cumstances, she was staying on Fifty-seventh Street instead of accompanying him to the capital for the legislative session; as often as possible, he hurried down by train to snatch a few hours with her. She and his mother both seemed to be enjoying excellent health and spirits during this waiting time.

Then in the second week of February, Mittie caught cold. But even she brushed off any concern—the impending great event was so much more important. Theodore did not have any idea that his mother was ill when he received a telegram announcing the safe arrival of a baby daughter. As he came hastening up to the front door some hours later, Elliott flung it open.

"There is a curse on this house," Elliott cried out. "Mother is dying and Alice is dying too."

It was true. Mittie's cold had developed into a virulent case of typhoid fever, and only two hours later, early on the morning of February 13, 1884, she died in the same bed where her beloved husband had breathed his last almost exactly six years earlier. She was forty-nine years old.

That same afternoon, Theodore's wife Alice died, too, of a previously unsuspected case of Bright's disease. She was only twenty-two.

The clergyman who presided over their double funeral told the assembled mourners that never in his ministry had he experienced any like occasion. Speaking in a voice faltering with his own emotion, he said it seemed strange and terrible for the young wife to have been taken. Of the other, he said, although she was not yet old, still her work could be regarded as done. Her children had been trained and educated; they had grown up; there were no special burdens lying upon her. So her task could be considered finished.

Alas, that was true, too.

Eliza Ballou Garfield

THE HARDEST ROW

Eliza Ballou Garfield

Nov. 13*th*, 1868
I will now write a brief sketch of my early life for the gratification of
my Children after I am laid in the Grave . . .

AT SIXTY-SEVEN, Eliza Ballou Garfield began thus to set down
her story, and no matter that her son has receded into the company of all but forgotten Presidents, she deserves better than a like
fate. She is the classic example of the poor widow whose solitary
battle against every adversity warms the hearts of the pious—yet
she adds a new dimension to the old platitudes. By the act of taking pen in hand, she contributed something of herself; and since
she was quite a person, she makes mere mythology dim in comparison.

Not surprisingly, her manuscript also has something biblical
about it—it suggests what the Book of Job might be if Ohio in the
nineteenth century were its setting. But in the case of Eliza, although her Lord did bless her later years more than her beginning, the greatest of her trials was saved till she was nearly eighty.

Then she had to endure a testing such as no other Presidential
mother ever faced. Just a few months after her son kissed her at his

inauguration, he was shot by a disgruntled office seeker; to the shame of American democracy, Rose Fitzgerald Kennedy was not spared a similar anguish. But Eliza Garfield's son lingered on the brink of death for eighty days, suffering unspeakably, before finally succumbing. He was forty-nine when he died, and she was within two days of her eightieth birthday. How she summoned the strength to bear that long and terrible vigil must be imagined, for she did not write about it; her venture into autobiography had been undertaken to please James, who no longer could read her words.

Even Eliza's childhood was hard. She was born on September 21, 1801, in Richmond, New Hampshire, not far above the Massachusetts line. An intellectual streak distinguished her father's family—there were distant Ballou relatives who became noted clergymen and educators—but when she was only six, her father died. Although she always kept in mind that she favored the Ballou side (a "French pony breed," the town called them, since they were small, compact, sensitive), Eliza, of necessity, had more exposure to her mother's sturdy Anglo-Saxon perseverance. Left alone in the world with five children, Mehitabel Ballou brought them over to western New York where she had relatives who might give her work. "My Mother was a Weaver," Eliza wrote much later. "She was not ashamed to labor."

So there was little schooling for Eliza, except learning the weaver's trade at a very early age. Her lack of opportunity to study any further must have oppressed her because she had in full measure that passionate regard for education which marks so many Presidential mothers. Somehow, probably from the Bible, she did acquire a more than average proficiency as a writer—her spelling was remarkably good, her punctuation delightfully erratic. She enjoyed sprinkling her letters with exclamation points, upside down, and that is one sign of what may be an unexpected source of her strength. Like Ida Eisenhower, Eliza was born with a sunny disposition.

She loved to sing—hymns, ballads, war songs inspired by the naval battles of the War of 1812. Her memory was prodigious, and her son once said he thought she could sing for forty-eight consecutive hours without repeating the same tune. While she dutifully helped her mother, she was storing up this amazing repertoire. She also found the time for joining other boys and girls at play, which she liked to remember. "I want you to know," she wrote to her children decades afterward, "that I was acquainted with your Father and played with him in Childhood more or less for four years."

These years in New York State, where a New England family by the name of Garfield had become neighbors, went swiftly for Eliza. Immediately after the war, at the urging of her oldest brother, the Ballous moved again, to Ohio. Settling in the vicinity of Zanesville, they were scraping along when a portion of the same Garfield clan arrived to renew old acquaintance. At twenty, Abram Garfield had in all likelihood never read a book through, but he was a fine-looking young man. Eliza never forgot how he appeared:

> Your father was five feet and eleven inches high, large head, broad shoulders and chest, high forehead, brown hair, blue eyes, light complexion, as beautiful a set of teeth as any man ever had. They were just as even as they could be and very white. Cheeks very red, lips tolerably full, but to me very handsome. His hands and feet small for a man of his size. His boots I think were eights, his bearing noble and brave, his bump of benevolence was fully developed, fond of his friends, everybody liked him, his judgment very good, more than common . . .

Before he was twenty-one, and when Eliza was eighteen—"so you see we started early in life to share each other's joys and sorrows" —on February 3, 1820, they were married. Then Eliza left her mother's house to move north with her husband:

> . . . Your father took up a piece of land on the Cuyahoga River, fifteen acres on the bottom and the rest on the hill. The amount of land was forty acres. Your father built a snug log house and in August we moved in . . .

But the tribulations of pioneering farmers were many, and on a site that is now suburban Cleveland, malaria was one of them. Within a month, Eliza was taken with "the Ague," and she "shook two weeks," by which time her complaint had turned into "the bilious fever" and her young husband was sick, too. They were both so weak that they had to abandon their cabin, then move in with relatives who kept them off and on for several years. "We was sick every fall regular," Eliza recalled. But that did not prevent her from bearing a baby every year or two. She had two girls and a boy before their father felt well enough to try making some money. In partnership with several other men, he became a sort of subcontractor, assuming responsibility for constructing portions of various canals. There was good money being made on such projects, and at first it seemed as if Abram Garfield might be in line for a profit.

But prices rose too fast for him and he ended up with hardly enough to buy a farm, somewhat to the east of their first location, on higher and healthier ground. Eliza, who had been helping along by doing some more weaving, had four children when they moved into their new log house. Here it did appear that they had come upon better days. Abram hired twenty acres to be slashed clear, then put in sufficient grain for keeping them all in fair style:

> . . . We lived as well as our neighbors [Eliza wrote]. For breakfast we usually had meat and potatoes, Bread & Butter & Tea sometimes Coffee & frequently pancakes, for dinner boiled Victuals or Baked Beans & baked pudding. For supper we had Tea, Bread & Butter or Biscuit, sometimes apple sauce, peach & Cold boiled Victuals which your Father was fond of . . .

On such a diet it was no wonder that Abram seemed to her able to do as much work in one day as any other man would in two. Eliza also worked hard, but she was content:

> . . . Our family Circle was unbroken. We enjoyed ourselves with our little Children as well as Parents ever did . . .

Then within less than a year the joys of parenthood yielded to sorrow, and Eliza had to add:

> . . . but Death loves a shining mark. It stole silently and suddenly into our Habitation and took from our embrace the pet of our Household, our Darling Jimmy . . .

Jimmy was the first boy she had borne, a plump and affectionate child who crept into her bed one evening to say he felt uneasy, then sank back into her arms and never breathed again. "I was then brought to exclaim, have Pity on me," Eliza wrote, "have

Pity on me, O ye my foe, the Hand of God hath touched me . . ."
She could not be reconciled to the death of her child, she "almost
frowned" on her Maker—until she was led to see her sinful dis-
obedience:

> . . . After awhile a Disciple Preacher by the name of Murdoch
> preached several times, it was the first Gospel sermon we ever
> heard. We were well pleased with the explanation of truth and the
> claims of the Gospel. Very soon Mr. Bently moved there & preached
> in the neighborhood & at his house, we attended Meetings almost
> every Sunday, we knew our duty, but like a great many postponed
> it . . .

Eliza's reason for the postponement must have been the fact
that she was pregnant again. Less than two years after the death of
the first Jimmy, she gave birth to another boy, on November 19,
1831, and she named this son James Abram Garfield for his departed brother as well as for his father, whose own days were
already numbered.

In time, though, Eliza and her husband both stepped forward
to be immersed, thereby becoming members in good standing of
the sect known as the Disciples of Christ. "It then seemed we were
perfectly happy," she wrote. Only a few months afterward, her
husband was taken from her.

Despite his susceptibility to the ague, Abram had appeared to
be almost as strong as an ox—he was famous as a wrestler. But he
pushed his strength too far trying to beat down a spreading fire
and caught a cold so violent that it killed him in two days. He is
said to have jumped from bed just before the end, and to have
gazed solemnly at his wife, saying, "Eliza, I have brought you four
young saplings into these woods. Take care of them."

So Eliza Garfield found herself on the edge of the wilderness,
with four children to care for, the youngest barely eighteen months
old. There were various Garfield and Ballou connections scattered
around Ohio who offered to help her. They told her she was too
frail herself even to think of staying on the farm, that her little
family should be broken up, that if they separated it would be
easier to house them. And since she was only thirty-one, who
knew? It was not beyond possibility that some decent widower
might sooner or later provide the means for reuniting them. But

the blood of fierce protesters, both French and English, coursed through her veins; Eliza instinctively chose independence.

A few days after the funeral, she called her son Thomas, who was not yet eleven, and together they inspected their property. A good stand of wheat was already up, but Abram Garfield had not been able to finish securing the field against roving animals—a pile of logs lay on the ground waiting to be split into fencing. The Widow Garfield and Tom between them completed the fence that day. Soon she sold off more than half her land, keeping just enough to make it possible, with frugality, for them to survive. She helped Tom plow, she taught her girls Mary and Hitty how to card wool clipped from their sheep, she sewed for the village shoemaker's family in return for shoes for her children.

Such invincible determination must feed on some exceptional source of energy, and Eliza discovered the reason for all this in her hopes for her youngest son—hopes which she communicated to the other children so that the whole family worked in order that James might reap advantage from their labor. James right from infancy had made a special impress on his mother:

> . . . James A. was the largest Babe I ever had, he looked like a red Irishman, a very large Head and Shoulders & Body equal to the Head and Shoulders. He was a very good-natured Child. He walked when he was nine Months old. When ten months old he would climb the fence, go up the ladder a dozen times a day. He never was still a minute at a time in his whole life . . .

But she had to admit when the time came for assigning him some chores that although he was quick to learn, he "did not like work the best that ever was." Nevertheless, Eliza made grand plans for him. When he was only three, she had Hitty take him by the hand a mile and a half to the nearest school; and how this mother must have rejoiced to find her faith in his exceptional intellect justified. Within a few months, he was, she always liked to remind him, already reading full sentences out of the Bible. Come Sunday, she would march the whole family three miles through the woods to church services, but the rest of the week, year after year, James was encouraged to keep at his lessons while all the others worked.

The arrangement apparently suited Tom, who took after his father in lacking any particular interest in books and who found sufficient reward in being treated so early as the mainstay of their little farm. And both sisters doted on James almost as fondly as their mother did; even after they married, they kept close ties with him. Yet the time had to come when Eliza's plans for James came up against another will besides her own—that time came when James was ten.

Then a man named Alfred Belding distracted her sufficiently to make her marry him. If this was surprising, the sequel was more so—six years later, she in some way provoked him to the extent that he divorced her. Nothing at all is known about this whole episode except the fact that it occurred; terse court records which go into no detail provide the only evidence of Eliza's brief interval as Mrs. Belding. Her absorption with her son must have had something to do with the failure of the marriage, and James certainly blamed whatever did happen on the mysterious Alfred— thirty years afterward, when James heard about the death of his one-time stepfather, he wrote in his diary that he still could not think of the man "without indignation."

Although this marital adventure, which Eliza herself never mentioned in her own writing, doubtless had a good deal to do with unsettling James during his adolescence, he probably would have revolted anyway. He was a large boy, strong and athletic although clumsy as could be with an ax; and he was too thoroughly good-natured to be quarrelsome, but somehow he had got the notion that other boys who had real fathers had an advantage which they were inclined to hold over him. So at the faintest sign of any slight, he would bristle, till he came to have the reputation of being a "fighting boy." This was a great grief to his mother, but worse was in store. Plowing and chopping wood and the odd jobs even he had to do made him so restless that about the time of her divorce, when he was sixteen, he ran away. He explained why some years later:

> I formed the determination to become a sailor. Nautical novels did it. I had read a large number of them, all I could get in the neighborhood. My mother tried to turn my attention in other directions, but the books were considered bad and from that very fact

were fascinating. I remember especially the "Pirates' Own Book" which became a sort of bible or general authority with me at that period . . .

Since Ohio offered such limited scope for piracy, James chose to sign aboard a canal boat instead, and spent twelve of the most crucial weeks of his life plying from Cleveland to Pittsburgh and back. Excepting perhaps a lumber camp, there was nothing rougher than the milieu in which he found himself, and he thought he was tasting depravity when he picked up some swear words. But being so thoroughly his mother's boy at heart, he could scarcely have been corrupted in so short a time; when he came to brag about his experience, he claimed only that he had been "ready to drink in every species of vice," not that he had actually done the drinking. Still he did get involved in a brawl with a bully almost old enough to be his father—which ended, thanks to his recent practice, with young Jim as the winner.

More significantly, though, he kept toppling overboard. Lacking even the slightest competence at swimming, he had to pray someone would throw him a rope, which did happen fourteen times in the few months he spent on the water. Being fearless but no fool, he eventually concluded that God was giving him a lesson. "I did not believe that God had paid any attention to me on my own account," he explained, "but I thought He had saved me for my mother and for something greater and better than canaling." So home Jim went, just in time to play out a scene dear to the hearts of every lover of melodrama:

> As I approached the door about nine o'clock in the evening, I heard my mother engaged in prayer. During the prayer she referred to me, her son away, God only knew where, and asked that he might be preserved in health to return to her and comfort her in her old age. At the conclusion of the prayer I quietly raised the latch and entered. I will not attempt to describe the scene which followed . . .

What he did for an encore was to fall seriously ill almost immediately, and for five long months Eliza Garfield nursed her boy until he was well again. When the crisis was past, a humbled James took the seventeen dollars his mother and Tom had managed to put aside, then set out to work his way through the seminary in the next town to the eastward. Thenceforth, his rise was not along one straight line, but it was steady.

From preaching, he veered off all the way to Massachusetts to attend Williams College, and then with an eastern degree he had the prestige to be appointed the principal of the Western Reserve Eclectic Institute in Hiram, Ohio; while there, he also studied law, and as soon as he was qualified to practice, he was elected into Ohio's Senate. The outbreak of the Civil War came just as he was considering opening a law office in Cleveland—so instead he mustered up a regiment of former students. He rose like a rocket after that.

It was not remarkable that he received a commission as a lieutenant colonel without the slightest soldiering experience; in the frenzy of getting an army organized, such incidents happened. But he proved to have the makings of a general—and he proved it fast. "Give 'em Hail Columbia, boys!" he hollered as he led his upstanding Ohioans into battle with the rebels. His sense of tactics turned out to be sufficiently acute for him to be promoted to the rank of major general, and he was assigned to serve as chief of staff for the Union forces in Tennessee.

His mother naturally dreaded the thought of his fighting, but she had to approve the high purpose which motivated him; it was she who had taught him to hate slavery. By now James was married to a sweet and steadfast former teacher who might have been Eliza's own daughter, and together the two women trembled for him while he was away. After not much more than a year, though, General Garfield returned to them, blessedly uninjured. Weakened by camp fever, he had been given leave to recuperate at home, and while he was resting, an interesting proposition was put to him. When he was thirty-one, he resigned from the Army to enter Congress.

During his eighteen years there, James Garfield was applauded more for the florid style of his oratory than for its intellectual content, which does not appear to have disturbed his mother. She had every confidence in his greatness, and his goodness needed no demonstration—there never was a more affectionate and devoted son. Although she visited often with her married daughters and with Tom, who had settled on a farm of his own in Michigan, her home was with James and his family. James even humored the whim of an old lady by accompanying her on a pilgrimage back to her birthplace in New Hampshire. "I cannot tell you how strange and touching it was to me to see her go back over the old ground which she left sixty years ago," he wrote to his wife. ". . . She hurried through the rooms of the old house where she was born with a strange mingling of the joyous romping child of eight and the sad gray-haired woman of seventy . . . I choked clear down to the heart and felt how great a joy it was to be able to help her to see the old place and be a girl once more."

Surely her pride in James was too fervid for Eliza Garfield to dwell on the manner of his elevation to the White House. It took thirty-six ballots for the Republican convention in 1880 to unite on him as a compromise candidate, and he defeated another former general—Winfield Scott Hancock—by only a slim margin in the popular vote that November. But such matters would not have been in Eliza's mind the following March when she sat on the flag-draped platform erected over the Capitol's steps watching her son take the oath of office as President of the United States. Although five women before her had lived till they had a son in the same position, she was the first to see the actual ceremony—and just four months later, she became the first who had to hear that her son had been struck down by an assassin.

The horror of the next eighty days survives in the files of that summer's newspapers. From the beginning of July till the middle of September, the United States drifted without a leader while James Garfield struggled desperately to stay alive. The best that medical science could do for him then was no help because infection sapped insatiably at his strength, but day after day false hopes were raised. Whether James Garfield might have made a good President can never be known, yet he certainly made a saintly patient—after a full month of agony, he even summoned the will to lift a pen and scrawl a letter to his mother.

She had left the White House in the spring to visit in Ohio, and it was there that she stayed during the whole ordeal. Perhaps they told her James preferred having her spared any needless shock, for right from the day of his injury he looked dreadful; within a few weeks, he lost more than a hundred pounds. But he wrote to her:

Dear Mother,

Don't be disturbed by conflicting reports about my condition. It is true I am still weak and on my back, but I am gaining every day and need only time and patience to bring me through. Give my love to all the relatives and friends and especially to sisters Hitty and Mary.

Your loving son,
James A. Garfield

When doctors could not ease his suffering, railroad men tried a spectacular feat. Washington in the heat of summer was undeniably aggravating the President's weakness, and yet it would be extremely dangerous and painful to move him; and so special railroad tracks were laid from the White House to Union Station, and from the depot in the New Jersey shore resort of Elberon right up to the door of a suitable cottage. Eliza's son survived being moved only to die by the sea two weeks later. Then she told a reporter that she prayed she might join him soon, but her prayer was not granted until January 21, 1888, when she died in Ohio at the age of eighty-six.

Nancy Hanks Lincoln   (PICTORIAL PARADE)

10

THROUGH NATURE'S
BACK DOOR

Nancy Hanks Lincoln

H<small>ER</small> <small>LOG CABIN</small> stood near a spring of icy water that came trickling out of a cave—most authorities agree on this. Two and a half miles south of the Kentucky village of Hodgenville, such a spring still drips from the same rocks; and so reverent tourists can gaze on the site of Abraham Lincoln's birth with some confidence, although not as much can be said for the particular cabin which has been enshrined inside a marble temple atop four tiers of marble stairs. Even less can be said for the legend enveloping the person of Lincoln's mother.

Her name was Nancy Hanks and she died when her son was nine years old; almost nothing else about her has the ring of positive fact. She may have been saintly—and a lot of good people have tried to give her a halo. On the other hand, there was a Nancy Hanks living around her time in her area who had the reputation of being a lewd woman. In either case, and the circumstance has, of course, only an indirect bearing on her character, she was probably illegitimate.

But her son probably was not. As the result of an extraordinary amount of painstaking inquiry by a scholarly parson and various pious scholars, it has been all but established that Honest Abe entered this world respectably—which he himself could never have proved. No written record certifying the marriage of his parents turned up till after his assassination, when an old settler provided the clue that led to the discovery of an itinerant preacher's personal ledger. A man in an excellent position to gain his trust thought the melancholy which marked the sixteenth President of the United States throughout his maturity stemmed from his belief in his mother's and his own bastardy.

That man was Billy Herndon, Lincoln's law partner before he moved into the White House. With only the best intentions, Billy Herndon raised a number of questions about Nancy Hanks Lincoln during the years immediately following her son's martyrdom —and these provoked one of the longest controversies in American history. For the most part, the story of Lincoln's mother is the story of prodigious efforts—both solemn and comic—to test the accuracy of Herndon's reporting.

Aside from his contribution, the sum total of reliable data about her life seems incredibly meager in the light of more recent publicizing practices. For campaign biography purposes, Lincoln prepared only one paragraph describing his ancestry:

> I was born February 12, 1809, in Hardin County, Kentucky. My parents were both born in Virginia, of undistinguished families— second families, perhaps I should say. My mother, who died in my tenth year, was of a family of the name of Hanks . . .

And that was about all the world knew until Herndon stirred up his hornet's nest. He did so out of love, not malice—when a covey of would-be Parson Weemses began hurrying to the printer with biographies of Lincoln portraying his hero as an insipid moralizer, he was infuriated. "Good heavens!" he exploded. "Shut out all light, freeze up all human sympathy from *this sacred man!* Never, no never."

Even before these other books started appearing, Herndon had conceived the plan of giving his dear friend a better memorial. At his own expense, he retraced Lincoln's early years, seeking firsthand recollections; to supplement what he remembered of Abe Lincoln in Illinois, he wrote hundreds of letters. But he had his living to earn, and it took him quite awhile to arrange for someone to help him boil his material down into a book. In the interim, by giving lectures and by sharing his findings with various people who appealed to him for information, he brought up the subject of Lincoln's mother.

As Herndon recalled, it had been 1851 or thereabouts when he and Mr. Lincoln had a bastardy case to argue, over at the circuit court in Petersburg, Menard County, State of Illinois. Mr. Lincoln, who would have been forty-two or -three at the time, appeared notably gloomy driving out of Springfield, which his young partner put down to his being occupied with trying the case in his mind. Then some three miles along the way, just where a swollen creek came lapping right onto the road under the wheels of their buggy, Mr. Lincoln all at once spoke up:

"Billy, I'll tell you something, but keep it a secret while I live . . ."

Herndon kept the secret until the unctuous process of sanctifying the nation's slain leader disgusted him; even such harmless vulgarisms as Lincoln's habit of saying "gal" for "girl" were being edited out of anecdotes. Then Herndon felt compelled to step forward and say Mr. Lincoln had confided that his own maternal grandmother, being poor and credulous in her Virginia girlhood, had been shamefully taken advantage of by a rich planter. Thus his mother had arrived on this earth through nature's back door.

It had struck Herndon originally, and he never changed his mind on this point, that Lincoln was moved to talk as he did because their impending court case required a discussion on hereditary qualities of temperament and so on. He said that Lincoln had gone on to remark that his own mother had inherited much from her unknown father, and that he himself had inherited in the same degree from her. The poignancy of a familiar quotation becomes genuine when it is quoted in its full context—according to Herndon, what Lincoln said next was: "All that I am or hope ever to be I get from my mother, God bless her. Did you never notice that bastards are generally smarter, shrewder, and more intellectual than others? Is it because it is stolen?"

Friends tried hard to dissuade Herndon from making any such confidences public, but he would not heed them. ". . . What makes Europe and America love Christ?" he demanded. "It is our sympathy that is at the root; and *shall I* strip Abraham of his crown and cross? It is criminal to do so. . . . What's the cause of his sadness, his gloom, his *sometimes* terrible nature? What made him so tender, so good, so honest, so just, so noble, so pure, so exalted, so liberal, so tolerant, so divine, as it were? It was the fiery furnace through which God rolled him, and yet the world must not know it, eh!"

Herndon's vehemence owed more than a little to his researches in Kentucky, for on the basis of what he heard from there he was tempted to accept the conclusion that Nancy Lincoln had done as her mother did. He certainly found quite a gamey collection of local gossip: that Nancy had favored one Abraham Enloe, who bragged often of having fathered her boy; that Tom Lincoln, discovering this Enloe with his wife, had jumped on the intruder and bit off his nose; that Tom Lincoln, before leaving Kentucky for Indiana and maybe much earlier, had been, as Herndon put it, "castrated, fixed, cut." There was more on the same order, all implying that even if Abe Lincoln had been born to a properly married woman, her husband had no part in the matter. Yet the charge could not be proved, and Herndon did not publish it; in the end, he summoned up the charity to give Nancy the benefit of every doubt.

Still the damage had been done. What he said publicly about her own paternity—plus such other startling episodes as Lincoln's fit of near madness after Ann Rutledge died, and his running off the first time his marriage to Mary Todd was scheduled—caused the forces of American nice-nellyism to mobilize. An atrocity had been committed, the *Chicago Tribune* trumpeted; at the very least, it was a crime against human decency. Herndon himself was vilified as a notorious drinker, which had been approximately the case at one time, and as a bitter office seeker who begrudged his former partner the glory he could never approach. That was certainly not true, as any reader of Herndon's letters can discover; Billy Herndon worshiped Lincoln.

In the long run, he did win the campaign that mattered most to him. Because he spread what he knew about Lincoln, and some-times what he only thought he knew, no Parson Weems has ever been able to replace the flawed human who became the Great Emancipator with a lifeless statue. Every book which so much as mentions the pre-Presidential Lincoln in more than passing refer-ence owes some debt to Herndon, for without him the earlier years would be practically blank. Not only the material he gathered, but also the frenzy of aggrieved inquiry he inspired can with some justice be included in the same category. Without Herndon, it is surely doubtful whether so much energy would have been spent in investigating the legitimacy and the chastity of Abraham Lin-coln's mother.

No matter that Herndon and his collaborator decided to leave out on the latter topic, there was extensive private correspondence about it which would not have stayed secret; and rumors based on the same gossip Herndon had gathered must have circulated on their own, particularly in the South. But lacking the opportunity presented by the open publication of his other revelations, the chances are that nothing much would have been made of this deli-cate question. As it was, scurrilous pamphlets with such titles as "The Sorrows of Nancy" began appearing in many parts of the country.

And then a lady named Mrs. Caroline Hanks Hitchcock stepped in where scholars still feared to tread. Having been born a Hanks, she was consumed by a strong passion to rehabilitate the good name of a possible connection, and when in the course of various genealogical explorations she came across a Nancy Hanks born in Virginia to lawfully wed parents at approximately the right period, she cried Eureka! The convolutions of her reasoning in the little book she published in 1899, purporting to prove that this Nancy was the Nancy who became the mother of Lincoln, need not be gone into in any detail; in brief, her Nancy was one generation too old, and probably an aunt of *the* Nancy. "The two surprising things about this slender book," said the bearded parson who became Mrs. Hitchcock's nemesis, "are, first, that so much misin-formation could have been contained in so small a volume, and, secondly, that so many usually discriminating people could have been deceived by it."

William Eleazor Barton, this patriarchal-looking pastor whose enthusiasm for Lincoln had led him on horseback up and down every hilly path his hero could have trod, undertook to settle the whole legitimacy issue once and for all. What he arrived at has not quite done so—the irate Mrs. Hitchcock tried to get her own pastor to sponsor a bonfire for burning every copy of the book Barton wrote, and Hitchcockians are still to be found; they probably never will surrender. But historians have generally accepted his conclusions.

These are that the mother of Nancy Hanks did stray, and so Herndon's account of his conversation with Lincoln can be trusted; but that if Lincoln brooded about the circumstances of his own birth, he did so needlessly. By the time Barton began his systematic search of courthouse records, there were more alleged fathers of Abraham Lincoln than just the short-nosed Enloe. "The woods are full of them," Barton wrote to a friend. But he was nothing if not methodical, and he traced down the contenders, one by one, till he had shown the patent impossibility of every claim except Tom Lincoln's. Carl Sandburg, who was then engaged in gathering material for his monumental biography of Lincoln, wrote admiringly to Barton that he had the feeling he was watching a champion bowler. "You set 'em up and knock 'em down with a short-arm, sure-shooting logic," he added.

Once this issue had been disposed of, Barton and others put their talents to constructing a more distinct framework for Lincoln's childhood than the simple setting of frontier hardship which had had to serve in the past. That turned out to be all but impossibly difficult, for neither the Hankses nor the Lincolns left any clear traces; they are the despair of the document-seeking school of biographer. Sandburg, with his gift for drawing lyric pictures from imagining a slender girl crooning in the moist evening twilight beside a cabin of logs, succeeded better than anyone else in breathing some life into the few poor scraps of information uncovered about the woman who became Nancy Lincoln.

It appears that for some five generations there were Hankses settled in Virginia, not very far from the fertile ground that produced George Washington and James Madison, James Monroe and Robert E. Lee. But being among the "second families," as Lincoln put it, the Hanks men filed hardly a land claim or a last will and testament, let alone won election to any public office; there do not even seem to have been many who served in the militia or saved family Bibles. Thus the tracing of relationships defies any rational genealogist.

But enough has been discovered to focus on a Joseph Hanks who had five sons and four daughters, the oldest being a daughter Lucy. During the years immediately following the American Revolution, just as after any war, some loosening of moral standards occurred, and perhaps this led Lucy down the primrose path. Who accompanied her nobody knows—he had his opportunity to accept the responsibility for his dalliance and failed to take it, as Brother Barton briskly commented, so even were the man's identity uncovered, it would serve him right to deny him any posthumous reward.

Despite the inferior status of the Hankses, it seems that Joseph felt the disgrace to his daughter deeply. From census records and land deeds, there is evidence that he moved to the western reaches of Virginia—to what is now West Virginia—just about the time Lucy's baby was born; it has been accepted that this occurred in 1784. Then only a year or so later, he sold the new farm at a loss and moved further—to Kentucky. Again, nobody can be certain, but it also seems that the infant Nancy lived the first twelve or thirteen years of her life under the log roof of her grandparents— who, it has to be supposed, did not fail to remind her of the stigma she bore. If she grew into a moody young woman, as some accounts suggest, who can wonder at this?

Her mother did not even stay by her side. During this period, at a town some distance from the Hanks farm, a Lucy Hanks was charged with fornication, but her case never came up for trial. One Henry Sparrow apparently had faith in her redeemability and he married her, forestalling the wrath of justice; as far as can be told, she made him a decent, God-fearing wife and gave him nine children. Yet his beneficence did not extend to keeping a living reminder of her youthful folly among his own children, so little Nancy remained with her grandparents.

Then when her grandfather died, and her grandmother expressed the wish of going back to her old familiar ground in Virginia for her last years on earth, the household was broken up; but if Nancy went to her mother, it was only briefly. One of Lucy's sisters, who also married a Sparrow, took her in, and, it has even been said, saw that she learned to read the Bible, although she never learned to write as much as her name. She did receive training as a seamstress, though, in order that she would be able to earn her own keep.

So she was probably sewing for a few weeks in the home of a a family named Berry when a young carpenter she may or may not have known from her younger days came into the settlement where she found herself. Because this was in another county from the area where she and he both had lived, nobody thought for years to look through marriage records there. Had it been done sooner, there would have been no doubt that on June 10, 1806, Nancy Hanks was lawfully wed to Thomas Lincoln.

He was black-haired and sturdy, with a history in general on the same order as her own. Neither of them could remember any shelter besides mud-chinked cabins, neither had seen beyond forest-rimmed farms and straggly little frontier villages, neither had any education to speak of. Somehow the impression that he was shiftless, but she was strong, has come to prevail; perhaps this was so, but comparatively recent findings of tax rolls and the like indicate he had some ambition, at least in his younger days. Whatever he did have he lost—before his death some forty years later, he slipped downhill to the extent that where once he had laboriously blockprinted his signature on official documents, he later became content with merely marking an X.

Nevertheless, in the nature of things he and Nancy must have cherished some hopes when they set up housekeeping together in the Kentucky village of Elizabethtown. Here Tom worked as a carpenter, and here eight months to the day after their marriage Nancy gave birth to a girl they named Sarah. But carpentry in a place where every man had to be able to use an ax, let alone a saw, must have been so unprofitable that he was soon looking for a farm.

Tom had bad luck, that much is certain. For the place he picked, though it had more than two hundred acres, proved mostly poor soil not worth trying to till, and in the bargain the title to it was unsound. The only attraction it had was a spring trickling out of rocks to drop and disappear into a sort of sinkhole. From this, it came to be known as the Sinking Spring. Because Nancy gave birth to Abraham Lincoln near this landmark, many thousands of Americans come every summer to stare at it; and because the trickling water has, as the National Park Service explains, become vulnerable to small boys, there is a warning sign: UNSAFE FOR DRINKING.

But it was probably pure when Abe Lincoln was born. The spring was one of the few conveniences his mother ever had. Till Abe was big enough to go fetch water for her, she had to do it herself and she never had an easier time than on this first farm. When her son was only about two years old, the family moved to another farm that had the advantage of better soil and a cabin facing right on the Cumberland Trail with its rumbling wagons and droves of livestock to break the solitude; but water had to be carried a further distance. Here Nancy bore and lost a second son, named Thomas for his father.

Then once more trouble over a clear title developed, and it would take more money than Tom Lincoln could muster to gain unchallenged possession. Over in Indiana, land was supposed to be easier to come by, so they picked up and moved another time, northwestward toward the Ohio River. It is likely that little Sarah, who was about ten, rode back of her mother on one horse, while Abe, who was around eight, sat back of his father. After crossing the river on a makeshift ferry, they pushed on through the heavy forest to the spot Tom had chosen on a solitary scouting trip. He had dug out the side of a hill to provide the most primitive sort of shelter, and this was all they had till he could get a cabin built.

Nancy Lincoln was not fated to move any further than that cabin. The very next summer her aunt and uncle who had kept her during her growing up came to join her, and the Sparrows brought along a few milk cows. New settlements in this part of the country were leery of cows, and with reason. Until the woods could be well cleared, foraging animals were tempted by a tall and succulent weed which very soon set a cow to trembling peculiarly. Anybody who drank the milk of such an afflicted cow turned sick and almost always died within a few days. This was no supersti-

tion; every wilderness family had seen it happen. And it happened to the Lincolns.

First both Sparrow relatives sickened, and Nancy nursed them.
But one and then the other died from the dreaded "milk-sick,"
which sometimes spread through a whole community. Other new
neighbors followed the Sparrows, and so did Nancy. On the fifth
of October in 1818, when she was about thirty-five, her husband
and her son nailed together the boards of a coffin for her.

No stone marked her grave, and when Billy Herndon came
searching for it in 1865 while still under the emotional shock of
her son's funeral, he had to find an eighty-two-year-old lady to
show him where to look. In his own notes on his trip, he wrote:
"There is no fence around the grave, no palings, enclosures, of
any kind, no headboard, no footboard, to mark the spot where
Abraham Lincoln's mother lies; curious and unaccountable, is it
not? All is dense forest, wild and grand."

The omission has since been remedied, but not grandiosely. A
decade later, a private citizen from South Bend caused a simple
stone to be set on the spot described by Herndon, inscribed:

> NANCY HANKS
> LINCOLN
> Mother of President
> LINCOLN
> DIED
> Oct. 5, A.D. 1818
> Aged 35 Years
> Erected by a friend of her martyred son 1879

Then in time, a park was created of the land that comprised the
Lincoln farm near the Indiana town of Gentryville, and some
attempt made to do homage to the woman who lived there so
briefly. On a rock at the base of the slope where her grave has
been presumed to be, visitors are informed: "You are facing the
wooded knoll on which sleeps Nancy Hanks Lincoln, mother of
the President who lived in this Hoosier environment during the
formative years of his life from 1816 to 1830. Beyond, to the north,
is marked the site of the humble log cabin where she led him for
a little while along the path to greatness." And that is all.

For there is really very little more that can be said. Was she tall or was she short? There are statements from those few who remembered her testifying either way. Was she cheerful or morose? Again, there is no decisive answer; she remains faceless, only a vague presence. Not unexpectedly, because of the aura that already surrounded her son by the time the statements were put down on paper, several of her old neighbors agreed that she was intelligent, deeply religious, and affectionate.

Yet no further evidence of what she provided, before a fortunately kindly stepmother supplanted her, was offered even by Abraham Lincoln. There are those who say his own glory would surely have dimmed had he not been cut down at a moment of triumph—and perhaps, like her son, Nancy Lincoln has acquired more honor by dying as she did than she could have won had she lived longer. How such a man as her son springs up, even in the most promising of environments, can, of course, never be explained. So the case must rest, after all, on his moving words to Billy Herndon: "All that I am or hope ever to be I get from my mother, God bless her."

Abigail Smith Adams

DEAREST ABBY
Abigail Smith Adams

It could not happen again. The march of progress has positively eliminated the possibility that such a light could be allowed to remain hidden. Were she to be reborn, Abigail Adams at the very least would make a lot of money by writing a daily newspaper column—not necessarily of advice to the confused, although she could do that splendidly. More likely, she would end up right back in the White House.

Even on her own she might get there, but if the United States ever has a female President, the chances are that she will arrive by the indirect route which would have suited Abigail best. Far from being unwomanly, she always put her husband's interests first, the way any good wife should; yet her interests were as political as his, which made her an ideal helpmate. So—to start with—were several of the widows who in the past half a century have managed to win elections beyond the ordinary feminine aspiration. Assuming that the reincarnated Abigail survived her spouse, she would be hard to beat.

Under the limiting conditions that prevailed during the early days of the republic, the original Abigail still did better than any other of her sex—without fanfare. Not till twenty-two years after

her death, when her grandson Charles Francis Adams apologet-
ically published a small volume of her letters, was the general
public let into the secret. That first edition sold out inside of two
months, and in one guise or another she has been diverting readers
ever since.

The trepidation felt by her grandson need not be imagined;
being an Adams in good standing, he was nothing if not articulate
and he expressed his misgivings plainly. "The present is believed
to be the first attempt, in the United States, to lay before the
public a series of letters, written without the remotest idea of
publication, by a woman to her husband, and others of her nearest
and dearest relations . . ." But one must beg to differ on the matter
of the remoteness of his grandmother's ideas concerning the publication of her letters. She and her husband both had a strong sense
of their duty to posterity, and just five days before he stood up to
make an impassioned plea for adoption of the Declaration of Independence, John Adams had written to Abigail informing her that
he had a new blank book in which he proposed keeping copies of
every letter he penned. He strongly urged that she do the same,
". . . for I really think that your Letters are much better worth
preserving than mine."

Charles Francis must have agreed, although uneasily, because
he chose to issue a selection of her letters before doing a similar
service on behalf of his grandfather. Yet he felt hesitant—with
sounder reason—at the thought that some readers might be
tempted toward a dangerous conclusion. "There were many persons, in the lifetime of the parties," he wrote carefully, "who
ascribed to Mrs. Adams a degree of influence over the public
conduct of her husband, far greater than there was any foundation
in truth. Perhaps it is giving more than its due importance to this
idea to take any notice of it at all in this place . . ." And then he
proceeded to notice it, meanwhile doing all he could in good conscience to demolish it, for the length of several long paragraphs.

He might have saved himself the trouble. The tactless, temper-
ish, and stubborn man Miss Abigail Smith had married also by
the grace of an inscrutable Providence possessed exactly the talents
urgently needed in Philadelphia after 1774. To say that anyone
softened his abrasive manner is to ignore the record left by other

contemporaries; the pity is that even Abigail was unable to influence him a little more. Then he might have made a more successful President.

But certainly she was the source of his strength, the inspiration that gave him the power to rise above his own weaknesses as often as he did. For theirs was, first and last, a love story—which has not escaped the attention of the true romances type of historian. It is piquant to discover that the only woman ever to wed one prospective President, and then become the mother of another, had a thoroughly timeless view of the female role. Yet Abigail Adams cannot be dismissed as merely the supporting domestic presence in the background of a Founding Father.

She had something close to genius, and her letters prove it. Whatever she embarked on, throughout her life, she accomplished with a sure knowledge of her own identity. Not for her the vaporous doubts as to the part she ought to play, which even in her time could dispose intelligent females toward some form of hysteria; and because she was so very intelligent, she stamped her personality wholesale, as it were, working her special alchemy on all she surveyed. At nineteen, she already had the wit to write to her betrothed:

> My Friend,
>
> I think I write to you every day. Shall I not make my letters very cheap? Don't you light your pipe with them? I care not if you do. 'Tis a pleasure to me to write. Yet I wonder I write to you with so little restraint, for as a critic I fear you more than any other person on earth, and 'tis the only character in which I ever did or ever will fear you. What say you? Do you approve of that speech? Don't you think me a courageous being? Courage is a laudable, a glorious virtue in your sex, why not in mine? For my part, I think you ought to applaud me for mine.
>
> *Exit* Rattle

Then on she went for another few pages of more solemn dissertation, until she ended sedately: "Adieu;—evermore remember me with the tenderest affection, which is also borne unto you by your A. Smith." Assuredly, here was no common garden variety of Puritan daughter, but upwards of a century of Puritan orthodoxy had produced her, with respected secular as well as religious figures along the way. Her mother's father was the Colonel John Quincy who had held an assortment of important posts in the colonial government; and her own father was the Reverend William Smith, minister of the Congregational Church at Weymouth, Massachusetts, for over forty years. Abigail was born into this worthy family on November 11, 1744.

It is a mistake to suppose that in the theocracy of young New England, the finer points of worldly status were overlooked. On the contrary, John Adams, whose father and grandfather and great grandfather had been farmers, was listed fourteenth in his class of twenty-five at Harvard—and he almost certainly would have been lower had his mother not been born a Boylston; for the students were ranked, not by their academic standing, but by their social position. Although Abigail's only brother did not even go to Harvard—he seems to have been quite an insignificant young man —if he had enrolled, he surely would have placed higher. To Abigail's mother, such considerations mattered.

Fortunately, that lady had comparatively little to do with her daughter's training. She already had one girl on whom to practice her maternal instruction, and another came after Abigail; so the future Mrs. Adams was allowed to spend months at a time with her Grandmother Quincy. Being deemed a sickly child, she did not have a day of formal schooling in her life, and yet she learned far more than was normally considered necessary or suitable for young ladies. Grandmother Quincy not only let her read Swift as well as Shakespeare—across the gap of two generations, these two carried on sprightly literary discussions.

Quite naturally then, Abigail grew into a girl old for her years, quaintly serious on the outside and a storehouse of pent-up emotions within. She was seventeen when John Adams first came calling, but already the signs of her superiority must have been clearly visible. Although he was nine years her senior, he never would be notably perceptive about any personal qualities other than his own, and even he saw that an exceptional prize might be within his grasp. She saw beneath his surface bluntness much more easily. From intellectual rapport, love bloomed swiftly.

But Abigail's mother took long months of persuading before she would agree to this match, and the wedding did not take place

till October 25, 1764, just a few weeks short of the bride's twentieth birthday. In his own sly way, Abigail's father demonstrated
whose side he had been on by his choice of the text for his sermon
—it was from Luke 7:33, and everybody knew what he meant
when he intoned: "For John came neither eating bread nor drinking wine, and ye say, *He hath a devil.*"

The subsequent life of Abigail Adams divides almost with the
neatness of a scenario into separate periods. For the first ten years,
her routine was domestic in the extreme. She gave birth to five
children, four of whom would survive to adulthood, and, whether
in the country, or later in Boston, occupied herself with seeing to
their welfare and their father's. There were ups and downs, depending in the main on John's volatile temper, but by and large
the tenor of these days brings to mind the Shakespearean observa-
tion on greatness: was Abigail born with it, or did she achieve it,
or did she have it thrust upon her? Were it not for the outbreak
of the American Revolution, she and John would have lacked the
great stage on which they acted so capably—but has an era ever
failed to provide some sort of a setting for heroes and heroines? It
does not really seem accidental that Abigail married a man with
John's desperate thirst for fame; modest as she truly was, she knew
her own worth too well.

So even if she wrote hardly a letter for a full decade, excepting
perfunctory notes when John was away briefly on legal business,
these were surely years of preparation. While she nursed her
babies, she could bide her time. John's impatience to be at the
summit of Boston's leadership, which at least in the eyes of Bos-
tonians would long remain the highest ambition a reasonable man
ought to entertain, ensured that sooner or later wider opportunity
would open to her. With the imposition of the misguided Town-
shend's tax on tea, her chance came rather sooner than it might
have. When she was thirty, her real career started.

It may be objected that Abigail Adams did not accompany her
husband to Philadelphia when he rode off to the First and then
the Second Continental Congress, that she stayed by her own
hearth as she would always profess she preferred to do. But self-
effacement was not within her power. Besides mothering, she made
politics her business, and the Boston of her day afforded only

slightly less scope than Philadelphia for practicing that fine art. No sooner had General Washington arrived to take up command of the city's defenses than Mrs. Adams was welcoming him—and her aptitude for diplomacy is reflected in the report she immediately wrote to her husband:

> . . . I was struck with General Washington. You had prepared me to entertain a favorable opinion of him, but I thought the half was not told me. . . . Those lines of Dryden instantly occurred to me:
>
> > "Mark his majestic fabric! he's a temple
> > Sacred by birth, and built by hands divine;
> > His soul's The deity that lodges there;
> > Nor is the pile unworthy of the God!"
>
> . . . As to Burgoyne, I am not a master of language sufficient to give you a true idea of the horrible wickedness of the man . . .

But beyond making friends for her dearest friend, Abigail also relayed to him a stream of news—about prices and taxes, about the temper of the city and its health problems. When she could not go in person to find out what she wished to know, she sent messengers, but during the terrible week in March of 1776 which shook Boston with the bombardment of battle, she managed to provide a running account based on her own observations: ". . . I have just returned from Penn's Hill, where I have been sitting to hear the amazing roar of cannon, and from whence I could see every shell which was thrown . . ."

Only for a few brief weeks during this ten-year period did Abigail have the boon of her beloved's companionship. For the latter part of it, when John Adams went abroad in his country's service, she lacked even the comfort of occasional hasty visits from him, and the sacrifice was not easy, as she showed when she gave vent to her feelings:

> Dearest of friends,
>   My habitation, how desolate it looks! my table, I sit down to it, but cannot swallow my food! O, why was I born with so much sensibility, and why possessing it, have I so often been called to struggle with it? I wish to see you again . . .

Nevertheless, the Puritan in her rejoiced at having found a

fitting cause to call forth self-abnegation on a grand scale. She could not but take herself seriously, and she solemnly wrote to John in Europe:

"If you had known," said a person to me the other day, "that Mr. Adams would have remained so long abroad, would you have consented that he should have gone?" I recollected myself a moment, and then spoke the real dictates of my heart. "If I had known, Sir, that Mr. Adams could have effected what he has done, I would not only have submitted to the absence I have endured, painful as it has been, but I would not have opposed it, even though three years more should be added to the number (which Heaven avert!) I feel a pleasure in being able to sacrifice my selfish passions to the general good, and in imitating the example, which has taught me to consider myself and family but as the small dust of the balance, when compared with the great community . . .

It was this tone, virtually unrelieved by flashes of gaiety, which prevailed in another correspondence Mrs. Adams entered upon during the same period—to her son. Her first child was a girl, named Abigail and always called Nabby, who grew into as kitten-ish a creature as might be expected under the circumstances. Both parents concentrated their perfectionist zeal on their first son, John Quincy, born on July 11, 1767. Thus he was not eleven yet when he began his travels, accompanying his father to Paris.

"Let me enjoin it upon you to attend constantly and steadfastly to the precepts and instructions of your father," his mother wrote to him, but she could not forbear adding page after page of her own preaching on the necessity of keeping a strict guard against the monster of vice rampant in foreign societies, despite their having certain undeniable cultural advantages. Along with such strictures came inspirational lectures—"These are times in which a genius would wish to live," she assured him, and she left no doubt that she would be disappointed if a son of hers privileged to watch great events from such close range failed to develop accordingly. Although genius still eluded John Quincy, he certainly repaid all the effort spent on his education with a high order of conscientious public service when his own turn came; that no more strictly self-righteous man ever dwelt in the White House is, however, hardly surprising.

Of her other two sons Mrs. Adams demanded less, but even so her disappointment was greater. Neither Charles nor Thomas could feel comfortable in the elevated moral climate that exhilarated the rest of their family, and Charles thrived so poorly as to die of alcoholism at the age of thirty. That unhappy day was still far in the future, though, when his mother energetically supervised his childhood schooling during the absence of her husband.

She also supervised the family's material wealth with more lasting success. From his father, John had inherited some land and a small house in the part of Braintree later known as Quincy in tribute to her own relatives. This property was less than impressive, and it could easily have gone further downhill in the decade that it lacked a master, but instead its mistress proved extraordinarily competent at running a farm. As her grandson delicately put it: "It is not giving [her] too much credit to affirm that by her prudence through the years of the Revolution and indeed during the whole period when the attention of her husband was engrossed in public affairs, she saved him from the mortification in his last days, which some of those who have been, like him, elected to the highest situations in the country have, for want of such care, not altogether escaped."

She looked after her husband's interests in other ways, too. No occurrence affecting him was unimportant enough to evade her notice—or her action, if she felt such to be merited. When the American Philosophical Society in Philadelphia saw fit to elect John Adams and John Jay into its select ranks, she was gratified by the tribute but not entirely so. For the announcement of the action referred to *Mr.* John Adams and to *The Honorable* John Jay. Mrs. Adams promptly addressed four closely written pages to the society's secretary, pointing out in some detail that her husband had served in the Congress just as long as the other gentleman, and had also been appointed to represent their country abroad at the same time. Since he was not present to lose his own temper over the slight, she did it for him.

After ten years of solitary responsibility, Mrs. Adams entered into the grandest phase of her career. At forty, she tearfully took her leave of relatives and neighbors, the parting from her husband's aged mother being painful in the extreme. As soon as the good old lady beheld her daughter-in-law in traveling garb, a fit of weeping seized her and she cried out: "Why did you not tell me you was going so soon? Fatal Day! I take my last leave; I shall never see you again. Carry my last blessing to my son." So reported the younger Mrs. Adams at the start of the remarkable diary she kept of her voyage from Boston to London in the summer of 1784. Because her husband had been prevailed upon to remain abroad even beyond the signing of the peace treaty ending the Revolution, she was finally joining him.

Her diary removes any possible uncertainty concerning the valor of all those who dared the Atlantic before the days of steam —even a summer crossing, lasting just one month, was almost unmitigated torture. No sooner had their vessel passed the harbor light outside Boston, according to Mrs. Adams's account, than the captain sent word to his passengers "to put on their Sea Cloaths and prepare for sickness. We had only time to follow his directions before we found ourselves all sick."

But this diary is interesting on other grounds besides its graphic detail about a thankfully departed mode of transportation. Ostensibly, it was written to provide the older sister of Mrs. Adams—the Sister Mary Cranch to whom she addressed many of her communications from Europe—with a running account of her adventures. Quite probably, Mrs. Adams enjoyed a Braintree celebrity as an excellent correspondent, and she may have expected that her letters to her sister would be passed from hand to hand. But surely she had an even larger audience in mind when she repeatedly penned such phrases as "You who have never tried the Sea can form no idea . . ." or, "To those who have never been at Sea . . ." At various times it was suggested to her that she ought to publish some of her letters and she always demurred vigorously. "A pretty figure I should make," she said in one such case. "No. No. I have not any ambition to appear in print. Heedless and inaccurate as I am, I have too much Vanity to risk my reputation before the public." Nevertheless, one must conclude that she had something quite like her grandson's project at the back of her mind as she composed during her European period—and would that not have made her one of the canniest writers who ever lived? At no personal inconvenience, she could still anticipate posterity's acclaim; what could be more pleasant?

But in Europe she acquired a notable contemporary admirer. Whatever Paris and London may have thought of Mrs. Abigail Adams of Massachusetts, Thomas Jefferson of Virginia was charmed. While he was representing the United States in one of these capitals, John Adams held the same rank in the other—and a three-way correspondence that must be one of the most appealing in diplomatic annals anywhere resulted. Having just returned to London after a stay in Paris, Mrs. Adams writes to Mr. Jefferson—". . . nobody ever leaves Paris but with a degree of tristeness." And then after some sharp comment on what the London newspapers have to say about Mr. Adams as an ambassador, she gets down to some business of her own. Would Mr. Jefferson be so good as to order a set of decorative figurines for her dining table? In teasing reply, Mr. Jefferson tells her he has secured not only Minerva, Diana, and Apollo as she requested, but also Mars which ought to grace any patriotic table after their nation's recent victory; and could he now trouble her to investigate the London price of two sets of tablecloths and napkins for twenty covers? Enclosing specimens of what is being offered in Paris, he puts himself at her judgment as to whether London can provide better and cheaper.

Soon she is ordering shirts for him in London, and he shoes for her in Paris; the computations on who owes whom how much become vastly complicated. Then when a young American gentleman secures the heart of her daughter, and a marriage results, Mrs. Adams proposes another sort of trade to Mr. Jefferson—the exchange of one of her sons for his daughter. "I am for strengthening the federal union," she explains. To which Jefferson is compelled to reply: "This proposition about the exchange of a son for my daughter puzzles me. I should be very glad to have your son, but I cannot part with my daughter."

For in close personal matters, Mr. Jefferson permitted no bantering or even well-intentioned interference, as Mrs. Adams discovered to her real dismay. The episode came about because the widowed Jefferson had another daughter, Polly, whom he had thought too young for him to bring abroad with him. But when she reached the age of eight, he determined on removing her from the relatives who had been keeping her; and he thought it suitable to have the child placed under the general care of a ship's captain bound for England. Then he wrote to Mrs. Adams: "I have taken the liberty to tell them that you will be so good as to take her under your wing till I can have notice to send for her."

Abigail Adams was appalled when Polly was delivered to her, for the child appeared utterly distracted by having been plucked away from every familiar surrounding. The mother in Mrs. Adams trembled to see how Polly clung to the ship captain, who was now the only remaining link with her past. But Mrs. Adams proved equal to the challenge, and a day later she could write to Jefferson: "Miss is as contented today as she was miserable yesterday." As was only to be expected, though, the arrival of a strange servant from Paris, commissioned to tear the child away from her new friend, set off another round of wailing. Mrs. Adams hastily wrote to Jefferson: "I have not the Heart to force her into a Carriage against her will and send her from me almost in a Frenzy."

But Jefferson replied that his plans were not subject to change, so Polly had to leave against her will, and Mrs. Adams wrote impulsively: "I never felt so attached to a child in my life on such short acquaintance. 'Tis rare to find one possessed of so strong and lively a sensibility. I hope she will not lose her fine spirit within the walls of a convent, to which I own I have many, perhaps *false prejudices.*" For it was the benefits of a Popish school, rather than his own Paris household, which Polly's father designed for her. Cutting off all further discussion on the subject, he told Mrs. Adams: "At this moment she is in the convent where she is perfectly happy."

If Jefferson's enchantment with Mrs. Adams melted somewhat as the result of her meddling in this matter, the occasion for a break between them was bound to arise anyway. Politics—the bitter political factionalism which started while Mrs. Adams was Mrs. Vice President and worsened during the four years she was First Lady—would separate them to the point where even perfunctory politeness became impossible. Those closest to the new national government thought the wife of John Adams exercised a marked degree of influence on the public conduct of her husband in this exalted portion of her life.

But that does not appear to have been precisely the case. Nobody, not even his dearest Abby, could sway Mr. Adams when his mind was set on a particular course. What she did instead was to assume more of an assisting role than the wives of statesmen were presumably intended to perform; in the novelty of organizing a federal republic, the framers of the Constitution, no less than their followers, had failed to notice that under any form of government known to man, woman had in one way or another exercised various powers. To Abigail Adams must go the distinction of inventing the American way of feminine politicking.

Martha Washington could not have done it. She was too much of a homebody at heart, too little interested in the intricacies of public affairs; and besides, George Washington stood so serenely above the need for what has come to be called political fence-mending that the plump, grandmotherly Martha lacked any motive to enter into an uncongenial occupation. Not so with Mrs. Adams. No sooner did she take up residence in New York in her Vice Presidential mansion overlooking the Hudson than she instinctively set about helping Mr. Adams.

"I took the earliest opportunity to go and pay my respects to Mrs. Washington," she wrote to her sister—and again, as she sets forth vivid detail about this and subsequent social events with the eye of a gifted writer, one must visualize her feeling the interested gaze of posterity over her shoulder. But she had another more immediate objective, which was the establishing of close, friendly relations with the wife of the President. Her assertions of how comfortably she enjoyed Mrs. Washington's society were surely sincere, and yet it is possible to wonder whether she would have as diligently cultivated the same lady's acquaintance were the lady's husband less eminent. After six months in New York, Mrs. Adams reported to her sister with profound satisfaction that at every public occasion her own place was "always at the right hand of Mrs. Washington." Should anybody else usurp her station, she added complacently, the President himself never failed of seeing that it was relinquished to her.

Winning the esteem of the Washingtons was not Mrs. Adams's

only wifely contribution. Political questions interested her so deeply that she paid more heed to all she heard on the subject than was expected of any lady, and she also talked more plainly. "The next question I presume that will occupy Congress will be the assumption of the State debts," she wrote to her sister, "and here I apprehend warm work and much opposition but I firmly believe it will terminate for the general good."

But there were more than political reasons why Mrs. Adams was happy to be in New York. Her married daughter lived near the city, and Nabby was not having an easy time, for the Colonel Smith she had married was proving distressingly improvident in money matters. Nabby's mother did all that high-minded advice could do under the circumstances, and she doted on the steady increment of grandchildren Nabby gave her. As for her sons, Tom was surely well intentioned, if at some loss about choosing a career, but Charles worried her much more; already his sad weakness for drink could not be blinked away. Only John Quincy of all her children afforded her complete satisfaction—without the suggestion of any improper efforts by either Mr. or Mrs. Adams, President Washington all on his own conceived the plan of sending the twenty-seven-year-old John Quincy as American minister to Holland. By happy chance, this had been one of his father's first diplomatic assignments; and from then onward, by his ability as well as such luck, this son would rise steadily toward the same pinnacle his father reached. (And John Quincy's son would be the diplomatically talented Charles Francis Adams, who in turn produced the historian Henry Adams.)

John Adams was still Vice President when John Quincy went abroad, but President Washington soon made it plain that he would not accept a third term. Then the senior Adams received his call to glory virtually as an expected inheritance, but the prize was tarnished by the time he got it. The amity prevailing at Washington's first inauguration had given way to discord, which the Constitution was not yet equipped to minimize. As the leader of an opposing political faith, Thomas Jefferson received the second highest number of electoral votes for the Presidency, and thus became his opponent's Vice President.

The intrigue, domestic and foreign, that marked the admin-

istration of John Adams cannot be dwelt on here except as it
affected Mrs. Adams. Beyond doubt, it undermined her health.
The national capital had removed to Philadelphia till the new
Federal City should be fit to receive residents, and the climate of
Philadelphia oppressed her; during two thirds of the year, she
grumbled to her sister, inhabitants of the Quaker city either froze
or melted. A recurrence of the rheumatic trouble which had
plagued her early childhood forced her to stay long periods in
Quincy, where her own provenance had made it possible for her
husband to purchase a fine old home on imposing grounds inferior
only to the estate of her grandparents. But one must suppose,
owing to the sturdiness of her health during so many other vicissitudes, that something other than the heat and cold of the Philadelphia weather disturbed her equilibrium. She gave a clue to her
trouble by quoting from Shakespeare to her sister:

> *Is Heaven tremendous in its frowns? Most sure*
> *And in its favors formidable too . . .*

Like many another striver after some worldly goal, she was, of
course, shaken by this realization. But Abigail Adams was too
much the Puritan to turn her back on duty, particularly her duty,
as she saw it, toward her dearest friend. After reviving up in
Massachusetts, she returned to Philadelphia repeatedly, ready to
foment confusion among his enemies. Sometimes more bitterly
than her own husband, she lamented the evil of their ways; and he
had no more articulate partisan than his wife when he tried to
circumvent their old friend Jefferson.

Her best known contribution was apolitical, though. When the
seat of the government moved southward in the autumn of 1800,
the honor of becoming the first mistress of the new President's
House in the city of Washington fell to Mrs. Adams—which she
indelibly impressed upon the national folklore by having laundry
hung up to dry in the East Room. For the executive mansion was
still unfinished, and its dampness was oppressive; only in one of
the state rooms, before a blazing fire, could any heat or comfort
be obtained. Mrs. Adams was not entirely sorry that her husband
failed of reelection to a second term.

But retirement to Quincy did not end her concern with matters governmental. As a grand old lady, imposing in her rustling black silk, she awed her grandchildren by the breadth of her interests; her letters continued no less encyclopedic. At the age of sixty-four, she penned the following to her daughter:

> . . . Providence has been so bountiful to us this season in the rich and ample supply of grass, that we can neither procure sufficient hands to cut it, or barns large enough to contain it. We have evenly cut fifty tons of English Hay, and shall nearly make an hundred. Such a grass season was never known before: the misfortune is that labour is higher than I ever knew it, it being now in such demand, and hay so low as to be sold at 7 Dollars per ton. We have employed 12 men for three weeks past, and for them were obliged to send more than twenty miles. I hope we shall finish in a week more—but the season has been so wet that the farmers have had bad luck in making their hay. Fruit will be very scarce, partly owing to the rain and partly to a late frost which occasioned it to drop from the trees. Corn looks well, barley not so good—whilst Heaven is pouring down upon us plenty and abundance, blessing us with a season also of health, we are murmuring and contending at our Rulers—and their laws and restrictions—that we have had a weak, timid cowardly administration is most certainly true—and that these measures have brought us into the present difficulties under which we are now suffering, I have no doubt. These led to the oppressive embargo, which has cut up our commerce, dispersed our seamen, and brought distress upon the whole country and will terminate I fear in disobedience to the laws, in insurrection and civil war, if a foreign war does not prevent it . . .

The letter, which went on to more than double the above length, was written in 1808. Ten years later, but no less mentally alert, Mrs. Adams was felled by typhoid fever; she died on October 28, 1818, at the age of seventy-four. It must be added that her dearest friend survived her by almost eight years—he was ninety when he died on July 4, 1826. So she failed to endure the pangs of widowhood, but were another such woman to come among her countrymen, and to have somewhat more staying power, would she not make a difficult candidate to defeat?

THE STRANGEST
MYSTERY
Mary Ball Washington

Her name was Mary, and since the house in which she gave birth to her son probably had only four rooms, on the main floor at least, it has been possible for some people to describe it as a mean hovel. Further developing the same theme, such observers have noted that the father in the case remains a shadowy, background figure. But his name was Augustine, and he seems to have been commonly called Gus. So much for the Holy Family myth.

Practically all of the myths about Mary Ball Washington deflate just as easily, despite the sad fact that her whole story can never be told; only a handful of authentic letters and courthouse records has rewarded generations of researchers in quest of the data on which to base a biography of her. Nevertheless, enough does survive to establish a charge of malicious mischief against Clio, the goddess of history. That divinity did not do right by American womanhood. *George Washington did not love his mother.*

Why a man with his lofty spirit was so lacking in filial affection has been labeled the strangest mystery in his life. But there are

Mary Ball Washington

clues that suggest a far more human tale than Parson Weems pro-vided—a tale of the natural antagonism between two commanding personalities. It starts with the arrival in Virginia, around 1650, of one Colonel William Ball of the British landed gentry, who preferred fleeing from Oliver Cromwell to fighting. So he brought his family across the ocean to settle on a plantation at the mouth of the Corotoman River, where he prospered as a tobacco grower.

His son Joseph married twice. Joseph had already reached a ripe age and had a large family of grown children when his first wife died, but single blessedness did not suit him and the young Widow Johnson did. Whether she had been his housekeeper be-fore they joined hands in matrimony cannot be proved, although there is a tradition to this effect; there is another that she was really a descendant of the ducal house of Montague. Cold-hearted scholars dispose of the issue by pointing out that no evidence of her high birth has lasted, while a document that she signed with an X has, and if illiteracy bore little stigma then, still a lady was likely to be able to write her own name. The presumption, in short, is that she accepted her elderly suitor for material reasons, because her own first husband had left her with two young chil-dren to raise.

High-born or low, the former widow was not welcomed as a stepmother by Joseph Ball's adult offspring. They already had quite definite ideas about what share of their father's property they could expect, and found changing these ideas difficult. To appease them, Joseph went through the legal motions of distribut-ing portions of his estate to each son and daughter before his health failed. He also fathered a new baby girl who became George Washington's mother.

Mary Ball was probably born on his plantation, Epping Forest, and 1708 has been set as the logical year for her birth. No matter that such details have defied proof, the fact that Joseph's older children had some cause for their concern emerges clearly. Within three years after his second marriage, he left his second wife a widow once more—but her circumstances were vastly improved. A substantial remnant of the Ball estate had, after all, been re-tained for her and, in the long run, her youngest daughter.

So little Mary grew up an heiress of sorts, but amid much

wrangling over who owned what, because it took years to solve various problems arising from her father's will. This was, of course, not unusual. Still the series of dislocations she endured compounded the turmoil; only a year after her father's death, her mother married a third husband who, ironically, did not even survive to see his wife's inheritance come into her hands, and then when Mary was twelve, her mother succumbed to a fever, leaving Mary a full orphan. Yet she was neither poor nor cringing. It seems that she was already used to having her own silk plush riding saddle.

Exactly how she spent the next decade cannot be told, but she surely lived with one or another relative, or perhaps in the household of the lawyer under whose "tutelage and government" her mother's will had put her. His name was George Eskridge, which forces the supposition that she thought of him, in lieu of the father she could not even remember, when it came to naming her own first son.

The myth-makers have a lovely, Tennysonian romance as a prelude to Mary's marriage. Naturally, she is alleged to have been a fair maiden—"The Rose of Epping Forest"—but it is necessary to report that not a single authentic portrait of her at any age has come to light; on the basis of later verbal testimony, she was tall, imposing, assuredly not delicate. Nevertheless, the fair Mary is said to have sailed to England to visit one of her stepbrothers who had gone there for business reasons, and, while demurely sitting by her window sewing, to have noticed a handsome gentleman struggling to calm his balky horse. When the horse reared, flinging its rider to the ground, and the gentleman was brought into her brother's house unconscious, did the young lady not nurse him tirelessly till he regained his health? Indeed she did. And did the fascinating coincidence that they were both visitors from Virginia not strike them as an omen from above? Certainly, and in a quaint old English church they were married, before sailing back to Virginia together.

There could be a shred of truth to this fantasy. For one of Mary's stepbrothers did spend much of his time abroad and several of his letters to Mary, dating from a later period, have been preserved. Augustine Washington also had business interests which took him periodically to England. Thus his meeting with Mary Ball in Britain must be accepted as a theoretical possibility, although there is every likelihood that the encounter occurred more prosaically in George Eskridge's parlor.

In either case, Mary was twenty-three when she was chosen—rather an unusually advanced age for the time and place, considering that she was neither sickly nor a pauper. Why she did not marry sooner is a provocative question. But if her temper had frightened other men, Augustine did not hesitate on its account; for he urgently needed a wife. He was a recent widower with two boys and a girl who required mothering.

Nearing forty, Augustine was a fine figure of a man and not otherwise remarkable. Like his father and grandfather, and no doubt their forbears in England, he played the part of a country gentleman creditably, serving his turn as justice of the peace and vestryman of his parish church; but the record divulges nothing suggesting singular talents, let alone genius. Although he indulged in the Virginian sport of amassing as much land as he possibly could, his accumulation could not compare with the enormous tracts acquired by several of his contemporaries. And although he put much effort into various schemes for making use of the iron ore discovered on one of his farms, he failed to show any profit. But he is supposed to have possessed great physical strength, which he sometimes demonstrated by lifting onto a cart an amount of iron two men ordinarily could hardly budge. He is also supposed to have been gentle in disposition, which would explain why he and Mary suited each other. They were married, according to a notation in his family Bible, on the sixth of March in 1731.

Augustine brought her then to his house set on a rise above a broad creek emptying into the Potomac, about a hundred miles south of the area where a city bearing his name would later be built. The house burned long ago, but diligent antiquarians have uncovered an assortment of foundations and broken bricks indicating that it was a comfortable if not magnificent two-story brick country seat, flanked by several outbuildings. During the 1930's, a committee of patriots constructed a presumed replica, which has since been certified as a national landmark. In its original, eleven months after marrying Augustine, Mary Washington gave birth to a large and well-formed baby boy; the date was, of course, February 22, 1732.

A more beautiful natural setting than George Washington's birthplace on Pope's Creek would be hard to imagine. The approach is through woods that have been allowed to revert to something like their first growth, with towering oak, hickory, and other forest giants lording over graceful dogwood and redbud; a glorious chorus of birdsong comes from the sun-dappled shadows. Closer to the house are cleared pastures and fields, beyond it the water—half a mile of glistening creek blending into the Potomac, which at this point stretches five miles to the distant Maryland shore.

Yet the serenity provided by nature must not be taken to prove that this hero's childhood was a true pastoral idyll. In fact, the household in which he grew up was crowded and probably contentious, despite the early departure of Augustine's children by his first wife. The two boys—Lawrence and Augustine junior—already entering their teens, were sent to school in England; and their frail little sister died when George was three. But by then the second Mrs. Washington had given birth, at intervals not much above a year, to her own daughter Betty and to another boy who was named Samuel. It appears that when her fourth baby was on the way the family moved, but to a less rather than more commodious house.

Possibly because the waters of Pope's Creek, pleasing as they were to the eye, were far too shallow to permit navigation by English trading vessels, Augustine took his wife and children up the Potomac to another of his properties. Here they occupied a farmhouse that would later be enlarged and improved and named Mount Vernon. As it was, they must have been cramped for space after the sturdy infant John Augustine arrived, then Charles, too.

Yet Augustine senior does not seem to have spent much time at home. His iron furnace near Fredericksburg, some fifty miles to the southwest, was consuming more and more of his attention, and after a few years on the Potomac the family moved again, to the outskirts of the young settlement on the Rappahannock. Only three years later, when George was eleven, his father fell ill of a sudden stomach ailment and died.

Augustine left his property, for all practical purposes, in three parts—precise bequests went to each of his older sons, and the rest was to stay under the control of his wife till their young children should reach legal age. After explaining how he would like the residue of his estate divided then, he hinted at what could be expected from his Mary: ". . . but if she should Insist Notwithstanding . . ."—and he proposed an alternate scheme for the apportionment.

By the loose terms of his will, Augustine all but guaranteed more of the sort of wrangling that had marked Mary's girlhood, yet he does not seem to have exerted any further influence on his family. Even after his death, he resisted deification; by the time the impetus arose to glorify him, just one witness survived who remembered him in person and that aged gentleman—a Mr. Withers —could not be prevailed upon to contribute any poetic detail beyond describing him as a blond giant. George Washington himself remembered his father merely as a tall, fair-complexioned man, well proportioned and fond of children. Allowances must be made for his reserve on private matters, but because Augustine was away so much his son may well have carried no deeper impression with him.

Mary Washington was thirty-five when she was left a widow in charge of rearing four sons and a daughter. The responsibility fell squarely on her shoulders and she did not shirk it; that must be said for her. She had a prodigious sense of duty—perhaps, after all, she did have some ducal blood, for she certainly behaved like a grand duchess. Still it is at this point in her career that pious nonsense begins to break loose of all restraint. Here is Washington Irving on the subject in 1856:

> Tradition gives us an interesting picture of the widow, with her little flock gathered around her, as was her daily wont, reading to them lessons of religion and morality out of some standard work. Her favorite volume was Sir Matthew Hale's *Contemplations, moral and divine* . . .

The volume in question, with her name in a firm hand on the flyleaf—directly beneath the signature of Augustine's first wife— has been preserved at Mount Vernon; there can be no disputing that she owned it, and she may even have read it. As for her religious and moral convictions, these were doubtless strictly orthodox. A stern belief in her own infallibility was, however, superimposed above all other principles. This appears to have irritated her son George, and from the age of eleven onward he spent as few hours in her company as he could possibly manage.

That he did stay at home sometimes was testified to by a cousin of approximately the same age. Toward the close of his long life this relative recalled that he had visited George at the Washington farm overlooking the Rappahannock—Ferry Farm, it was called, from the presence of a ferry landing down below the breezy slope on which the house stood. The visitor's characterization of Mary Washington struck exactly the right note to thrill the nineteenth century, although it may appall the twentieth. "Of the mother," he said, "I was ten times more afraid than of my own parents."

In her vicinity, proper tall boys stood meek as mice. Presiding over her household, she displayed an air and manner so awe-inspiring as to leave scant chance of her commands going unobeyed; certainly she set an example that, tempered by time and his own tact, George would follow, to the inexpressible benefit of his countrymen. But even during his own youth, he was too much like his mother to be able to obey willingly. Thus he sought refuge for months on end in the homes of his two elder half-brothers, who had married and set up establishments of their own shortly after returning from school in England. Portions of their father's property, plus good marriages, made them both more than capable of welcoming him; and from Lawrence in particular, who had inherited the Potomac acres which now were named Mount Vernon, George secured incalculable advantages in the way of exposure to books and polite society—his formal schooling was to be limited to brief periods of tutoring with various country pedagogues.

Not that Mary Washington was illiterate like her own mother. Somewhere she had picked up the rudiments of reading and writing, and her spelling was no worse than normal then; but she lacked the passionate commitment to education that marked so many other Presidential mothers. She surely did not propose sending George to school in England, and if the idea came up she must have opposed it as she did a number of other programs for taking her oldest son entirely out of her control. The first of these was an elaborate scheme to enlist him in the British Navy.

Lawrence Washington and his father-in-law—the cultivated Colonel William Fairfax—and a Dr. Spencer, who apparently had some designs of his own involving the Widow Washington, all cooperated in the plot to secure her assent to the adventurous step when George was fourteen. But she stood out alone against them all, and who is to say she was wrong? Her "trifling objections," as one of the disgusted men put it, did keep George Washington from donning the uniform of a British seaman. Instead he took up surveying—and soldiering. Two of his letters to his mother when he went into the wilderness to fight the French and Indians have been preserved; one is a matter-of-fact recital of battle prospects, but the other is amusing:

> To Mrs. Washington
> near Fredericksburgh
>
> Hon^d. Madam,
>
> I was favoured with your Letter, by Mr. Dick, and am sorry it is not in my power to provide you with a Dutch Servant, or the Butter, agreeably to your desire; We are quite out of that part of the Country, wherein either is to be had; there being few or no Inhabitants where we now lie encamped; and butter can not be had here, to supply the wants of the Army.
>
> I am sorry it was not in my power to call upon you as I went to, or returned from, Williamsburgh—The Business that I went upon (viz. Money for the Army) would not suffer an hour's delay . . .
>
> There is a Detachment of 500 men marched from this camp toward the Alegany, to prepare the Roads etc. and it is imagined the Main Body will move in about 5 days time.
>
> As nothing else remarkable occurs to me, I shall conclude (after begging my love & compliments to all Friends)
>
> Dear Madam,
> Your Most Aff. &
> Dutiful Son,
> GWashington
>
> Camp, at Will's
> Creek, 7th June, 1755.

Cool as the tone of this missive is, it is still warmer than any other of the letters George Washington wrote to his mother; although he was away from her almost constantly, and he method-ically kept copies of virtually everything he wrote, only six letters to her—over a period of more than half a century—have been found in his papers, exhibiting a steadily mounting exasperation. The cause is not hard to discover. Instead of urging her firstborn onward toward ever greater triumphs, Mary Washington did all in her power to clip his wings: ". . . thear was no end to my troble while George was in the army but he has now given it up," she wrote to a relative in 1759; this letter is one of the four or five extant that scholars accept as the genuine productions of her own pen.

Furthermore, if she had a ruling passion as she grew older, it was greed. Besides being self-willed and domineering, she became insatiably grasping in money matters. She still owned a farm her own father had left her, and Augustine had provided enough to live on comfortably if not luxuriously, but she was not content. From his early manhood, George was constantly embroiled in financial argument with her, growing out of his agreement to manage her farm and pay her rent for the privilege—while she stubbornly held on to Ferry Farm, too, although legally it belonged to George as of his twenty-first birthday.

Dozens of notations in her son's expense ledgers during the 1760's confirm this unpleasant picture beyond any reasonable doubt. After the early death of Lawrence Washington and his widow, George had acquired Mount Vernon and he had no need of Ferry Farm as a place to live; but the unfairness rankled. While he was, in effect, dutifully supporting his mother, she kept him from realizing any return on a piece of his own property. In addi-tion, she must have nagged him for money every time he visited her on his way through Fredericksburg and eventually he took to jotting down the name of any witness present when he handed her a sum in cash, obviously to forestall convenient lapses of mem-ory on her part. His diaries also show that he much preferred stopping at the home of his married sister Betty when he passed through Fredericksburg going to or from sessions of the House of Burgesses in Williamsburg.

The eyes of dedicated historians have naturally not been closed to such evidence, and the monumental work on George Washington by Douglas Southall Freeman which is the standard of excellence in American historical biography even uncovers the unsavory local tradition that the mother of his hero would keep a joint of lamb so long in her larder that she was obliged to lean over her plate and smell each slice before conveying it to her mouth. During the free-thinking 1920's, other writers boldly described her as a slovenly pipe-smoking hag. She was also blamed—or credited—with beating her house slaves over the head with her household keys when they dared to displease her. But still the saintly image endures.

Indeed the cottage in Fredericksburg where she spent her last years has been restored as a shrine for tourists, but the circumstances attending her move there from Ferry Farm are not dwelt on by the charming ladies who act as hostesses. Cryptic jottings in George Washington's notes indicate that by the early 1770's he could no longer contain his own temper at the constant financial drain her odd sense of business entailed; for he had also inherited her temper—which she gave him much practice in the art of governing—along with more than a trace of her closeness when it came to money. In any case, he convened a family conference to decide what could be done about her.

Among the participants were his brother Charles, who would not have been of much help, he being the drinker in this Presidential family; and his brother-in-law, Colonel Fielding Lewis, husband of his only sister Betty. These latter two bore the brunt of the arrangement that was arrived at, which was the purchase by George of a small house within convenient walking distance of the Lewis mansion, Kenmore. A brick path stretching from Betty Lewis's garden steps to the more modest garden of her mother was put down; its remnants still touch the sentimental hearts of visitors to both restorations.

Doubtless by dint of extremely delicate negotiations, George then secured his mother's assent to the sale of Ferry Farm. It is likely that his favorite brother Jack—a prospering planter in Westmoreland County—also took some part in all this. But Samuel would hardly have been consulted; his profligacy was George's despair. Samuel married five wives before he was finished—and he is alleged to have resembled Henry VIII in other ways as well.

His own brothers could scarcely keep track of the assorted nieces and nephews he provided them with, nor could George fathom how a man could get his financial affairs into such a tangle. "In God's name, how did my brother Samuel contrive to get himself so enormously in debt?" he wrote to Jack.

Sensible as their cottage plan for their mother seemed, it still did not solve the problem. Even George's departure onto the great stage of history in 1775 did not stop her complaints. He had left a distant cousin at Mount Vernon as his agent, charged among all of his other duties with the task of keeping up the maternal payments, and this kinsman inherited her nagging, too. "I never Lived soe pore in my Life," she wrote to him in 1778—with nary a word about the portentous struggle her son was leading. Three years later, her voice grew shrill enough for Virginia's General Assembly to hear that the mother of the commander in chief needed a public pension to prevent her starving.

George Washington's anguish when he received a letter from a legislator friend telling him that a plan to provide such a pension was being considered does not have to be imagined. The lady did not have a single child, he wrote back immediately, who would not divide his or her last sixpence "to relieve her from *real* distress."

If it is remembered that Mary Washington was past seventy by this time, her avarice may possibly be excused as the vagary of an old woman. Discovering grounds for dismissing her earlier rapacity is more difficult. Once one has said that she meant well, in a regal sort of way, the catalog of her amiable characteristics is almost completed; singularly little evidence of any endearing qualities has been preserved, except the testimony from a grandson that she often took him walking to her favorite spot above the foaming Rappahannock, where two large rocks provided a natural bench for viewing the grandeur of nature. Here she would point out the different forest trees visible on the hills across the river, and impress on him the majesty of the Creator of all things.

Only in the recent past has loving God seemed less important than being lovable; and there is no precedent requiring a duchess to behave lovably. Nor does any older civilization expect the son of a duchess to feel real affection for a termagant of a mother, even in her old age. Certainly George Washington felt no such emotion when he wrote to his mother in her eightieth year, after she had provoked him unbearably by still another appeal for money:

. . . my sincere and pressing advice to you is to break up house-keeping, hire out all the rest of your servants except a man and a maid and live with one of your Children. This would relieve you entirely from the cares of this world, and leave your mind at ease to reflect undisturbedly on that which ought to come. . . .

My house is at your service & would press you most sincerely & devotedly to accept it, but I am sure and candour requires me to say it will never answer your purposes in any shape whatsoever, for in truth it may be compared to a well resorted tavern, as scarcely any strangers who are going from north to south, or from south to north do not spend a day or two at it. This would, were you to become an inhabitant of it, oblige you to do one of 3 things, 1st to be always dressing to appear in company, 2d to come into [company] in dishabille or 3d to be as it were a prisoner in your own chamber. The first you would not like, indeed for a person at your time of life it would be too fatiguing. The 2d I should not like because those who resort here are as I observed before strangers and people of the first distinction—and the 3d, more than probably, would not be pleasing to either of us—nor indeed could you be retired in any room in my house; for what with the sitting up of Company; the noise and bustle of servants—and many other things you would not be able to enjoy that calmness and serenity of mind, which in my opinion you ought now to prefer to every other consideration in Life . . .

In short, he saw no objection to her moving in with Betty, but neither his mother nor his sister agreed with him. Mary Washington stayed exactly where she was, becoming ever more querulous after her strength was sapped by a cancer of the breast, until she died in her own cottage on August 25, 1789; she was then in her eighty-second year.

One week later the son, in whom so many of her strong traits had been modified by some marvelous alchemy, received word of her death. He was President Washington now, acclaimed as one of the noblest men ever to have lived, but he mourned his mother only perfunctorily; ". . . it is the duty of her relatives to yield due submission to the decrees of the Creator," he wrote to Betty. "When I was last at Fredericksburg, I took a final leave of my mother, never expecting to see her more." Then he skipped a line, started a new paragraph, and began a discussion of the provisions of his mother's will.

If Parson Weems and others have prevented Washington's countrymen from seeing any such flaws in the character of their first President, it is possible that these myth makers have done the United States a major service. Historians with a flair for psychology have come to believe, in fact, that the imaginary cherry tree filled a real need—that any new nation must have a national hero—and that this nation wanted a marble god. In that case, perhaps the good ladies of the nineteenth century who raised money to memorialize his mother have also served us well.

Till the time of Grover Cleveland, she had received only limited homage. Although patriotic writers and orators had long since found the inspiration for referring to her as a sacred mother figure, she had, as it were, no temple. She had been buried near her favorite spot above the Rappahannock in Fredericksburg but if any stone had been placed there it had already disappeared. Finally, in 1894, the holy sanctity of American motherhood was fittingly symbolized by the unveiling of a classic shaft of marble on the site of her grave. Carved at the base were just these words:

MARY THE MOTHER OF WASHINGTON

AND, IN BRIEF...

Hulda Minthorn Hoover
1848-1883

WHENEVER IT SEEMS that there is no such thing as progress, there may be some consolation in considering the case of Herbert Hoover's birthplace. During his own lifetime, this humble cottage was remodeled twice—first into a hot dog stand, and then into a shrine. Furthermore, a fact about his mother which once caused much embarrassment has become bearable.

She was born in Canada. To a certain number of one hundred percent Republicans, this made sad news back in the 1920's when her son was nominated to run against Al Smith for the Presidency. Nobody talked then about the image projected by a candidate, but somebody at the Republican National Committee thought it would not look right if any foreign taint was admitted; and so the biography of Hoover circulated as campaign publicity ignored his mother's Canadian past. Naturally, the truth came out, though, and a small scandal resulted. Yet the whole truth was so thoroughly respectable that one must doubt whether many votes could have been lost.

Hulda Minthorn Hoover was indeed born on an Ontario farm, on May 4, 1848; but her parents were Quakers of decent New England stock, and when she was only eleven they moved to Iowa. There she lived all the rest of her life, which was not long. But all that high-minded piety could do in so short a time she did—her son was just eight when she died, yet she left him with the memory of having spent an entire day at the polls with her during an early anti-liquor crusade. That she strongly supported a local womanly effort aimed at convincing men voters to vote themselves dry must have impressed him when he came to take his own position on Prohibition.

Nevertheless, she was no fierce-eyed Carrie Nation. On the contrary, Hulda Hoover had the gentle, sweet-faced sort of righteousness that characterized so many intelligent Quaker girls. Still if she was gentle, she was not retiring—dissatisfied with merely speaking at meeting, she became an ordained minister of the Society of Friends two years before her death.

"She was such a gifted girl," her sister said of her, and perhaps she was; in an environment where higher education for females was uncommon, she attended the University of Iowa till the death of her father compelled her to come home. Then she taught school for several years in the town of West Branch, where at the age of twenty-two she married an ambitious blacksmith named Jesse Clark Hoover. She gave him two sons and a daughter, the middle child, born on August 10, 1874, being her claim to fame; the tiny frame cottage in West Branch which witnessed the event has as a result gone through its various transformations.

But neither she nor her husband was destined to know what they had wrought. After just ten years of marriage, Jesse died of typhoid fever; after two hard years of widowhood, Hulda died of pneumonia on February 24, 1883, a few months short of her thirty-fifth birthday. Then relatives took over the upbringing of her three orphaned children. Only because of the honor that came to one of them, she achieved the wish with which she ended a mournfully schoolgirlish letter she had written at the age of fourteen:

> *Remember me when death shall close*
> *My eyelids in their last repose*
> *Remember me when the wind shall wave*
> *The grass upon your schoolmate's grave.*

Victoria Moor Coolidge
1846-1885

O NE MISFORTUNE that Calvin Coolidge shared with Herbert Hoover was maternal—they both lost their mothers in early boyhood. At least partly because Victoria Coolidge lived till her son reached the more impressionable age of twelve, he felt her departure more deeply; almost every investigator who has had any occasion for inquiring into the probable reasons for his odd personality has concluded that he suffered all his life from what is popularly described as a mother complex.

His spareness with conversation, which went far beyond the bounds of the quaint taciturnity expected of New Englanders, must have owed something to a second shock just a few years after his mother's death. Then the little sister who was his only other close female relative—and by all accounts, a delightfully playful and pretty redhead—died suddenly of appendicitis. Thenceforth, he sometimes seemed to have forgotten how to talk. Yet it was his mother's passing that made him what he was, as he himself recognized. "The greatest grief that can come to a boy came to me," he wrote in his autobiography many years later, and with a rare impulse toward self-revelation, he added: "It always seemed to me that the boy I lost was her image."

On the other hand, though, after he had won several elections he once admitted to a close associate that the boy within him had not perished—far from it. In a confession of startling candor, he explained:

> Do you know, I've never really grown up? It's a hard thing for me to play this game. In politics, one must meet people, and that's not easy for me. . . . When I was a little fellow, as long ago as I can remember, I would go into a panic if I heard strange voices in the

kitchen. I felt I just couldn't meet the people and shake hands with them. Most of the visitors would sit with Father and Mother in the kitchen, and the hardest thing in the world was to have to go through the kitchen door and give them a greeting. I was almost ten before I realized I couldn't go on that way. And by fighting hard I used to manage to get through that door. I'm all right with old friends, but every time I meet a stranger, I've got to go through the old kitchen door, back home, and it's not easy.

This, too, undoubtedly stemmed from his dependence on his mother. The woman who caused him such trauma was a rather ethereal creature. She is supposed to have had a drop of Indian blood, although her people were for the most part staid farm folk of Scottish ancestry; she was born on a farm near the Vermont hamlet of Pinney Hollow on March 14, 1846. But someone in her family had romantic tendencies, and she was named Victoria Josephine—for two empresses.

Yet there is hardly a clue to her own character. At an early age she moved a few miles with her family to the somewhat less isolated little settlement of Plymouth Notch, where one of her schoolmates was an upstanding boy named John Coolidge; like him, she had the benefit of a few terms at a private academy in a neighboring town. When she was twenty-two, and he was a year older, they were married, on May 6, 1868. He kept the country store attached to the frame cottage in which they lived; here their son John Calvin Coolidge was born on July 4, 1872, and their daughter Abbie three years later. In the larger house right across the road—later to be celebrated as the scene of her son's oath-taking when the death of Warren Harding made him President of the United States—Victoria Coolidge died on her thirty-ninth birthday, probably of tuberculosis. That is almost all one can say about her.

For she made only a vague impress among her matter-of-fact neighbors, who remembered her later as being comely and liking flowers; they could think of nothing else to say. Only her son, despite his tendency to silence, could find words to describe her. "She was of a very light and fair complexion with a rich growth of brown hair that had a glint of gold to it," he wrote. And although by the time he could recall her, she was practically an invalid, she lavished all the strength she had on caring for him and his sister. Moved to an exceptional flight of lyricism, he added:

> There was a touch of mysticism and poetry in her nature which made her love to gaze at the purple sunsets and watch the evening stars. Whatever was grand and beautiful in form and color attracted her. It seemed as though the rich green tints of the foliage and the blossoms of the flowers came for her in the springtime, and in the autumn it was for her that the mountain sides were struck with crimson and with gold.

No matter that Calvin Coolidge thought he had buried his own strain of poetry, and grim competence propelled him to be governor of Massachusetts—from which post he went beyond his depth in Washington—along the way he dropped his guard long enough to win a warm, utterly charming wife. But when he died not long after leaving the White House, it was discovered that within the case of his old-fashioned watch—in a pocket right over his heart— was a picture of his mother.

Phoebe Dickerson Harding
1843-1910

ON A FINE SPRING MORNING in 1864, a farm boy of nineteen hitched up a pair of horses and mentioned that he planned to take two of the neighboring Dickerson girls out for a ride. That he did—right to the home of the Methodist preacher in the next town, where he married one sister while the other served as witness. Riding back from town, the bride borrowed her husband's watch and she scratched a little verse inside the case:

> *Phoebe Dickerson is no more*
> *May 7th 1864*
> *Phoebe Harding now it is*
> *Didn't we fool Mal and Liz?*

Thus did the future mother of Warren Gamaliel Harding record her elopement. Those who were fooled, beyond the two other sisters she cited, included the whole of two large families—both the Dickersons and the Hardings ran to continual procreation. Phoebe herself was the youngest of nine living children, all but one of them female; and she must have been the pet of the lot.

"We are all well and hearty, getting fat on clear Consciences," she wrote saucily to her only brother while he was off fighting the rebels. It was because young Tryon Harding aimed to do the same —and was loath to leave the lively Phoebe unattached during his absence—that he prevailed on her to elope. Then that same evening he started for the camp where another Ohio regiment was training, but marriage softened him to the extent that he signed up as a drummer instead of a soldier.

Keeping their secret, Phoebe stayed with her own family on the farm where she had always lived, in central Ohio near the hamlet of Blooming Grove; she had been born there on December 21, 1843, and thus was twenty when she married, about six months older than George Tryon Harding II, the imposing full name of her husband. But in deeds he was less impressive—by autumn he was back with her, discharged owing to "general debility" incurred from a bout of typhoid fever. Then both families accepted accomplished fact, and the new couple set up housekeeping on a small farm adjoining the Harding homestead. Tryon's condition did not prevent his becoming a father a year after his return from the war. On November 2, 1865, Phoebe gave birth to the first of her eight children—the one who became President of the United States.

Warren G. Harding was indisputably the least qualified man ever to live in the White House, and so there is no need to ponder the mystery of how his parents could produce a hero. Not that they disgraced their plain farm forbears—not at all. Phoebe settled down to domesticity, and if one must surmise that she let at least her oldest run too free for his own good, she set a high example by taking her religion seriously, so much so that she became a devout Seventh Day Adventist in her later years; and her husband was sufficiently ambitious to study medicine—although then and there that merely meant dogging the steps of a country doctor for a few years, before finding a school up in Cleveland which would

award a diploma following just two or three semesters of attend-
ance. After that, Doc Harding moved his wife and children off the
land and he practiced his healing arts in the small city of Marion.
By now he was slow and patient and he could look wise, so he
managed all right when farmers and their families stopped in to
consult him. But he never attracted much business or attention
either, and his firstborn was another Mama's boy—every Sunday
during the last several decades of her life, he brought or sent her
flowers. Unlike so many other Presidential mothers, though,
Phoebe Harding had no particular strength of character.

Nor did her son, although he had the nerve to tell a press club
dinner in Washington some years later that one day his father had
said to him: "Warren, it's a good thing you wasn't born a gal."

"Why?"

"Because you'd be in the family way all the time. You can't
say no."

It was, of course, true, and had Warren Harding stayed in
Marion, where he rose to be the publisher of the local daily, he
might have saved his country quite an embarrassment. But he had
his father's bland manner, plus his mother's light-hearted faith,
along with a splendidly handsome facade probably derived from
both sides of his family—although no picture of Phoebe Harding
has ever come to light and thus the presumption of her beauty
must rest on hearsay. In any case, men shrewder than her son were
satisfied with his appearance, and lured him into politics.

Phoebe lived to see him as lieutenant governor of Ohio; she
died on May 20, 1910, at the age of sixty-six. He certainly had no
business going any further, but it is unfair to blame only him for
his sad performance in the Presidency. And one must admit he
was not all that incompetent—didn't he fool sixteen million voters?

Nancy Allison McKinley

1809-1897

WHEN THE REPUBLICAN PARTY picked William McKinley to run for President, it got an unexpected bonus—Will's mother was like a twin of Whistler's, and twice as religious. What's more, she was eighty-six, meaning she had been born in exactly the same year as Abraham Lincoln. Although the art of spreading such tidings was still in its infancy, Mother McKinley's obvious usefulness to the cause did not escape attention.

In the absence of television, the private enterprise system mobilized the railroads, and special excursion trains converged on the small Ohio city of Canton throughout the summer of 1896. Every Sunday morning, crowds of visitors watched as the candidate called at his mother's house, then emerged with a surprisingly perky figure beside him; in black coat and bonnet, she was all ready for church. At other times, interested bystanders were rewarded with a view of mother and son comfortably rocking on either his or her front porch.

The value of such wholesome scenes was enhanced by the unfortunate disability of the candidate's wife. Ever since the shock of losing two infants in rapid succession many years earlier, she had been subject to epileptic seizures, and she avoided public appearances. But her mother-in-law would have shone even if Ida had offered her any competition—as a testimonial for her son, Nancy Allison McKinley was almost too good to be true.

Although it was no longer plausible to claim that a candidate had been born in a log cabin, at least his mother had this credential; on April 22, 1809, she had made her appearance in a cabin every bit as primitive as the most devout Republican could wish. Her people were appropriately simple farmers, Scottish a few generations back, who had crossed over from Pennsylvania to settle on the Ohio frontier. Anxious for their children to have some schooling, Nancy's parents moved into the town of Lisbon during her girlhood, and there she met a stocky young man named William McKinley; they were married on January 6, 1829.

Instead of farming, the first Will McKinley was interested in the steel business—he became the manager of a small ore furnace in the Ohio village of Niles, just northwest of Youngstown. Meanwhile, Nancy devoted herself to childrearing and Methodism; except for the preaching, she ran the local church, her old neighbors testified. Somehow the full fervor of both of her preoccupations focused on the seventh of her nine children, who was born in Niles on January 29, 1843. She named this boy for his father, and set her heart on his becoming a bishop.

To give him the right start, she packed up and moved to the larger town of Poland when he was ready for school; her husband was tied to Niles by his work, and for some years saw his family only on Sundays. But he lived to understand the logic of his wife's fierce drive to educate young Will—before he died at the age of eighty-five, this son was governor of Ohio. Nancy McKinley still felt a lingering pang, though, because her boy had failed to become a preacher.

Otherwise, he was exemplary in her eyes. He neither drank intoxicating beverages nor used foul language, and he cared for his ailing wife with a tender solicitude his mother had to consider saintly. Only his unhealthy habit of smoking cigars, which he had acquired from his political associates, disappointed her; and although she thought she had resigned herself to his choice of politics as a career, she feared the temptation to which he was exposed when he was nominated for the Presidency.

On the night when the votes were counted, as soon as the trend of the returns became clear, she had both Will and Ida kneel to pray with her in her bedroom. A distracted nephew, trying to get the President-elect to take an important telephone call, had to report that his uncle could not be disturbed. "Oh, God, keep him humble," Mother McKinley was imploring.

Yet she had the verve to ride the Presidential Special to Washington for his inauguration. The glint of her bright eyes behind their steel-rimmed spectacles struck sparks of human interest then in the florid prose metropolitan newspapers poured forth for the occasion; only the *Canton Repository* had had a correspondent at the Presidential suite earlier that morning, though, to hear her son Abner reassuring her: "Mother, this is better than a bishopric."

Abner was the black sheep of her family, inasmuch as his business transactions in New York City involved the sale of various stock certificates not worth any more than the paper on which they were printed—but one way or another, she was spared any open scandal about his activities. Among the rest of her children, one son died in California, another became minister to Hawaii, and her daughters married respectably or taught school till it was time to keep her company in her old age.

So she had much for which to be grateful before she was called to another kingdom on December 12, 1897; she was then eighty-eight years and 234 days old. Dutiful as ever, Will had arrived in time from Washington, leaving affairs of state in other hands while he sat by her bedside. In its obituary notice, the *Repository* paid due tribute to Mother McKinley's strong influence on this son:

> Those who knew her best say that to her the President owed the qualities which rendered him so eminently successful as a public man. He was in all respects a "mother's boy," and he was as proud of her as she was of him.

Ann Neal Cleveland

1806–1882

NOT ALL PURITANS are born austere, nor do they even recognize their stoic nature early. Ann Neal was the daughter of a prosperous Baltimore publisher of law books, and she grew up accustomed to luxury. One may even wonder whether she would ever have lost her taste for it if she had not met a young theology student named Richard Falley Cleveland.

He was a thin, pale, and intellectual New Englander who had graduated from Yale with honors and was taking his religious training at Princeton. Deacons and ministers, including a few of some prominence, abounded in his ancestry; it seemed only logical that he was on the verge of a distinguished career. Ann certainly thought so when she married him on September 10, 1829—she brought along her Negro maid and her jewels and a stylish city wardrobe when she went with him to assume his first pulpit in the village of Windham, Connecticut.

There the good Congregational ladies swiftly let Ann know that nobody from a slave state could bring a colored servant into their midst without arousing suspicions; and that furthermore no decent clergyman's wife wore jewelry or bright colors if she valued her husband's reputation. Ann humbly sent her maid back to Maryland—it was as if she accepted the interference as an omen from on high. Thereafter, she took her religion possibly even more seriously than the Reverend Cleveland did.

She was twenty-three when she accepted her destiny; she had been born on February 4, 1806. From Windham on, she never gave the slightest sign of missing her soft silk gowns or the graciousness of Baltimore society, and she never knew another day of ease till she died at the age of seventy-six, on July 19, 1882. For her husband failed utterly to live up to his promise, but she did her duty as she had come to see it.

Throughout the twenty-four years that he remained with her, although he preached diligently in a succession of small churches, he made no impress such as a more ambitious man would have done; he never had so much as a pamphlet of his sermons published. At best, ministerial wages were slim—his could scarcely feed the nine children he managed to beget. Ann Neal Cleveland and her children never starved, but Yale, let alone Princeton, was out of the question for her sons.

From Windham, they moved briefly to Virginia, then to Caldwell, New Jersey, where the fifth of her babies was born on March 18, 1837. Why this boy, who was named Stephen Grover Cleveland after the minister his father had recently succeeded, assumed so close a place in her heart it is impossible to say; perhaps his birth coincided with her realization that not only material success but also distinction in his chosen profession was beyond her husband. Although she had turned her back on frivolity, she still could not settle for mediocrity. With her new strictness, she gave this son no leeway at all for human weakness.

In Caldwell, which was then an isolated country village, and after that in the various hamlets of central New York State where the Reverend Cleveland served out his days, all of his children were required to memorize huge chunks of dogmatic writing; and their mother sternly limited their other activities. But the conditioning weighed heaviest on Grover. When his father died in 1853 at the age of forty-nine, Grover was only sixteen, and he had two older brothers—but for the next thirty years, he willingly assumed the martyrdom of supporting his mother and unmarried sisters.

He had help, of course, while he picked up the rudiments of law by clerking for a Buffalo firm; and then he stayed in Buffalo practicing his profession and dabbling in local Democratic politics, spending only his vacations with his mother over in the village of Holland Patent where she remained throughout her widowhood. But he dutifully provided for her all this time—at the expense of his own needs. It was the saddest of ironies that if he had felt free to marry, this intensely moral man would almost certainly not have fathered the illegitimate child whose existence came to light when he was running for President. Although he won anyway, after manfully admitting his transgression, he had to endure a terrible celebrity as the hero of:

> *Ma! Ma! where's my Pa?*
> *Gone to the White House,*
> *Ha! Ha! Ha!*

Fortunately, Ann Neal Cleveland did not live to shudder at this —she had died just as her son was contemplating running for mayor of Buffalo. Cold as he seemed on the surface, he missed her, of course, and despite the austerity she had taught him, he expressed his loss touchingly. "Do you know that if Mother were alive I should feel so much safer," he wrote to one of his brothers right after winning the mayoralty. "I have always thought her prayers had much to do with my success. . . ."

Elizabeth Irwin Harrison
1810-1850

The MOTHER OF Benjamin Harrison was a strict Presbyterian who distrusted cucumbers. When it is added that she died at forty while giving birth to her tenth child, there is not much more that can be said about her; like her son who happened to become President, she defies the interest of posterity.

But the family into which she married cannot be dismissed so easily—from colonial Virginia onward, Harrisons have run for so many offices, and won so many elections, even in the absence of any particular talent, that they probably outpoint every other dynasty in American political history. It was Elizabeth Irwin's misfortune, if not her country's, that the Harrison she married was too modest to aim higher than Congress.

Her husband was a serious-minded lawyer named John Scott Harrison. Following the early death of his first wife, who left three children, he chose Elizabeth within a year; she was twenty-one at her wedding on August 12, 1831. Being the granddaughter of a Scottish gentleman whose profit instinct had led him to establish a flour mill in Pennsylvania—she had been born in Mercersburg, on July 18, 1810—she had an entirely respectable background. Her own father was a Captain Archibald Irwin, who had seen the sense of removing to the promising new state of Ohio. But her husband's father had been President of the United States, albeit only for thirty-two days.

As William Henry Harrison's sole surviving son, John Scott had a claim on the Whig Party—it owed a lot to Old Tippecanoe—but he refused to cash in on his name. Despite this diffidence, he ended up with the unique distinction of being both the son and the father of a President. How much his wife contributed toward this end must remain open to question, although she certainly did her share of pious exhorting in the time she had on earth.

"I pray for you daily that you may be kept from sinning and straying from the paths of duty," she wrote to Benjamin and his older brother Archibald when they went away to school together. Archibald, her firstborn, served as a lieutenant colonel during the Civil War and died soon afterward; there is no way of assessing his potentialities. Benjamin, who was a year his junior—he was born on the Harrison's farm homestead near North Bend, Ohio, on August 20, 1833—proved himself to be as prudent as his mother would have wished. "I hope you will be prudent in your Diet . . . and abstain from cucumbers," she had written to him. In the war, he displayed sufficient courage to be made a brigadier general; and later in the Senate, he showed sufficient regularity to avoid antagonizing his party's leadership.

By then the Harrisons were, of course, Republicans, and Benjamin on his marriage had settled in Indianapolis to practice law. Thus it came about that Indiana gave the nation a President who was certainly not distinguished, but he was not a disgrace either. Had his mother lived to see him in office, she could have taken pride in his prudence. On the matter of producing children, however, she had been unable to follow her own precept, and she had died on August 15, 1850, more than thirty years before her son succeeded in settling the main issue of the 1888 election. "Grandpa's pants won't fit Benny," the Democrats chanted. "Yes, Grandfather's hat fits Ben—fits Ben," the Republicans sung right back, and although Grover Cleveland got the popular vote, Old Tippecanoe's grandson got the electoral vote, and the United States got four whole years of another Harrison.

Malvina Stone Arthur
1802-1869

In THE CASE OF Chester A. Arthur, not only his mother was alleged to be Canadian. During those tense days when James Garfield clung to life after being shot, and his Vice President waited nervously in the wings, a plot worthy of Gilbert and Sullivan unfolded as comic relief. Its theme was that a British subject stood an excellent chance of becoming the next President of the United States.

Greatly to his credit, Vice President Arthur kept a dignified silence while the drama was being played—he left it to the *New York Sun* to deal with the matter, which that worthy journal did at the crucial moment. The morning after Garfield's death, it published three columns on its front page describing an intrepid reporter's expedition to the northernmost reaches of Vermont; and it concluded that Arthur was fully entitled to all of the rights and privileges of American citizenship, including the Presidency.

Yet the hoax certainly was more interesting than the plain truth. Whatever personal papers Chester Arthur may have had were destroyed by fire and so all that can be said with any assurance about Malvina Stone, who became his mother, is that she was born on April 24, 1802, in Berkshire township, Vermont, to the wife of a farmer named George Washington Stone; and he, despite his patriotic nomenclature, a few years later moved his family just across the Canadian border. In the Quebec village of Dunham, only fifteen miles from the line, Malvina married an Irish lad on April 12, 1821, shortly before her nineteenth birthday.

This William Arthur of County Antrim was teaching school there at the time—he is supposed to have been a graduate of the University of Belfast, recently arrived to seek his fortune in the

New World. But soon the young couple crossed back into Vermont, where a Baptist revivalist set William on the path toward the ministry. While Malvina was giving her husband one baby girl after another, he was preaching and teaching in several Vermont hamlets; there seems no question that they were safely within the United States when she finally produced a son on October 5, 1830.

Even the promoters of the anti-Arthurian libretto did not dispute this. What they offered instead for the edification of the American electorate was a gruesomely inventive farce in which this particular male infant died; but the death was never recorded because the baby's body was sold to a medical school in Burlington. Then about two years later, while Malvina Stone Arthur was staying with her parents up in Quebec, she gave birth to another boy —so the story went—and when it became politic for this son to be a citizen of the United States, he assumed the identity of his dead brother. "The evidence upon which this theory is based is very insufficient," the *Sun* commented dryly.

But there were no written records to confirm Chester Arthur's birth, either; only the oral testimony of old settlers supported the more prosaic tale. By the time it had to be told, the President's parents had long since left Vermont to live in western New York, and they had both already died there, Malvina on January 16, 1869, and her husband a few years later. Thus those disposed to believe the worst of Chester Arthur could still do so with impunity. British or not, he made a somewhat better President than his previous career as a stalwart Republican spoilsman would have promised—for the sake of Anglo-American solidarity, though, it is just as well that Vermont was willing to claim him.

Sophia Birchard Hayes
1792-1866

Dɪᴅ ʏᴏᴜ ᴇᴠᴇʀ ᴏʙsᴇʀᴠᴇ this singular trait in her of being rather disposed to look on the dark side when others are joyous, & rising as others are depressed . . . thus preserving the equilibrium in our family?" When Sophia's daughter wrote this, she was not exaggerating. Her mother had a lugubrious streak of awesome dimensions, along with the bounce of an India rubber ball.

Considering the number of funerals at which Sophia Birchard Hayes had to sit on the front bench, it is no wonder that she habitually looked for the doleful point of view—and yet, even if the fates had been kinder to her personally, she probably would have tended in the same direction. Owing to her strictly Presbyterian predisposition toward gloom, she instinctively made the worst of any happy state of affairs. Nevertheless, her cheeks were so pink that they seemed almost painted, and her spirits were so naturally buoyant that disaster could not crush her. "She is grand company!" another relative once told Sophia's son. "She talks a perfect hailstorm, faster and faster, and never is tired. Oh, it did me good to hear her!"

This incorrigibly cheerful pessimist was a Vermont product; she was born in the village of Wilmington on April 15, 1792. Her father, a farmer with the shrewdness but not the stamina for making money as a merchant, died of consumption when she was thirteen. Within the space of only a few years, her mother married again, was divorced—this must have happened to strong-minded widows more often than is usually remembered—and then died of the spotted fever. Six months later, on September 13, 1813, Sophia married a young man whose hair was even redder than her cheeks; she was nineteen then.

Rutherford Hayes had come up from the Brattleboro area as the managing clerk of a new branch of a general merchandise emporium. With Revolutionary forbears every bit as doughty as Sophia's own, he also had bold ideas—he thought in terms of brick houses and expansive business interests. Vermont was too staid for his taste, and he convinced Sophia that the West would be better.

So they set out, not as poor folk by any means; they brought along three wagons stocked with furniture and such, and Ruddy Hayes chose a brick house right away, not a mansion and yet a perfectly comfortable dwelling in the central Ohio town of Delaware. This was a respectably religious settlement of transplanted New Englanders, where even Sophia allowed that she could feel quite at home helping to organize Bible classes and temperance lectures while her husband went about making their fortune with fruit orchards. She soon had three healthy babies to occupy her more fully, after having lost her first; and the future seemed so auspicious that Sophia must have shuddered with uneasy foreboding.

It turned out that her worst fears were justified. During the sickly season—which, only too aptly, was the name for summer in Ohio then—five years after their arrival, everyone in her house came down with fever. One of her darling daughters died first, and then her beloved husband. When Sophia buried him that July, she had two frail children standing by her, only barely recovered as she was herself, and she was pregnant. Two months plus two weeks afterward, on October 4, 1822, she gave birth to a boy so feeble that nobody expected him to live. Instead of despairing, Sophia Hayes named this child for his father, and she hovered over him and encouraged and scolded and cherished him with such dauntless energy that he became the sturdy comfort of her old age; he also became a safely conventional President of the United States.

Sophia had more anguish along the way—just three years later, her oldest child fell through the ice when he was out skating, and at the age of nine he drowned. That left her only little Ruddy, and the lively Fanny, but around these two she built a marvelously protective wall. She was so careful with Ruddy that he almost never played with other children; but he and his sister sewed together and studied French together and even after their paths separated they remained the closest of friends.

That Ruddy eventually escaped from his cocoon was at least partly because he did have an independent male example provided by a brother of Sophia's. A long-faced and laconic Yankee, Sardis Birchard had come out from Vermont with the Hayes caravan, and although he could not stand living with Sophia—he liked to take a drink now and then, for one thing—he never married, and he made it his business to do all he could for his sister's children. Being gifted at turning a smart trade, he ended up a banker in the small city of Fremont, and he paid the bills when Sophia wanted to send his nephew to college, besides giving Rud and Sophia both the benefit of much good advice.

But she managed her own property just as shrewdly as any man, nor was she shy about expressing opinions. "Had we not better support good schools than many needless wars with the Indians?" she wrote to Sardis. Political questions interested her to the extent that her letters were sprinkled with staunch Whiggery, and she must have turned Rud's mind in this direction. Yet these letters to her children and her brother for the most part make dolorous reading. When she took up a pen, it was usually to communicate anxiety or worse—even her announcement to her son, while he was away at school, that his sister Fanny had become engaged was tinged with melancholy:

Dear Rutherford,
. . . Seventeen years this day since your dear Father left this world of pain and sorrow. . . . Your Uncle's health I fear will never be restored and what will be still more strange, Fanny intends to leave her Mother's house and go to Columbus. What do you think of that? If you are angry about it, you must reconcile yourself to it before you come home. You will then see Mr. Platt and *try to like him well enough for a brother*. He is as much undersized as Fanny and of course a pretty good match. For further particulars, I refer you to herself . . .

Fanny's own letter to her brother provided more of a clue as to the true state of affairs within their family:

. . . Well, verily, Mother has told a doleful tale of my intentions—

trust you will bend the sympathizing ear & enter fully into the sad horrors of the case. The base ingratitude of a daughter leaving her mother's house—a proper brick one, too—& going to this vicious place, Columbus, than which Sodom & Gomorrah would be more tolerable!

Now you perceive that the sin lieth in leaving the *house,* for the Mother has agreed to go with the daughter whithersoever she goeth. And now comes the exhortation. . . . You will be required to *"try to like him well enough for a brother"*—mark the expression and draw consolation from it—your conscience may be quieted by *trying to* like him—only think how much more dreadful the requirement would have been if that one little word "try" had been omitted!

But poor Fanny had to pay for her gaiety. Although she seemed more than content as the wife of the undersized Mr. Platt—a storekeeper who turned into quite an astonishingly good provider—with the arrival of the first of her babies, she sank into a severe depression which happily subsided of itself. Then after her second baby, the malady reappeared in even worse guise; she turned so violent that she had to be confined in a lunatic asylum for the better part of a year. Thereafter, she regained her health only to suffer something of a relapse each time she gave birth, and yet she became pregnant every year or two. In between her seizures, she doted on her children, as did their grandmother, who, of necessity, took over their upbringing when Fanny, at the age of thirty-five, died a few days after producing stillborn twins. "My only support and comfort," Sophia wrote to Rutherford then, "is that she is happy and free from care and pain in the Mansions of the Blessed with my Husband and Children, a happy family in the bosom of their Savior."

For ten years more, Sophia kept on dutifully teaching manners and listening to lessons while her son-in-law attended to his business, and her only remaining child rose steadily on life's ladder. With a dear, sweet Prohibitionist wife Sophia had almost literally picked for him, Rutherford was a successful lawyer down in Cincinnati at the start of the Civil War.

Then his mother could no longer hold him back, and he galloped into the fray like the daredevil boy he must have yearned to be with one part of his personality. Commissioned as a major, he advanced to major general, achieving a glorious record on the field of battle in West Virginia. After that he was content to reap his laurels more sedately. But his mother survived only to see him elected to Congress; on October 30, 1866, when she was seventy-four, she went to join the rest of her family up in those mansions which she had discussed so often during her time on this earth.

Hannah Simpson Grant
1798-1883

THERE IS NOTHING particularly appealing about either parent of Ulysses S. Grant—in their separate ways, they repulse every effort to admire them. Still, one can at least sympathize with this hero's mother, for she had many crosses to bear, among them none more galling than a boorish, bragging, opinionated husband. Since her own sins were of omission, especially when it came to language, he could not have suffered as much as she did.

Taken together, Hannah and Jesse Grant provide a dreary example of early American Gothic domesticity; no wonder their son was tempted to drink. But even so, and although he failed sadly as a President, it must not be forgotten that he made a very good general. Surprisingly enough, the same habits of mind which marked his silent, fatalistic mother were the basis of his strength— this bearded avenger was another Mama's boy.

She had been scarred young, having lost her mother at the age of three; she was born on a farm not far to the north of Philadelphia on November 23, 1798. Her father, an unhurrying sort of man one generation removed from the North of Ireland, waited four years till he found a suitable stepmother for his four children. Even though he made a decent choice when he did get around to it, it seems that Hannah had already been hurt seriously. With approval, because quiet obedience was valued so highly then, John Simpson's second wife some years later bore witness that this girl at the age of seven had "as much the deportment of a woman as most girls at twenty."

Hannah was twenty-three when this testimonial was given—to a brash young man who came calling in search of a wife. Only a few years earlier, the Simpson family had moved out to Ohio; approaching fifty, Hannah's father got the Western bug, and sold his thriving farm to begin again with six hundred choice acres southeast of Cincinnati. At school back in Pennsylvania, Hannah had seemed clever enough, and strong-minded beneath her outer docility, but her prim exterior had not attracted any suitors on either side of the mountains until Jesse Root Grant appeared. Hence, even he was welcomed.

Being twenty-six, he was already one year beyond the deadline he had set himself for marrying. But he had been delayed by assorted buffetings of fate which certainly helped to explain, if not excuse, his crudities. For all practical purposes an orphan since the age of eleven, when his mother had died and his Revolutionary captain of a father had dissolved in drink, he had been taken in by neighbors who saw that he got a little schooling; it was his own idea that because his father had started with property, then lost everything, he himself would reverse the pattern and, starting with nothing, end up not just comfortable, but rich. As a first step, he applied himself fiercely toward learning the tanner's trade, but a long bout of malaria had kept him from lifting a finger after he first went into business. Now he was trying again in a new community, and wanted a wife.

As far as can be known, romance was totally lacking in Jesse's courtship of Hannah. Having heard there was a marriageable daughter out on the fertile Simpson farm, Jesse rode by to look her over, and, being so much of a talker himself, he found her silence attractive. As for Hannah, she already was religious to the point of mysticism, but she lacked the option of entering a convent —in that part of Ohio, she could not even find the comfort of a Presbyterian church, and she had to embrace Methodism. So she took it as God's will that she dutifully marry; and since her family seemed satisfied with Jesse Grant, she made no objection.

That the prosperous Simpsons were willing to give her to an upstart tanner with hardly a dollar to his name did cause some headshaking in the neighborhood, and yet it had to be remembered that Hannah might not have another chance. Furthermore, Jesse for all his bluster was ambitious to better his mind, which pleased Hannah's stepmother. She loaned him books from her own stock of the classics, and these two spent companionable hours discussing literature. Whether Hannah contributed so much as a word was never mentioned later—but she did make the proper responses when she and Jesse were married on June 24, 1821.

Their first home was Jesse's two-room frame cottage in the nearby Ohio River village of Point Pleasant. Here Hannah gave birth to a large boy just ten months later, on April 27, 1822. It almost seems as if she had vowed to assume the pain of bearing children without any thought of pleasure—she did not even care about naming this baby. The ceremonial selection of a fitting appellation took place a month afterward at the Simpson farm, when every relative present was asked to state a preference on a slip of paper. Hannah did favor Albert, a popular name in the West then because of the road-building program of Albert Gallatin; but Grandfather Simpson wanted Hiram; and Jesse and Hannah's stepmother, both inspired by their recent reading, agreed on Ulysses. As a politic gesture toward his well-off father-in-law, Jesse compromised with Hiram Ulysses Grant.

What they actually called the boy, though, was a short form of his middle name—rendered in writing as Ulyss. But despite Jesse's eventual victory on this front, and despite his loud claims of authority in every area, he was far from an idol to his son; and even on this matter of a name, his triumph was accidentally diluted. When in the course of events Ulyss packed up for West Point, he shuddered at the initials H.U.G. on his trunk, and arbitrarily reversed the first two, only to find in the East that the Congressman who had signed his appointment papers—an old acquaintance of the Simpson family—had put him down as Ulysses Simpson Grant. Although Ulysses tried to get Hiram back on his record, the Army proved inflexible, and owing to his new initials, he got plenty of the sort of attention he had dreaded, but after a spell as Uncle Sam, he managed to become plain Sam Grant.

That he could dread being the butt of cadet horseplay was more than ordinary adolescent sensitivity—Ulyss had his mother's dispo-

sition. Throughout his childhood, he kept to himself to the extent
that neighbors commented about how much he favored her, and
they also commented about her remarkable way of child-rearing,
which undoubtedly had more effect on him than anything else did.
Being positive that God determined even the smallest happening
on earth, she would not interfere with His will. When Ulyss was
still an infant, she let him crawl about where horses could trample
him, and if neighbors came running to warn her that her boy was
in danger, she calmly thanked them and went about her business.

Not that she neglected him altogether—if his stomach got upset,
she gave him castor oil and put him to bed before leaving the rest
to the Lord; and once when he came in from sledding with his feet
frozen, she thawed them out in smouldering hay and bound them
in bacon to ease his pain. But what she was unable to offer him or
her other children or her husband was a cheery smile, a warm
word, any evidence of human concern. She fed their other needs
dutifully, but she must have starved their spirits.

Considering the kind of man Jesse Grant was, her steady retreat
into religious mysticism is not too hard to understand. Just about
the only ingratiating touch in the picture he presented to his neighbors was a bit of doggerel he wrote when a Buckeye bard sent an
open verse to the local newspaper, confiding that he badly needed
a new pair of shoes. This provoked Jesse to reply:

> *Backwoodsman, sir, my aged friend,*
> *These lines in answer back I send,*
> *To thank you for your rhyming letter,*
> *Published in The Castigator.*
> *The story of your worn-out shoes,*
> *Is, to a tanner, no strange news . . .*
> *And though I have not much to spare,*
> *I can, at least, supply a pair . . .*

Otherwise, conceit and bombast marked the man as his own
worst enemy. For even though he must have antagonized a good
many people whose paths crossed his, and he failed utterly to advance his own political ambitions, he did manage to build a solid
business reputation. From his small start, he expanded with a chain
of harness and leather supply stores that amply fulfilled his promise to himself; before he was finished, he was worth about $150,000.

Ostensibly because he could not stand the smell of leather curing, Ulyss stayed as far away from his father's tannery as he could—being so good with horses, he did his share of helping by hauling supplies and making deliveries. For a strong-looking boy, Ulyss had more than his share of oddity; he could not stand his mother's favorite milieu either. Because he insisted that any kind of music at all grated unbearably on his nerves, he was excused from accompanying her to church.

Yet he raised no objection when his father proposed West Point as a good way for getting a free education. Just before departing, Ulyss stopped in at a neighbor's to bid the family farewell, and the emotional reaction he encountered caused him to say: "Why, Mrs. Bailey, you must be sorry I am going. They didn't cry at our house." That and the greeting he received when he returned to Ohio for his first visit two years later tell all that needs to be added about the Grants' home life. "Ulysses, you've grown much straighter," his mother observed before resuming her preparations for her family's next meal.

It does not appear that Hannah's other children felt their deprivation so keenly; she brought up five more to maturity, and Ulyss's two brothers went uncomplainingly into their father's business while the girls lived unremarked lives which must be presumed to have been unremarkable. Only Hannah's first son was noticeably affected by the uncongeniality of his early environment. After West Point, he saw his parents as infrequently as possible, and yet his mother's obsession with predestination colored his whole career.

When he was asked to resign from the Army despite his fine record in the Mexican War—because of an excessively alcoholic tour of duty in Alaska—it seemed that his chance for success was blasted. But after floundering almost into ruin as a farmer, and being forced to come to his father for a clerking job, the Civil War gave him his second chance. With the audacity of a man who knows that even the best laid plans are subject to change by some mysterious force, call it God or call it fate, he proved himself a brilliant improviser then.

While Jesse gained renown among his neighbors as a man who would stop anybody in the rain to brag about his son, Hannah not only held her peace—she ran from the room in a discomfited blush if she ever heard her son's praises spoken in her presence. "She thought nothing you could do would entitle you to praise," one of her relatives suggested; ". . . you ought to praise the Lord for your opportunity to do it."

Although she lived through his two terms of office as President, she attended neither inauguration; she never even visited the White House. Because she had succeeded in thoroughly alienating her St. Louis daughter-in-law, the impetus for keeping apart doubtless was mutual. But Hannah did have enough pride or some similar emotion to regret the separation, or at least there is one justification for assuming this was the case. In the only product of her pen that found its way into the Library of Congress collection of Grant papers, she wrote in 1880, when she was almost eighty-two, to an old neighbor:

> Dear Sister King,
>   How I would like to see you . . . U S Grant paid us a short Visit he received your letter he Seldom Writes to any of us. . . . May the Lord bless and protect you is my prayer
>
> Hannah Grant

A little more than three years later, after Jesse had died and she was living in Jersey City, New Jersey, with a married daughter, Hannah departed this world at the age of eighty-four on May 11, 1883, only two years before her cancer-stricken son, disappointed in his hopes for a third term, also succumbed.

Mary McDonough Johnson
1783-1856

WHEN Andrew Johnson began running for Congress, he felt obliged to write an open letter on the subject of his parentage. Being no mincer of words, he called his enemies "ghouls and hyenas" because they were spreading the story that his beginnings could not possibly have been as humble as he claimed. In short, he declined to take it as a compliment when people doubted whether such a man as he could truly have sprung from the union of a porter and a chambermaid.

On this matter, no less than on his intransigence in fighting the radicals within his own party when he accidentally reached the Presidency, posterity has supported him. The best that conscientious scholarship has been able to come up with concerning his early life is that he was indeed born to a pair of servants who were poor and illiterate and, as far as can be discovered, utterly lacking in family connections.

His mother had started life as Mary McDonough on July 17, 1783, but where and how she spent her childhood is, and probably always will be, veiled in mystery. Her first traceable appearance occurred in September of 1801, when she was eighteen; she turned up then before the appropriate authorities in the North Carolina capital of Raleigh to certify her intention of marrying one Jacob Johnson, porter at the inn just opposite the State House. Perhaps she was already working there herself, but be that as it may, she helped the landlord's wife from that time on—diligently enough to be remembered by a decade of travelers as Polly, the porter's wife.

In the yard near the inn's stables was a small cottage, and here Polly gave birth to a girl who died, then to a boy named Bill who left no impress except a vague tradition that he ended as a ne'er-do-well in Texas. The same modest shelter was the setting for the arrival of another son on December 29, 1808; he became the seventeenth President of the United States.

According to local folklore, a merry party marking the holiday season was in progress in the inn's taproom when word came that Polly had just produced a boy—and a contingent of revelers who admired General Jackson down in Tennessee suggested giving the general a namesake. So Andy Johnson it was, and a less promising candidate for success would have been hard to find. When this Andy was just three, his father died of the aftereffects of rescuing a few gentlemen who had been celebrating some other occasion at a mill on a creek outside of town, which left poor Polly to support her two sons all by herself as best she could.

She had no easy time. Because one of the gentlemen Jacob had succeeded in fishing out of the creek was the editor of the *Raleigh Star,* that newspaper published a warm tribute to the departed porter's honesty and industry; but when it came to feeding her boys, Polly barely managed with the money she earned by weaving and spinning. After a few years, she felt unable to carry on alone any longer, and she married a man named Turner Dougherty. Yet he, it seems, had even less talent than she for making money. Soon they bound out young Bill to a tailor, and right after Andy turned thirteen he joined his brother as an apprentice to this same Tailor Selby.

How much hindsight marked Tailor Selby's testimony nobody can say, but many years later he remembered that Andy had seemed a natural leader who resented his own low status even that young. Being also "a wild, harum-scarum boy with no dishonorable traits, however," he got into plenty of mischief. When an old lady threatened to prosecute him for some sort of minor vandalism, he ran away at fifteen; and Selby advertised a ten-dollar reward for Andy in the newspapers.

Although he returned after a year or so of tailoring on his own down in South Carolina, his dubious situation as far as his apprenticeship was concerned made it politic for him to leave Raleigh for good. With his mother and stepfather, and all of their earthly belongings loaded in a two-wheel cart, Andy Johnson set out for Tennessee in 1826. There he opened a tailor shop on the main street of Greeneville, which brought him to the attention of the village shoemaker's daughter; he was eighteen and she sixteen when they married on May 17, 1827.

That his wife taught him how to read is practically the only fact about Andrew Johnson assimilated by most schoolchildren—until they have to consider the shameful chapter about his impeachment proceedings. No matter that he deserves better than his accusers, he still has gone down in history as the only President ever to be put on trial for dereliction of duty. Yet the real lesson in his career has been all but overlooked.

No other President started from quite such a disadvantaged position as he did, and it is too bad that there is no way of discovering what else besides just plain luck operated in his favor. The thoroughbred school of thought would hold that he must have got good blood from somewhere—thus the rash of stories, to the effect that he was sired by at least a banker, which spread through Tennessee after his prowess as a village debater brought him into local then state then national politics. Perhaps his mother herself had unsung qualities, but if she did, she left no hint of them; she and her shiftless second husband stayed put on a farm Andy bought for them till she died at the age of seventy-two on February 13, 1856. So the source of his inspiration must remain, as the King of Siam said, a puzzlement.

Elizabeth Speer Buchanan
1767-1833

> *Monarchs, we envy not your state*
> *We look with pity on the great*
> *And bless our humbler lot . . .*
> > *Wrote by me*
> > *E.B.*

I᛭ DOES SEEM as if the mother of James Buchanan meant exactly what she said in her poem, which she entitled "The Fireside," and so she was fortunate. Had she lived to see her son in the White House, her emotional conflict would have been fearful. Between pride in him and pity for him, she could have enjoyed no peace.

During a calmer era, he might have made a reasonably competent custodian of the national interest, but it was his fate to win the prize he had been seeking for more than a decade at a time when sectional animosity cried out for a political Solomon, which he was not. Being a bachelor, he even lacked the comfort of wifely solicitude—if ever a man needed his mother, this President did.

Whatever was likable about him he had already learned from her, along with a taste for untroubled rural retirement that much better suited a poetically inclined lady than the chief executive of a nation on the brink of civil strife. The ambition which had propelled him into "the giddy dance," as his mother described the preoccupations of the great world, derived undoubtedly from his father.

As a girl of sixteen, Elizabeth Speer had quite understandably been fascinated by James Buchanan senior. She was born in 1767, on a date that was not recorded, near Lancaster in Pennsylvania, and she must have received more than just a rudimentary schooling because she could repeat long stanzas of Milton from memory. But after a dispute with his pastor, her Presbyterian father had moved his family onto a farm further to the west, where it was lonelier, although the next farm along the wagon trail that went on through the mountains had a wayside tavern for the convenience of travelers.

Here a nephew of the tavern keeper turned up one fine day, right off a boat from Ireland and filled with determination to make his fortune in America. The glamour of that exciting world she later dismissed clung to him, enchanting Elizabeth. But he had to earn a place for himself before he could take a wife; she was twenty-one and he twenty-seven when they married on April 16, 1788.

Then the place he took her to was rough enough, but it hardly qualified as lonely. In a mountain gap forty miles to the west of her family's farm—at a place called Stony Batter—her James had become the owner of a busy trading post. Often there were a hundred horses stamping about the corral while their drivers transferred goods destined for Pittsburgh from wagons to pack trains. So noise and flurry gave a semblance of civilization, even if the best accommodation available for the bride consisted of a mud-chinked log house. Within its shelter, Elizabeth gave birth to a daughter the year after her marriage, and then on April 23, 1791, she produced a son who was named for his father.

Circumstances conspired to make this boy the best hope of both of his parents. Shortly after his birth, his older sister died, causing Elizabeth to cherish the child who remained with her extravagantly. Then her next child and the next and the next were all girls, until their father despaired of having another son and focused all his paternal zeal in one direction—not till young James was almost ready to leave for college did he acquire a brother, then another and another. In all, Elizabeth had eleven children.

But her first son grew up surrounded by adoring females, and with a father who demanded perfection of him. So it is easy to see how a doctrinaire analyst would explain why he never married; and yet it is much harder, of course, to give any pat explanation for his achieving the Presidency. From his father, James Buchanan got a go-getter outlook, from his mother a disposition to compromise, and with these qualities he might well have made a successful country lawyer, which in the long run would have been the right niche for him. His further advancement simply must be accepted as a lesson in humility by would-be seers, although it is pertinent to note that during the two decades preceding the Civil War, Presidential mediocrity was almost guaranteed by the facts of political life; in order to avoid antagonizing either the South or the North too much, parties striving for national status of necessity tended to nominate weak men.

Well before Buchanan began his rise via Congress and the diplomatic service, his father had moved his family from the rowdy discomfort of Stony Batter to a gentlemanly farm just outside the pleasant little town of Mercersburg. With the proceeds of his assorted business interests, James senior could well afford squiredom, and his wife rejoiced in the blessings of her own warm hearth where she contentedly quoted poetry to her children and grandchildren. After her husband died in 1821 at the age of sixty, she still had many loving hearts to keep her company, although she missed her son James as he journeyed farther and farther away from her. It was from St. Petersburg that he wrote to her in the summer of 1833:

> My dear Mother,
> I can now write to you with some degree of certainty in relation to my return to my native land. With God's blessing I hope to be able to leave St. Petersburg at the beginning of the next month. . . . You may rest assured that I shall then lose no time in paying you a visit; when I trust in Heaven you will still be in the enjoyment of your usual health. Inclination & duty—affection & gratitude all render you the first object of my affections . . .

The letter never reached her, however, because she had already died quietly by her fireside. Two months earlier, on May 14, 1833, Elizabeth Buchanan had departed this life at the age of sixty-six. Owing to the irregularity of transatlantic mail service, James Buchanan did not discover his loss till he returned to America; and so he had only his sisters and his nieces to pity him when he moved into the White House two decades later.

Anna Kendrick Pierce
1768-1838

In one respect, Anna Kendrick Pierce differs from every other Presidential mother. She drank. Nor is this a matter of only limited pertinence, because her son Franklin had the same failing —and he attributed it to maternal example. Since there was nothing else that particularly distinguished New Hampshire's sole occupant of the White House, the weakness he shared with his female parent can hardly be overlooked.

It was, as far as scholarly inquiry has been able to determine, a weakness in the literal sense. Both mother and son were constitutionally incapable of imbibing even small amounts of alcohol without ill effects—they were allergic to liquor, a sympathetic biographer has concluded. Be that as it may, neither of them resisted taking a few drops anyway from time to time.

Not unexpectedly, Miss Anna Kendrick was a lively girl, noted for her mercurial temperament. The youngest in her family, she had been born in Amherst, New Hampshire, on October 30, 1768; she was twenty-one when a forceful newcomer to nearby Hillsborough took her as his second wife on February 1, 1790. Although he was only thirty-three, Benjamin Pierce had fought through most of the Revolution, ending up a captain, and then, dissatisfied with his prospects back in settled Massachusetts, he had decided to try his luck in the more open spaces to the north. His recent first attempt at matrimony having terminated abruptly when his bride of a year died giving birth to a daughter who survived, Ben needed a stepmother for the baby right away, and Anna was willing.

All he could offer at the moment was a log house beside a little stream that ran through his farm, but already he had grander ideas. With his soldiering experience, he aimed to be a leader in the local militia, and soon he did enjoy the pleasure of being called General Pierce. Although he had only a rough sort of education, this fazed him not a bit; he also pushed ahead with the politicking that eventually brought him two terms in New Hampshire's gubernatorial mansion. Well before then, he had built a mansion of his own in Hillsborough which, alas for Anna, had a tavern attached to it.

The village talked, naturally, about her tendency to seek alcoholic stimulation; it was local gossip passed down diligently through the years that called her frailty to the attention of her son's biographers. Yet there is no reason for doubting the substance of these stories because members of her family discussed the same subject, albeit guardedly, in some of their letters. Anna Pierce's fondness for showy dress also found its way from the sewing circle onto the printed page in the same manner—they say she once appeared in church wearing a gown so short that it displayed ankles encircled with red ribbons.

Nevertheless, she managed not too badly at bringing up her own eight children, plus the stepdaughter who married another militia officer and became Mrs. General McNeil during the War of 1812. Of her own children, her oldest son gained some distinction in the same combat and her youngest acquired a respectable local name for his civic services; another died at twenty-five over in Utica, New York, of an unspecified malady. Her daughters, as is not unusual, have faded into decent obscurity. Only the sixth of her offspring preserved her from the same respectable fate.

He thought she was a good mother. "She was a most affectionate and tender mother," he wrote to his brother-in-law McNeil right after her death, "strong in many points and weak in some but always weak on the side of kindness and deep affection." Exactly the same could have been said of him. Neither first nor last among the progeny in his family, he stood out because of his amiability; except for his oldest brother, he was the only son General Pierce could be prevailed on to provide with higher education. One must assume that his wife encouraged him to grant Franklin this boon.

For of course she must have been charming during her younger days, and that was something else in which Franklin took after her. When he went off to Bowdoin College up in Maine, it happened that one of his classmates was a rather strange young man from Salem, Massachusetts, named Nathaniel Hawthorne who later wrote: "At this early period of his life he was distinguished by the same fascination of manner that has since proved so magical in winning him unbounded personal popularity."

Certainly Hawthorne's anxiety for a political appointment clouded his judgment; in truth, his friend was an amiable mediocrity whose candidacy appealed mainly to those hoping the North-South troubles would somehow blow over if ignored. But it was undoubtedly true that Franklin Pierce got as far as he did mainly on charm, plus the fact that a Democrat hailing from New England had something of a novelty appeal; Franklin inherited his political coloration from his father, a bluff Jacksonian Democrat who even looked a lot like Old Hickory. But in the White House the little that Pierce had to offer was not enough, and his own party would not even pay him the ritual compliment of nominating him for a second term; he died in obscurity twelve years after leaving office. Much before then, but many months after descending into what was charitably called senility, his mother had preceded him. She died in Hillsborough on December 7, 1838, at the age of seventy.

Phoebe Millard Fillmore

1780-1831

She was sickly and she died of dropsy at a comparatively early age, but before she did she saw to it that her first son got the chance to rise out of grinding poverty by studying law. Hardly

anything else is known about the mother of Millard Fillmore—
which cannot be considered a great loss. He compels almost no
interest, and it does not appear that she would either.

What little survives about her suggests a sad picture. Her own
girlhood had been rather comfortable; the daughter of a doctor,
she was born in Pittsfield, Massachusetts, on an unrecorded date
in 1780. But when she was about sixteen, she fell in love with an
adventurous farmer in his early twenties whose boldness out-
stripped his ability or at least his luck. For he convinced her to
dare the wilderness with him instead of staying in tame New
England and, sight unseen, he bought a piece of land over in
central New York State from a traveling promoter.

Nathaniel Fillmore could scarcely have done worse. After the
labor of clearing a few acres and building a cabin, he discovered
that his part of the forest had a hard clay soil worth virtually nothing—and that, in the bargain, it was not really his to keep. Owing
to a tangle of conflicting claims, he had to give up and accept the
mean status of being just a tenant farmer plowing somebody else's
ground in the same general area near the village of Summerhill.
Bare subsistence was all he could hope for then, but he could find
no way to do any better.

From the time she married her bumbling adventurer, Phoebe
knew only hardship and yet she does not seem to have surren-
dered to it. With the birth of her first son on January 7, 1800—she
had eight children in all, sickly though she was—she made this
boy's success her goal. By giving him her family's name, she certified her faith in his higher destiny.

Although her husband was more than willing to join her in
disparaging backwoods farming, he could not help Millard improve himself. Phoebe had carried a Bible, a hymnbook, and an
almanac from Vermont—with these she taught her boy to read, but
he saw no other books till he was seventeen and tending the machinery in a cloth mill in the next county. Then he discovered a
circulating library, and he read enough after hours to qualify for
enrolling on a part-time basis in a local academy.

One thing more Phoebe could do for her son. When he came
home on a visit a few years later, she told him his father had gone
to see their landlord, who was a lawyer, and had convinced this

gentleman to try out his tenant's son as a clerk. Millard was so overcome with joy that he broke into tears right at the dinner table.

After that, he went ahead on his own, mastering sufficient law to be able to begin practicing when he was twenty-three. As a representative of that odd splinter group known as the Anti-Masons, he reached the New York State Assembly within the decade—before she died on May 2, 1831, at the age of fifty-one, Phoebe Fillmore had the pleasure of seeing him depart for Albany in a fine new suit and sporting a cane.

Later he traveled on to Congress as a Whig, and he reached the Vice Presidency when that party won in 1848 with General Zachary Taylor at the head of its ticket; because the old general was defeated soon afterward by typhoid, Fillmore spent almost three years in the White House, and he did not do too badly. But he never did manage to win the Presidency in his own right although he tried several times, even as the standard-bearer of the belligerently chauvinist Know Nothings. If for no other reason than his willingness to accept their rickety platform, he deserves the obscurity that thereafter descended upon him and his family.

Sarah Strother Taylor
1760-1822

I was born in Orrange County, State of Vig. Nov. 24th 1784. My father Richard Taylor was appointed an officer in the first Regiment of continental troops raised by the State of Virginia to oppose the Brittish at the commencement of the Revolution & remained in the service in the Continental Line until the close of the war & quit the Service as a Lt. Col. In the Spring of '85 he emigrated to this state, settled in the neighborhood of Louisville where I was raised. In the Spring of 1808 I was appointed a first Lieutenant in the 7th Regiment United States Infantry . . .

THUS DID Zachary Taylor start a fifteen-page autobiography—without so much as mentioning his mother. Since he was interested in very little besides soldiering, this is not especially surprising, and yet it is not really fair because he owed quite a lot to her. Whatever learning he had came from her, and one must doubt whether he would have been able to write even one page if she had not taught him his letters.

As Sally Strother, she herself had tutors from Europe when she was growing up on a plantation to the west of Fredericksburg in Virginia; she had been born there on December 14, 1760. During the Revolution, Old Zack's father must have taken some time off from fighting, for Sally married him on August 20, 1779, when she was eighteen, and she soon began producing children—her eventual total was nine. Zachary, who was named for his paternal grandfather, had two older brothers, three younger brothers, and three sisters of whom almost nothing is known.

By the time he made his appearance in 1784, the war was over and his father had determined on a great step. Coming of a respectable family but one of no particular distinction, he did not have any grand prospects in the settled area of his birth, and so he decided to take advantage of the land bonus due him over in Virginia's western preserve, which would soon become Kentucky. After a scouting trip by himself, he came back to escort his gentle wife and three infants down the Wilderness Trail early in 1785.

Although eventually Richard Taylor had a fine and comfortable plantation going in the Louisville area, the first years there were not gracious. Sally must have had plenty of stamina in addition to her gentility because at the outset she had to make do with a log cabin just the same as any poor man's wife. While her menfolk toiled with ax and brute strength, it was up to her to keep alive a vestige of civilization.

About her accomplishments nothing else can be said except that she raised a boy who learned to read even as he was dreaming of becoming a soldier. He never did reach any notable rank intellectually, but when his country craved a noncontroversial hero as its President after the Mexican War, Old Zack was ready—at least partly owing to her forgotten patience. But she did not live to see him a general, let alone President; she had died on December 13, 1822, a day before her sixty-second birthday, when this son, like his father before him, was only a lieutenant colonel.

Jane Knox Polk

1776-1852

ALTHOUGH he was not a likable man, James K. Polk made a strong President. While a number of other factors undoubtedly played some part in bringing about this state of affairs, one cause stands out—and it very definitely has to do with his mother. She was the great great grandniece of the founder of Scottish Presbyterianism.

Even if Jane Knox lacked the force of John Knox—who had a strength of will only rarely encountered in all history—she certainly took the tenets of her illustrious ancestor with the deepest seriousness. So she only naturally instructed her first son to consider time spent on mere amusement as time wasted; as a result, he accomplished a great deal but he never did learn how to smile.

Whether she herself was quite as dour as this son cannot be stated with any assurance because only one of her letters to him has been preserved, and since it was written not long after she became a widow, her mournful tone may not be typical. "Mother until death Jane Polk," she signed it. There is, however, one bit of evidence hinting that, at least in her younger days, her gloom was slightly leavened—for they called her Jenny then.

The daughter of a hard-working farmer in western North Carolina, she had been born near Mecklenburg on November 15, 1776; not long afterward, her father went off to fight in the Revolution and came home a colonel. Thenceforth, besides his distinguished name he also had a brave record to set him apart in the community; but above all he was known for his piety, as was Jane.

Yet she married an ambitious young fellow with a chip on his shoulder when it came to churchgoing, which he got from his outspoken Scotch-Irish grandfather. Of course, she must have thought she would help her Samuel to see the light, and he submitted meekly for the first year or so after their wedding on Christmas night in 1794. But Sam Polk rebelled soon enough, right after she gave him a son on November 2, 1795. Although he agreed to name the boy James Knox Polk after her father, he positively refused to have the boy baptized a Presbyterian if doing so meant that he himself would have to stand forth and profess his own faith first. When the parson insisted there was no other way, Sam Polk contradicted him. How Jane must have suffered can only be imagined but she never did convince her husband to yield—young Jim Polk grew up a strict Presbyterian in everything except actual fact.

It might seem then that as far as strength of will was concerned, Jane Polk took second place in her own home. Nevertheless, as does happen rather often, the silent partner carried more weight, after all. From early childhood, James was clearly his mother's boy. Almost girlishly delicate, he deprived his father of the sturdy helper the latter craved—especially after Sam Polk decided North Carolina was stagnant and took his family down to the wilds of Tennessee.

James was eleven then, and when he was about fourteen somebody concluded that without surgery to remove stones from his gall bladder, of all unlikely things, he would never do a man's work. Since there was a renowned lithotomist over in Kentucky, Sam Polk brought the boy to him to be operated on; and the drastic treatment must have done some good. After surviving the knife, James was no longer troubled by his health.

But the sense of purpose that drove him from then on owed more to his mother than his father. In Tennessee, Sam had raised his sights to include surveying and storekeeping besides farming, and he had plenty of opportunities to offer; what James wanted, though, and what his mother wanted for him, was schooling. This time Sam gave in, and he sent his son all the way to the University of North Carolina.

By assiduously devoting himself to all work and no play, James Polk rose from being a backwoods lawyer to become the Speaker of the House of Representatives. As far back as Mecklenburg, Polks had been acquainted with Jacksons, and President Andy Jackson found this Polk a more than useful lieutenant; as a result, the Democratic Party passed over a profusion of other candidates to make Old Hickory's favorite the first dark horse nominee for the Presidency. But when Polk won election in 1844, he swiftly proved he was his own man—and a miserable politician. He admitted Texas, he fought and won the Mexican War thereby gaining California, and he settled the Oregon question, all of which he had methodically set out to do; in the process, though, he made so many enemies by his self-righteousness that his own party refused to put him up for a second term.

Only his mother, who did live to see him in the White House, had no cause for complaint against him. Less than a year after he left office, when he sank into a strange decline and was dying, he is said to have told her: "Mother, I have never in my life disobeyed you." There is no reason to doubt this, but another of her sons had done what he could to balance the record by drinking himself into his grave at the age of twenty-eight. Yet only one of Jane Polk's ten children failed her so dreadfully and so she had no reason to anticipate reproaches from on high when she died two years after James, on January 11, 1852; she was seventy-five then.

Mary Armistead Tyler

1761-1797

ONCE IT HAS BEEN SAID that John Tyler was the first Vice President to achieve the Presidency on the death of an incumbent, and that when he was in the White House as a widower of fifty-four he married a delightful girl thirty years his junior, his claims on the attention of posterity are extremely small. Because his family papers were destroyed during the Civil War, even less can be said of his mother—practically all that is known of her is that she was a Virginia gentlewoman who died in April of 1797 when he was only seven.

Having been born on an unrecorded date in 1761, she was

thirty-six then. The daughter of a prominent planter named Robert Armistead, she was married, if fragmentary documents are to be trusted, when she was just sixteen. Then she and her distinguished husband, a lawyer and later a judge who was to serve three successive terms as the governor of Virginia, took up residence at a gracious tidewater establishment they named Greenway. Her sixth child and second son, who was born on March 20, 1790, for a reason unfathomable at this distance was given his father's name and went on to surpass his father's purely Virginian fame. Being too ardent a states' righter for the North to admire, President Tyler won no more national elections after he left the White House, nor did any other Virginian till Woodrow Wilson.

Elizabeth Bassett Harrison
1730?-1792?

ABOUT HALFWAY between Williamsburg and Richmond, ideally situated for the convenience of tourists, the lovely mellow brick plantation house where this lady reigned as hostess still stands commanding awe—and an occasional chuckle. That a man born and raised here could be sold to the American electorate as a log cabin President does beat almost anything in the line of political humbuggery. If the mother of William Henry Harrison had a sense of humor, and if she had managed to live to see the Presidential campaign of 1840, she might have died laughing.

But there is no reason at all to suspect her of any such proclivity. Absolutely the only information that has survived concerning her own person fits into a single sentence. She was born on a neighboring plantation owned by Colonel William Bassett, probably in 1730; when she was about eighteen, she married the fifth Benjamin Harrison of Virginia; and after producing seven children, she died on the Harrison plantation known as Berkeley when she was about sixty-two, in 1792 or the following year. With somewhat less assurance, it can be added that she is supposed to have been a niece of a sister of Martha Washington, and noted for her beauty and benevolence. Otherwise, her life is a blank.

And yet Berkeley itself fills in many details. Overlooking a particularly pretty reach of the James River, it is advertised as one of the finest examples of early tidewater elegance to have survived intact; and although the hand of the restorer did have to make certain repairs, the job has been done unobtrusively enough to preserve a feeling of comfort rather than any stiff museum atmosphere. To live there must have been extremely pleasant.

Besides her house, there is also Elizabeth Harrison's husband to provide a few clues. From the year of their marriage, he served uninterruptedly in Virginia's House of Burgesses—till he went up to Philadelphia, where in due course he signed the Declaration of Independence. He was also a militia colonel, and governor of Virginia from 1781 to 1784. The wife of such a man surely would have been familiar with the best drawing rooms of Williamsburg in their original incarnation.

He was, of course, following but also improving on the unbroken record of public service compiled by other Benjamin Harrisons going back to the 1630's. But her own first son—Benjamin VI—died at forty before he could add any further luster to the name; at least partly accidentally, the youngest of her seven children became the most famous Harrison of all.

William Henry was born at Berkeley on February 9, 1773, and doubtless because he was so far down the line he was encouraged to look for another profession besides that of planter. Whether or not medicine was his own choice, he was enrolled as a medical student at the University of Pennsylvania when something that suited him better turned up—he quit to join the Army and fight the Indians out in the Northwest Territory. Thereafter, he made his own personal headquarters in what soon became Ohio, and since this was rough enough to start with, he knew how it felt to seek shelter within a cabin of logs.

Yet he had at least some Berkeley tastes, and by the time the Whig Party seized on him as its Presidential candidate he had a perfectly civilized country estate on the Ohio River. Still it struck a Baltimore newspaper as a good idea to say that the aged winner of the Battle of Tippecanoe should be allowed to live out his days peacefully in his log cabin, drinking hard cider and mulling over the War of 1812. The Whigs merely took advantage of the opportunity thus opened to them—Old Tip became the log-cabin-and-hard-cider nominee, while poor Martin Van Buren, who could truthfully have boasted of humble beginnings, but dressed like a dandy, had to watch his bid for reelection go down amid an uproar of raucous song:

> *Old Tip he wears a homespun suit,*
> *He has no ruffled shirt-wirt-wirt;*
> *But Mat he has the golden plate,*
> *And he's a little squirt-wirt-wirt.*

At the final "wirt," tobacco chewers, of course, took their cue to spit, which certainly would not have amused the candidate's mother. But Old Tip still retained some feeling for the finer things which she had taught him; on his way to Washington, he made a sentimental pilgrimage back to Berkeley where he wrote his inaugural address right in the room where she had died. Being sixty-eight when he delivered the speech, which was exceptionally long, he got pneumonia as the result of standing out in the cold for such a length of time, and so after just a month in office he went to rejoin her in another sort of mansion.

Maria Hoes Van Alen Van Buren
1747-1818

ONLY IN THE CASE of the mother of Martin Van Buren can an out-and-out feminist take real comfort. This lady married twice, and she bore sons by both husbands—with her first spouse she produced a member of Congress, then the second time she did a little better and contributed a President to the United States. Since the rural Dutch community where she lived was not otherwise noted for political fertility, she may well have been a remarkable woman.

But there is a sad lack of fact to bolster any such supposition. Her more famous son, when he came to write his autobiography, dismissed her quickly after describing her family background: ". . . & she was regarded to all who knew her as liberally endowed with the qualities & virtues that adorn the female character." Even the painstaking compilers of several marvelously digressive local histories treating her part of the Hudson Valley offer no personal information about her except her epitaph: "Her long life was adorned by domestic virtues of the most useful kind . . ." It does not appear to have struck any of her contemporaries that her talent extended beyond the ordinary bounds set for good wives.

Still, the bare outline of her life suggests this. She was the daughter of a respected family, originally written as Goes but pronounced, Dutch style, as Hoes, until the change in spelling finally was adopted to end confusion among the English-speaking authorities who succeeded the Dutch rulers of New York. Maria's grandfather had been among the first settlers of Kinderhook, about twenty miles south of Albany; she was born in the neighboring village of Claverack on an unrecorded date in 1747.

Twenty years later, she married a young man whose name was Johannes Van Alen, but nothing else is known of him. Because the area abounded so richly in Van Alens who not uncommonly bestowed the name of Johannes on their progeny, even expert genealogists have had to glide past him with only the terse mention that he gave Maria two sons and a daughter before dying early in the 1770's. The older of these boys grew up to be a lawyer and a judge and a Congressman for one term; although he was willing to move with the times and become James Van Alen instead of another Johannes, he apparently was less flexible when it came to abandoning Federalism, which soon became a lost cause, so he went no further politically.

Maria's first son by her second husband—she bore him two girls and three boys—proved to be much more adaptable. Martin Van Buren had no difficulty about embracing Jacksonian Democracy, and after following in his half-brother's footsteps, getting generous help from him at every turning, he advanced bravely on his own up the rungs of state and national office to the White House itself. But if it seems that perhaps Martin Van Buren's father may have contributed something toward this greater staying power, there is no justification for any such claim. Quite the contrary.

For Abraham Van Buren of Kinderhook was that rarity among the Dutch, an improvident waster. His people were thrifty, and he started with a good piece of land plus a thriving tavern along the old Post Road between New York City and Albany; but he did not marry till he was thirty-nine, and by the time he chose Maria with her three fatherless children, he must have needed a stabilizing influence. Already he had succeeded in reducing his inheritance to a poor portion of his original property.

They said it was amiability that prevented his holding onto what he had—his son Martin put it tactfully when he wrote that his father, being "utterly devoid of the spirit of accumulation, his property, originally moderate, was gradually reduced until he could but illy afford to bestow the necessary means upon the education of his children."

This meant there was some truth in the snide comment made by the *New York Herald* soon after Martin Van Buren's inauguration. He was, that paper opined, just "a common country lawyer who began life trundling cabbages to market in Kinderhook." But if he was not all that common, it was because his mother saved the pennies to send him to the Kinderhook Academy. Then when he was fourteen, and further schooling was beyond her resources, she saw to it that his half-brother, whom she had already given a good start, helped this boy survive during a long and laborious clerkship, leading to a license to practice law.

Whether or not Maria herself had any part in a change involving her own heritage—and it is doubtful if she did because one thing her neighbors remembered was that she recited the Psalms for mental sustenance, but she recited them in Dutch—by the time it was necessary to raise a gravestone for her, at least Martin referred to her as Mary. When she died on February 16, 1818, he was already attorney general of New York State, and it suited him to honor his mother with a more readily acceptable first name. That, perhaps, was his sincerest tribute to her.

Elizabeth Hutchinson Jackson
17??-1791

ANDY JACKSON'S MOTHER had red hair and blue eyes, in both of which respects he resembled her. And she was wonderfully plucky—almost unbelievably so. Although her husband may have provided similar genes, he could not have influenced the seventh President by the force of example because this father died a few days before his son was born. But Betty Jackson had more time to make her personality felt; she did not leave Andy utterly alone in the world till he was fourteen.

No other Presidential biography has quite the starkness of Old Hickory's story, and inasmuch as he was unquestionably one of the great figures in the larger American drama, a lot of effort has gone into investigating his early days. Nevertheless, the rewards have been small, which is not surprising; the society from which he sprang was not given to recording its progress in writing. Even so basic a detail as the place of Andrew Jackson's birth has never been established positively, nor is it likely that this will ever be done.

The best that scholarship has been able to come up with assigns the honor to South Carolina, which was what Andy himself believed. But after he shot to fame as the hero of the Battle of New Orleans, Ireland and England and Pennsylvania and Virginia also claimed him, and another tale had it that he had really arrived at sea, aboard the ship carrying his parents to the New World. The strongest challenge came, though, from North Carolina, which did not surrender for many decades.

To help adjudicate such a case, a mass of hearsay and only a few facts are available. These point toward the conclusion that in 1765 an Andrew Jackson who was a tenant farmer in the North of Ireland decided on crossing the ocean, and with him he brought his wife Betty who showed her mettle right then. She embarked on this hard voyage despite having an infant boy to care for, and another who was only two—her sons Robert and Hugh. Whether or not the young family landed in Charleston defies proving, and yet there is no question about their eventual destination.

This was a sparsely settled area on the border between North and South Carolina which had been poetically described to them as "the Garden of the Waxhaws." Betty had two sisters already living there and two more were soon to come—the Irish spinner named Hutchinson who fathered five such adventurous girls must have been quite a man, or perhaps the courage in this family was transmitted through the female line.

Betty faced a call for stoicism soon enough. Although no Eden, the Waxhaw area proved no desert either, and the newcomers were welcomed by kinfolk with a warmth most pioneers missed; so the task of carving a home out of wilderness did not demand more of her than of her sisters. But only two years after arriving, she suddenly found herself a widow—they say her husband strained himself lifting a log, and died in fierce pain. Just two or three days later, Betty gave birth to her third son.

She bore this second Andrew Jackson on March 15, 1767— somebody marked down the date. But which sister Betty had visited in her hour of need nobody can say positively, and when the boundary line between North and South Carolina was finally set beyond any further haggling a few years later, it worked out that Betty had sisters in each state. Mainly because she spent the next several years with her South Carolinian Sister Crawford, that state has won out in the record books.

It must have been crowded at Sister Crawford's, where there already were eight children, but until the Revolution life went on with no more upheaval for the Jacksons. Then young Andy, who had taken to reading at the age of five as soon as he got a few lessons from the Waxhaw pastor, became more or less the public reader for the community; when newspapers arrived by mail, he was selected as often as any grown man to shout out the whole contents, sentence by sentence, to an assembled crowd of his elders. But as soon as the fighting lapped right up into their own area, he lost interest in reading—at thirteen, he became a message carrier for a local militia company.

Betty wanted him to be a preacher, but she herself had told him glorious stories about his grandfather at the seige of Carrickfergus; he remembered as an old man how she had stirred him by her talk of that fight against the nobility who were oppressing the laboring poor. And she did not try to stop any of her boys from emulating their grandfather's example in this new struggle against tyranny. They—and she, too—all did their part for the patriot cause. Before the Revolution ended, all but Andy were dead as a result.

Betty's son Hugh was killed in action at eighteen, and her son Robert died of smallpox at sixteen after he had been taken prisoner for defying a British officer. That unnamed dragoon gained renown of a sort by slashing at both Robert and Andy when they refused to polish his boots—Andy carried the sword scar on his face for the rest of his life, but he survived the subsequent imprisonment that brought death to his brother. Yet Andy might have succumbed, too, if his mother had not hurried forty miles by pony to seek clemency for her thirteen-year-old son; that was his own memory of the episode.

Then no sooner was Andy safe than his mother decided she was needed more elsewhere. Several of the Crawford men were on a prison ship in Charleston Harbor where some sort of plague was killing patriots mercilessly, and she determined to go aboard as a nurse. Understanding the risk she was taking, Betty Jackson said a formal farewell to her sole remaining son before she left him. Wiping her eyes with her apron, she gave him her last advice, which Andy Jackson later repeated to a friend: "Andy, never tell a lie, nor take what is not your own, nor sue . . . for slander. *Settle them cases yourself.*" A few months later, after she had been buried in an unmarked grave with other victims of the epidemic, her son received a small bundle containing her spare clothes.

They said of her then that she had been so "fresh-looking," and "very conversive." Always busy, "she could spin beautiful," and even read and write a little. And somehow she had given her youngest boy a good start on the path to greatness. But for some years afterward, finding life with her relatives too chafing, he almost disgraced her—"Andrew Jackson was the most roaring, rollicking, game-cocking, horse-racing, card-playing, mischievous fellow that ever lived in Salisbury," said someone who knew him when he arrived to study law over in North Carolina. He never did get over some of this, but he never got over his mother's death either. When he was running for President in the particularly scurrilous campaign of 1828, and a newspaper printed an ugly, entirely unfounded rumor about his mother, the bluff old general burst into tears. He could defend himself and he could defend his wife, who had already been subjected to unprecedented vilifying, but it thoroughly unnerved him to see his long-departed mother under attack.

Elizabeth Jones Monroe
1 7??-?

WITH THE MOTHER of James Monroe, the absolute nadir of maternal information is reached—even the years of her birth and death went unrecorded. Like practically everybody else who has ever referred to her on paper, her famous son wrote more about her brother than about the lady herself. For her brother was a judge and later a member of Congress, and unquestionably the main ornament on the escutcheon of this particular Jones clan.

Besides the fact that the "very amiable and respectable woman" who gave birth to him happened to be the sister of Judge Joseph Jones, the fifth President of the United States mentioned only that her father had emigrated from Wales to Virginia. Elsewhere, this Welsh arrival was described as an "undertaker in architecture," but the profession did not command the status of planter by any means. Even so, it seems that the Monroes were no more affluent than these Joneses.

For the father of James Monroe besides being a farmer was a joiner, which is a word that Virginia genealogists prefer over carpenter. No matter if social distinctions in the colonial days were less rigidly drawn, the marriage of Spence Monroe and Eliza

Jones could not have been treated with anything like the ceremony that accompanied a wedding in, for instance, the Randolph family. Although not very much more is known of the mother of Thomas Jefferson, at least the crucial dates in her life were diligently written down.

Yet it must be added that Eliza, after all, had a major influence on the career of her first son, born on April 28, 1758; he was, as has only sketchily been indicated for posterity, the oldest of five children. However, the Monroe farm in Westmoreland County to which Eliza had gone as a bride was hardly palatial—merely a highway marker remains to show where it was located, but the sandy scrub growth by the side of the road suggests that this soil could never have supported any lush vegetation.

Although Spence Monroe did do well enough to send his James to William and Mary College at sixteen, and although James on his own in the Third Virginia Regiment and thereafter displayed quite exceptional talent, the money to make him a gentleman came from the Joneses. When Eliza's eminent brother died, he instructed that his estate be divided between the children of his late sisters, "allowing my nephew Colonel James Monroe the first choice."

Nelly Conway Madison

1731-1829

NATURALLY, James Madison felt some apprehension when he was summoned home to Virginia early in 1783. His mother had been ailing again, and at her age the worst was to be feared; she was fifty-two already. But he need not have worried, as it turned out—she put off dying for quite some time. Not till a month after her ninety-eighth birthday did she finally leave him.

Yet she did not live long enough to savor a marvelously silly controversy which swirled some years later around and about her own name. When the sensitivities of the South had been excited by other matters, it suddenly struck fastidious Dixie as exquisitely painful to have a Nelly in such a position of honor. Owing perhaps to the popularity of "Darling Nelly Gray" among the darkies, Nelly had acquired too lowly a connotation to be acceptable for James Madison's mother; and so a suitable substitute had to be provided. The nod went to Eleanor.

Eleanor Rose, for good measure, was what one school of genealogical research offered. There does seem to have been some basis for the Rose—R was the middle initial of the monogram on her silver. Yet nothing except wishful thinking justified the new first name, and an assortment of evidence supported the original Nelly, including the lady's own signature on her will; a neatly written signature it was, too. And the spoons in the drawer of her sideboard had been marked N.R.C., presumably for Nelly Rose Conway.

If it appears that those spoons should have ended this teapot tempest, any such appearance is deceiving. Not only in the Old South, but also in the most unemotional reference books, the mother of James Madison still can be discovered as Eleanor. Doubtless the no-nonsense quality of the name Nelly has something to do with the impression, but she does seem the sort who would have laughed heartily at the whole fuss.

Born in the Virginia town of Port Conway on January 9, 1731, Nelly was the daughter of the owner of a tobacco warehouse. The gentleman who has gone down in history as James Madison, Sr., had dealings with this establishment, and he must also have been on a friendly footing with its proprietor's family; on September 13, 1749, when Nelly was eighteen, she married him.

Although the Madisons were not yet in the top rank socially, they had a very decent position; James Sr.'s great grandfather had been a carpenter but his grandfather was more ambitious—he had begun putting together the plantation in Orange County that became Montpelier. By adding judiciously to what he had inherited, Nelly's husband was able to pass on some four thousand acres.

But he and Nelly lived in homey style, particularly during the first years of their marriage before the regular arrival of babies— she had twelve in all—required a larger domicile than the modest wooden house the original proprietor of the estate had left for them. Even the new dwelling they built on a knoll affording a pleasing vista of the Blue Ridge Mountains was no mansion—until President James Madison remodeled it some years later.

He was the first of Nelly's children, born on March 16, 1751, or so it seemed sensible to state after the present calendar was adopted; before then, under the old Julian calendar, the last day in the year was March 24, and March 25 started the new year— March 24, 1750, was followed by March 25, 1751. (And, it must be added, December 31, 1749, was followed by January 1, 1749.) So the original birthday of the fourth President was March 16, 1750, which was subsequently pushed ahead a full year in order that persons unaccustomed to the old calendar would not count on their fingers and conclude that he arrived just six months after the marriage of his parents; in actual fact, he was born eighteen months later.

Nelly's influence on this son, or for that matter on any of her children, is difficult to estimate. Although she was certainly not illiterate, the Madison family papers include no letters that she wrote—she is only written about, or in a few cases, written to—and the picture that emerges thus indirectly is merely of an unpretentious lady who sews shirts for young James while he studies at Princeton, who sends tubs of fresh butter to him when he goes on the public's business to Richmond.

For a number of years, she suffered from chronic malaria, and James was constantly noting that he had dispatched "bark of Vitriol" for the relief of her symptoms. Frequently in the course of his correspondence with his father, he has occasion to describe other commissions he has carried out for her, and sometimes the window thereby opened casts an amusing light on plantation life, as for instance in the letter from James Jr. to James Sr. which begins:

Richmond, May 13, 1784

Hon^d Sir:

The spectacles herewith enclosed came to my hands yesterday with the information that the Pr. first sent were forwarded by mistake. It will however give my mother a double chance of suiting herself. I wish the pr. which may not be preferred to be sent down to me by the earliest opportunity, unless they should suit yourself & you choose to keep them. . . .

When Nelly was sixty-eight, her husband died and his property went mainly to their first son. But even though her daughter-in-law—the famous Dolley—then became the mistress of Montpelier, and the house had to be expanded in order to accommodate hordes of guests, Nelly was discommoded hardly at all. A separate apartment just to the right of the central hall was reserved for her private domain, and Dolley Madison catered to her mother-in-law most kindly.

According to a guest at Montpelier during this period, it was considered a great favor by the visitors who thronged to Mr. Madison's hospitable mansion to be admitted to pay their respects to his venerable mother. Just a year before Nelly's death on February 11, 1829, this guest won admission to the inner sanctum, and one must rely on her for the only firsthand description of Nelly Madison:

> She lacks but 3 years of being a hundred years old. When I enquired of her how she was, "I have been a blest woman," she replied, "blest all my life, and blest in this my old age. I have no sickness, no pain; excepting my hearing, my senses are but little impaired. I pass my time in reading and knitting." Something being said of the infirmities of old age, "You," said she, looking at Mrs. M., "you are *my* mother now, and take care of me in my old age." I felt much affected at the sight of this venerable woman. Her face is not so much wrinkled as her son's who is only 77 years old.

Jane Randolph Jefferson
1720-1776

*March 31st—My mother died about eight o'clock
this morning. In the 57ᵗʰ year of her age.*

THAT WAS THE SUM TOTAL of what Thomas Jefferson had to
say about his mother in his diary, and except for a few perfunctory financial notations, he left only one other reference to her in
his voluminous writings. As an old and honored sage setting down
his autobiography, he spent half a sentence on her marriage to his
father, then added wryly in regard to the Randolphs: "They trace
their pedigree far back in England & Scotland, to which let every
one ascribe the faith & merit he chooses."

Clearly, he himself did not ascribe much of either to the school
of thought which glorifies the maternal role. Why a man of his
polish had so little, graceful or otherwise, to say concerning his
female parent—who became his sole parent when he was only fourteen—has baffled some of his admirers. To others, the explanation
is simple: because he kept silent about his wife, too, they are willing to believe his reticence stemmed purely from a disinclination
for any exposure of his personal feelings.

Perhaps, and yet there is a chance that a deeper current ran
beneath this passion for privacy. More than in the case of any
figure in American history with anything like his stature, his domestic life has been preserved from prying. No matter that tourists
by the tens of thousands peer at his ingenious dumbwaiter and
sliding doors when they visit Monticello, they fail to discover
there or elsewhere whether he could even stand the sight of his
mother.

Any patriot can sympathize with George Washington's lack of
warmth toward the unpleasant lady who bore him; terse as the
record is concerning her, it contains more than enough to make his
unfilial behavior understandable. But so little can be told about

Jane Randolph Jefferson that nobody really knows if her son's outer coldness was justified.

Because she was a Randolph, at least her pedigree can be traced —she was the daughter of an Isham Randolph who had mercantile interests which took him to London from time to time, in addition to his ample lands in Virginia. While he was temporarily living abroad, he met and married an English girl named Jane Rogers, and the first child she gave him was a daughter who was baptized in the London parish of Shadwell on February 20, 1720.

Nineteen years later, a tall and personable young man named Peter Jefferson, who was no aristocrat but far from a pauper either, claimed the young Jane Randolph as his bride; they were married in Virginia on October 3, 1739. Much has been made of Peter Jefferson's inferior status, compared with the eminent family into which he married, altogether too much, for Peter had a talent for amassing land, despite his less elevated start in life, and he already had several parcels of substantial size. Although largely self-educated, he was also a competent surveyor.

After a few years in the more settled neighborhood where Jane's family lived, years during which she produced two daughters in quick succession, Peter brought his wife and children to a promising but still wild westerly tract he had purchased, about five miles from Charlottesville. Wolves still roamed the woods here, but he named his new farm Shadwell after Jane's more civilized birthplace. In a small house on this property, Thomas Jefferson was born on April 13, 1743.

Not long afterward, the death of a close friend of Peter Jefferson's compelled him to move again—he had promised to supervise the education of his friend's sons. So his own son Tom enjoyed the advantages of a gracious James River plantation during much of his childhood, while his mother went on giving him more sisters; the two infant boys she gave birth to died almost immediately.

But the Jeffersons were back at Shadwell when Peter Jefferson sickened and died in 1757. Thenceforth, Tom spent almost no time in the same house with his mother. The necessity for his acquiring an education accounted for his absences at the beginning, but as soon as he decently could—well before he married the young widow whose own health was worn down by repeated pregnancies till she died after only ten years as Mrs. Jefferson—Thomas felt the need for an establishment of his own and he began building Monticello atop a mountain on the other side of Charlottesville.

He had not completed more than a room or two when his mother's home at Shadwell burned to the ground in 1770. Only in the reminiscences of one of his great granddaughters have any clues to his domestic habits been provided, and although this polite lady had only good to say of her illustrious ancestor's mother—"His mother, from whom he inherited his cheerful and hopeful temper . . . was a woman of strong understanding . . ."—she illustrated his filial solicitude with an anecdote of no doubt unintended harshness.

For she was the source of the chilling little tale that tells how Thomas Jefferson was informed of the awful fire by a Negro servant who raced to him with the news. The blurted intelligence that Shadwell had been destroyed brought an instantaneous question from the young master: What of his books? Oh, they were all gone, came the sad response—"but ah, we saved your fiddle." There was apparently no upset about the almost total destruction of his mother's not inconsiderable property, let alone the possibility of her having been injured.

Before her husband died, Jane Jefferson had given birth to ten children, of whom eight survived to maturity. In this number was one other son she named Randolph, who on the basis of several letters to his older brother that have been preserved has been given the benefit of every doubt and labeled merely simpleminded. Among the daughters, there was a girl who wandered more seriously both physically and mentally; as the result of an escapade which was never described in any detail, she died in her late adolescence.

Furthermore, there were other instances of instability in Jane Jefferson's branch of the Randolph family. Gossip two centuries removed is certainly not to be relied on, but a lady whose present home borders on the boundary of the vanished Shadwell had no doubt of why Thomas Jefferson stayed as far as he could from his mother. "She was crazy as can be," said this lady. "She tried to burn down that house three times, and finally she succeeded."

Be that as it may, after Shadwell burned, and Monticello at no great distance was being improved into a showplace of America, there is no evidence at all that Thomas Jefferson invited his mother to move in with him. It seems, on the other hand, that she and her younger children stayed in her cramped little out-buildings which had survived the conflagration. Only when it came to burying her, after she suffered what is supposed to have been a stroke three months before her first son wrote the Declaration of Independence, did she find refuge on his property. She is buried in his shaded family cemetery at Monticello with an old stone marker above her grave for the tourists to photograph.

Susanna Boylston Adams

1709-1797

WHEN THE PROPER Bostonian grandson of President John Adams published the diary of his illustrious grandfather a century ago, certain passages were omitted. One of these provides a price-less antidote for an overdose of maternal platitude—while it applies specifically to the case of Susanna Boylston Adams, in all probability its pertinence is not that limited.

To understand what follows one must keep in mind that John Adams was twenty-three at the time he wrote it, and obviously an intense young man; he has just returned home after spending some months living in a distant town, in the household of some people named Putnam, while studying law. Thus his impressions of his own family are subject to a new basis of comparison when he finds that his father, a plain farmer who is also on the local board of selectmen, has provoked his mother by undertaking all on his own to board two girls who are town charges. Now here is John:

> How a whole Family is put into a Broil sometimes by a Trifle. My P. and M. disagreed in Opinion about boarding. . . . My P. continued cool and pleasant a good while, but had his Temper

roused at last, tho he uttered not a rash Word, but resolutely as-
serted his Right to govern. My Mamma determined to know what
my P. charged a week for the Girls Board. P. said he had not determined what to charge but would have her say what it was worth.
She absolutely refused to say. But "I will know if I live and breathe.
I can read yet. Why dont you tell me, what you charge? You do it
on purpose to teaze me. You are mighty arch this morning. I wont
have all the Towns Poor brought here, stark naked, for me to clothe
for nothing. I wont be a slave to other folks for nothing." And after
the 2 Girls cryed. "I must not speak a Word [to] your Girls,
Wenches, Drabbs. I'll kick both their fathers, presently. [You] want
to put your girls over, to make me a slave to your Wenches."

After observing sagely that the above could properly be described as "a conjugal Spat, a Spat between Husband and Wife,"
and after bemoaning that he had lacked the presence of mind to
observe the "faces, Eyes, Actions and Expressions" of both participants more fully, in order that he could draw a general conclusion
from the episode, he proceeded to do just that anyway:

> M. seems to have no Scheme and Design in her Mind to persuade
> P. to resign his Trust of Selectman. But when she feels the Trouble
> and Difficulties that attend it she fretts, squibs, scolds, rages, raves.
> None of her Speeches seem the Effect of any Design to get rid of the
> Trouble, but only natural Expressions of the Pain and Uneasiness,
> which that Trouble occasions. Cool Reasoning upon the Point with
> my Father, would soon bring her to his mind or him to hers.
>
> Let me from this remark distinctly the Different Effects of
> Reason and Rage. Reason, Design, Scheme governs pretty con-
> stantly in Put[nam]'s house, but, Passion, Accident, Freak, Humour,
> govern in this house . . .

But, of course, it was from the passionate Susanna that John
Adams inherited his own disposition, and perhaps even his intellectual strength. Before her volatile addition, several generations
of Adamses had done their duty stolidly, then after her time, the
spark of genius ignited. How much credit she deserves can never
be measured accurately, but there is no doubt that she was at least
socially her husband's superior. For she was born a Boylston.

The daughter of Peter Boylston of Muddy River (which later
became better known as Brookline), she was born on March 5,

1709, into a family that already lived in fine houses and contributed notably to their community. Her uncle was the Dr. Zabdiel Boylston who introduced the first method of smallpox inoculation in the colonies. Susanna grew up in a hilltop mansion commanding a grand view of Boston and its environs—". . . the islands, the rivers, the ponds of water, the orehards and the groves were scattered in . . . profusion over this great scene." How she came to marry Farmer John Adams of Braintree—who was eighteen years her senior—cannot be explained, but two facts suggest at least part of the story. She was already a spinsterish twenty-five when she became a bride on October 31, 1734, and one of her older sisters had married a clergyman brother of her forty-three-year-old husband.

One day short of one year after Susanna's wedding, on October 30, 1735, she gave birth to the son who became the second President of the new nation he had done so much to establish. Her two other sons appear to have lived respectably if not outstandingly; but it must be remembered that both of them were told from early childhood that only their oldest brother could expect an education. For the farmer who has gone down in the Adams genealogies as Deacon John Adams—to distinguish him from his famous son—promised this firstborn boy a chance at Harvard even before young John could have had much chance to demonstrate that he deserved it. One may reasonably assume that John's mother had something to do with this decision.

How else she helped him cannot be described, except fictionally, because even the immense bulk of Adams Papers contains surprisingly few revealing references to her. Her son and his letter-writing wife mentioned her from time to time in their correspondence— there is no evidence that they felt anything less than warmly cordial toward her. And yet she does not receive quite the extensive attention one would have expected in such a discursive family. Probably the reason is that her second husband antagonized them in some unknown way.

For John Adams's father died in an epidemic of something like influenza in 1761, when Susanna was fifty-two; and five years later she married a Lieutenant John Hall. No matter how diligently Adams scholars have tried to investigate this gentleman, no other fact except that he kept Susanna company for fourteen years before dying in 1780 has rewarded their pains—leading to the suspicion that Susanna's children at the very least did not like him.

Susanna survived the mysterious Hall by seventeen years. Despite her plaintive cry when her daughter-in-law took leave of her in 1784 and went to join John Adams in Europe, despite the aged lady's piteous weeping at the thought that never again would she see either of them, she was still alive in 1797 when her son took his oath as the President of the United States. But she was so feeble then that Abigail Adams felt obliged to remain with her instead of going to New York for the inauguration ceremonies, and she stayed by Susanna's bedside till the end came six weeks later on April 17, 1797. Susanna was eighty-eight then, and had been in failing health for some years, but her children mourned her sorrowfully. Yet no matter that her name was legally Mrs. Hall, they could not bring themselves to remember this; on her tombstone they identified her only as an Adams.

Notes and Bibliography

THE RESEARCH PROBLEMS involved in gathering material for this book were varied, to say the least. But instead of attempting a ponderous essay on the subject, I would rather just mention that I have tried to search out letters, diaries, and the like as the basis for each chapter; and to provide specific references for those readers who may be interested in such matters. Thus a chapter-by-chapter listing of sources follows:

Rebekah Baines Johnson

The main sources for this chapter were personal interviews in Johnson City, Texas, and Austin from December 26–30, 1966, and the material Rebekah Baines Johnson herself provided in the private memoir subsequently published as *A Family Album* (New York: McGraw-Hill, 1965); as well as in *The Johnsons, Descendants of John Johnson, A Revolutionary Soldier of Georgia, A Genealogical History* (privately printed, 1956). Among those whose personal reminiscences proved most helpful were Mrs. Lyndon Baines Johnson, Mrs. Mary Stribling Moursund, Mrs. Stella Gliddon, Mrs. Kittie Clyde Leonard, Mrs. Gene Barnwell Waugh, and Mr. and Mrs. Stuart Long. In addition, I went through the files of *The New York Times* for material relating to the Johnson family; among the articles of most value were several by Nan Robertson printed in May of 1965, and one by Max Frankel on January 2, 1967. Other journalistic pieces of some interest were "His Mother's Story of LBJ" in *U.S. News & World Report,* February 15, 1965; "The First Lady Bird," *Time,* August 28, 1964; "A Reminder of Rebekah Baines," by Hugh Sidey in *Life,* December 16, 1966; "Lyndon Johnson's Mother," by Isabelle Shelton in the *Saturday Evening Post,* May 8, 1965; a profile of Mrs. Lyndon Johnson by Daniel Greene in *The National Observer,* April 24, 1967; an obituary of Rebekah Baines Johnson in the *Dallas News,* September 13, 1958; and an interview with President Johnson's sister, Mrs. Rebekah Johnson Bobbitt, distributed by The Associated Press on December 7, 1966; although I tried to see Mrs. Bobbitt while I was in Austin, she gently but decisively declined over the telephone to be interviewed again. I might add that my appointment with Mrs. Lyndon Johnson, who most graciously spent an hour with me in her husband's boyhood home in Johnson City on December 27, 1966, was arranged through the good offices of Mrs. Elizabeth Carpenter, Mrs. Johnson's press secretary. Mrs. Carpenter was unfailingly patient and efficient about arranging for this meeting and providing copies of letters and pictures I requested, but she drew the line when I subsequently asked to see the President, informing me that seldom if ever was the same reporter granted access to more than one member of the Presidential family. Thus for President Johnson's own recollections of his mother I am indebted to the National Broadcasting Company's television program, "The Hill Country," on which Mr. Johnson spoke freely and feelingly of his childhood; this program appeared on May 9, 1966, and was rebroadcast on December 11, 1966.

The specific sources for quotations in my chapter are as follows: "I am a Baptist . . ." from a biographical sketch of Joseph Wilson Baines by his brother George W. Baines, reprinted in RBJ's *Family Album*, p. 80; "At an incredibly early age . . ." *ibid.*, pp. 28–9; "I asked him a lot of questions . . ." *Dallas News*, September 13, 1958; "It was daybreak . . ." *Family Album*, p. 17; "the deep purposefulness," *ibid.*, p. 18; "Linden isn't so euphonious . . ." *ibid.*, p. 18; "Get up, Lyndon . . ." President Johnson on NBC television program, "The Hill Country," broadcast May 9, 1966; "Honey, I want you to get this paper out," Mrs. Lyndon Johnson to author; "I'd Rather Be Mama's Boy," *Family Album*, p. 19; "I have a mighty fine grandson . . ." *ibid.*, pp. 18–19; "Notice Lyndon's protective air," *ibid.*, picture caption, p. 34; "I think he thought he was papa," Mrs. Rebekah Johnson Bobbitt, quoted by The Associated Press in *New York World Journal Tribune*, December 7, 1966; "She was a gentle lady," various residents of Johnson City to author; "Rebekah, we should have married those preachers," Mrs. Mary Stribling Moursund to author; "My darling Boy . . ." RBJ to Lyndon Johnson, undated, attributed to April of 1937, photocopy provided by Mrs. Elizabeth Carpenter; and "She was quiet and shy . . ." President Johnson, quoted by Mrs. Isabelle Shelton in the *Saturday Evening Post*, May 8, 1965.

Rose Fitzgerald Kennedy

On June 15, 1967, I visited Mrs. Joseph P. Kennedy, as she prefers to be called, in her New York City apartment; that interview is the basis of my chapter about her. But I had naturally read a good deal in advance preparation, and was much helped by having done so. Among the books I found most useful were *John Kennedy: A Political Profile* by James MacGregor Burns (New York: Harcourt, Brace, 1959), which contains many family letters that have not been made available elsewhere; *Life and the Dream* by Mary Colum (Garden City, N.Y.: Doubleday, 1947), for an account of school days at the European convent where Rose Fitzgerald was a fellow student; *"Honey Fitz": Three Steps to the White House* by John Henry Cutler (Indianapolis: Bobbs-Merrill, 1962), an anecdote-filled biography of Mrs. Kennedy's father;

Front Runner, Dark Horse by Ralph G. Martin and Ed Plaut (Garden City, N.Y.: Doubleday, 1960), a study of two candidates for the Democratic Presidential nomination in 1960, which gains interest from the fact that the then Senator John F. Kennedy and his family cooperated fully with the authors; and *The Founding Father* by Richard J. Whalen (New York: New American Library, 1964), the fascinating and authoritative study of Joseph P. Kennedy. A more general picture is provided in *The Kennedy Family* by Joseph F. Dineen (Boston: Little, Brown, 1959) and *The Kennedy Years,* edited by Harold Faber (New York: Viking, 1964). Concerning Mrs. Kennedy herself, a bland work entitled "A Personal Memoir," which was serialized in the *New York World Journal Tribune* of October 2–6, 1966, offers not much information; but "Rose Fitzgerald Kennedy" by the late Marguerite Higgins in *McCall's* of May, 1961, does. The best kaleidoscopic view of Mrs. Kennedy's public career comes, however, from the files of *The New York Times.* Because of this superabundance of material, and most particularly because in this case it was possible to speak with the subject of my inquiry, I might mention that I made no effort to seek additional data from other members of her family beyond initiating negotiations for an interview with Senator Robert F. Kennedy. Then right after I received a cooperative reply, that storm over another literary project involving his family broke onto the front pages, and no appointment was forthcoming, after all; it seemed to me that my chapter would not suffer seriously if I let the matter drop.

As to specific quotations in that chapter, "Now I'm grateful to Mother . . ." and "Come on, Mother . . ." Mrs. Kennedy to author, confirming various newspaper references; "I want my home to be a place . . ." quoted in Cutler's *"Honey Fitz"* on pp. 170–1; "Not exactly," Mrs. Kennedy to author; "Honey Fitz can talk you blind," Cutler, p. 57; "My heavens! It's my friend . . ." Mrs. Kennedy to author; "Pink teas bore me," Whalen's *Founding Father,* p. 41; "in the world," Mrs. Kennedy to author; "We loved it," Mrs. Kennedy to author; "My theory is . . ." Mrs. Kennedy to author; "I made a point each day . . ." Cutler, p. 244; "You have to tend to the roots . . ." Cutler, p. 244; "Second best is a loser," *Kennedy Years,* p. 16; "When the going gets tough . . ." Whalen, p. 169; "She was the glue . . ." Martin and Plaut's *Front Runner, Dark Horse,* p. 122; "Why are those cities . . ." Mrs. Kennedy to author; "When they grow older . . ." Mrs. Kennedy to author; "When Jack spoke . . ." Whalen, p. 89; "In all the years we have been married," *New York Herald-Tribune,* December 12, 1960; "Well, Rose . . ." Whalen, p. 205; "At last I believe in the stork," Whalen, p. 258; "I told him that he was right about Boston . . ." John Powers quoted in Martin and Plaut, p. 177; "Hello, I'm John Kennedy's mother," *The New York Times,* October 17, 1960; "We had a daughter . . ." *The New York Times,* various dates 1961 on; "the woman who started it all . . ." *The New York Times,* December 7, 1962; "I used to say . . ." Mrs. Kennedy on television, quoted in *Newsweek,* July 17, 1967.

Ida Stover Eisenhower

On a narrow road winding uphill from the Virginia hamlet of Mount Sidney, a rural mail deliverer who is a distant relative of General Eisenhower pointed out the farm where Ida Stover was born; in Kansas there was much more to see that cast some light on her life. Her Abilene house has been preserved down to the last doily exactly as she left it, and right across the street in the splendid new Dwight D. Eisenhower Library are several folders of documents pertaining to her. Without General Eisenhower's express permission, these are not yet available for research purposes—I am most grateful to him for giving me this permission. Yet the record is still slim because many of his family papers were lost when he returned to this country from the Philippines shortly before the United States entered the Second World War. As a result, I tried to supplement it when I was in Abilene on July 17–19, 1967, by various interviews; those with Mrs. Florence Etherington, an Eisenhower cousin, and Mrs. J. Earl Endacott, who is in charge of keeping up the Eisenhower home, were the most helpful. Although an assortment of scheduling problems prevented my visiting General Eisenhower as planned, I found his reminiscences in his recent *At Ease: Stories I Tell to Friends* (Garden City, N.Y.: Doubleday, 1967) rewarding, as was his television appearance on a CBS News Special entitled "Young Mr. Eisenhower," broadcast on September 13, 1966, and an interview with him entitled "What I Have Learned" in the *Saturday Review* of September 10, 1966. Dr. Milton Eisenhower, whom I visited on January 20, 1967, in Baltimore, insisted genially that he and his brother got on so well because they never spoke for each other, but was good enough to clear up many details about their mother. Otherwise, the only extensive published interview with Mrs. Ida Eisenhower may be somewhat highly colored but is still interesting; published originally as a magazine article—"The Mother of General Ike" by Kunigunde Duncan in *The Woman* for July, 1944—it was later expanded by Miss Duncan into a book, *Earning the Right to do Fancy Work: An Informal Biography of Ida Eisenhower* (Lawrence, Kans.: University of Kansas Press, 1953). For Stover genealogy—Mrs. Eisenhower's mother was a Link—Paxson Link's *The Link Family 1417–1951* (privately printed, 1951) is helpful; for Eisenhower anecdotes, the same can be said of Bela Kornitzer's *The Great American Heritage: The Story of the Five Eisenhower Brothers* (New York: Farrar, Straus, 1955) and Kenneth S. Davis's *Soldier of Democracy: A Biography of Dwight D. Eisenhower* (Garden City, N.Y.: Doubleday, 1945). Henry Jameson, Abilene's newspaper publisher and unofficial historian, more than generously provided me with local lore.

Sources for quotations in the Eisenhower chapter include: "because I was a girl . . ." from Kunigunde Duncan in "The Mother of General Ike," *The Woman*, July, 1944; "We would make for the woods . . ." *ibid.;* "The Lord deals the cards . . ." General Eisenhower in "What I Have Learned," the *Saturday Review*, September 10, 1966; "I was a great bawler . . ." General Eisenhower on CBS program "Young Mr. Eisenhower," broadcast September 13, 1966; "There's no rest for the wicked," quoted in letter from Dwight Eisenhower to his mother, November 28, 1945; "The answer lies, I think . . ." General Eisenhower in *At Ease*, p. 37; "about a half hour later . . ." General Eisenhower on "Young Mr. Eisenhower"; "It is your choice," *At Ease*, p. 108; "Which one?" Milton Eisenhower to author; "Mother, what did we have for dinner?" Milton Eisenhower to author; "Her serenity . . ." *At Ease*, p. 76; "She was the salt of the earth," interviews in Abilene.

Martha Young Truman

By sharing her own recollections of her grandmother and going out of her way to pave the way for me in Independence, Margaret Truman Daniel provided invaluable help on this chapter. In an interview in New York on April 12, 1967, she added to the stock of anecdote offered in her book *Souvenir* (New York: McGraw-Hill, 1956) and undertook to check several points with her parents; for health reasons her father no longer was going to his office in Independence. But his secretary of long standing, Miss Rose A. Conway, welcomed me to the Harry S Truman Library there on July 19, 1967, and arranged for me to see former President Truman's sister, Miss Mary Jane Truman, at her home in nearby Grandview the following day. Miss Truman's memories of her mother were exceptionally interesting. Material at the Truman Library that I also found useful included the transcripts of tape-recorded interviews with Mary Ethel Noland, a Truman cousin, and with Mize Peters, Nathan Veatch, and Ted Marks, all old associates of Harry Truman. Mr. Truman's *Year of Decision* and *Years of Trial and Hope* (Garden City, N.Y.: Doubleday, 1955–56) not only told his story in his own words, but also offered the text of several family letters; apart from these, family correspondence has not been made available for research purposes. However, a variety of excerpts from personal papers and also introspective statements by Mr. Truman are embodied in William Hillman's *Mr. President* (New York: Farrar, Strauss, 1952). *The Man of Independence* by Jonathan Daniels (Philadelphia: Lippincott, 1950) is a good biography with much detail about Mr. Truman's early life; Alfred Steinberg's *The Man from Missouri: The Life and Times of Harry S Truman* (New York: Putnam, 1962) is even better. For contemporary material about Martha Truman in her last years, the files of *The New York Times* and the *Kansas City Star* are particularly rich.

Sources for specific quotations in the Truman chapter are as follows: "Boys, if you ever pray . . ." Steinberg's *Man from Missouri*, p. 239; "Oh, fiddlesticks . . ." Mary Jane Truman to author; "Anyone who could live . . ." Steinberg, p. 19; "I was what you might call . . ." Margaret Daniel to author; "I never did milk cows . . ." Mary Jane Truman to author; "Don't call him Harrison . . ." Mary Jane Truman to author; "I was blind as a mole . . ." Steinberg, p. 23; "She didn't scare easy," Daniels's *The Man of Independence,*

p. 53; "Mama couldn't get a lasso . . ." Steinberg, p. 26; "It was on the farm . . ." Daniels, p. 86; "It was quite a blow," Steinberg, p. 42; "Well now, Mrs. Truman . . ." Ted Marks's oral history transcript, HST Library; "I'd have gotten eleven thousand dollars . . ." Steinberg, p. 97; "I can't really be glad he's President . . ." *The New York Times,* April 17, 1944; "Well, *The Washington Post* . . ." Truman's *Year of Decision,* p. 63; "It isn't neighborly," Steinberg, p. 251; "Just belong to the key of B-natural," Mary Jane Truman to author; "Be good and be game," *The New York Times,* September 17, 1945; "I'd rather stay on the ground . . ." *The New York Times,* November 25, 1945; "I'm glad Harry decided . . ." *The New York Times,* August 15, 1945; "She sat up with me . . ." *The Washington Post,* May 26, 1947; "She's wonderful . . ." *Kansas City Star,* June 30, 1946; "Judge not . . ." Mary Jane Truman to author.

Sara Delano Roosevelt

At the Franklin D. Roosevelt Library in Hyde Park, there are seventeen manuscript boxes filled with material about F.D.R.'s mother—and Sara Roosevelt's letters from her son are not included in this collection. But access to them has been easy since the publication in book form of a large number of F.D.R.'s personal letters. Mrs. Roosevelt's scrapbooks up at Hyde Park and *FDR: His Personal Letters,* edited by Elliott Roosevelt (New York: Duell, Sloan & Pearce, 1947), were the basic sources for my chapter about this lady. In addition, there is a wealth of maternal anecdote in Eleanor Roosevelt's *Autobiography* (New York: Harper & Row, 1961); somewhat different perspectives are provided by Frances Perkins in *The Roosevelt I Knew* (New York: Viking, 1946); Robert Sherwood in *Roosevelt and Hopkins* (New York: Harper & Row, 1948); James A. Farley in *Jim Farley's Story* (New York: Whittlesey House, 1948); and Joseph P. Lash in *Eleanor Roosevelt: A Friend's Memoir* (Garden City, N.Y.: Doubleday, 1964). For background about the Roosevelt family, Karl Schriftgiesser's *The Amazing Roosevelt Family 1613–1942* (New York: Funk, 1942) and Allen Churchill's *The Roosevelts: American Aristocrats* (New York: Harper & Row, 1965) are useful. Standard biographies which include interesting material about F.D.R.'s relationship with his mother include Frank Freidel's three-volume work—*FDR: The Apprenticeship* (Boston: Little, Brown, 1952), *FDR: The Ordeal* (Boston: Little, Brown, 1954), *FDR: The Triumph* (Boston: Little, Brown, 1965); and James MacGregor Burns's *Roosevelt: The Lion and the Fox* (New York: Harcourt, Brace, 1956). Besides these, there are three books of varying quality which must be consulted to complete the record on Sara Roosevelt. *My Boy Franklin* (New York: Ray Long and Richard R. Smith, Inc., 1933) is described as Sara Delano Roosevelt's own story as told to Isabel Leighton and Gabrielle Forbush; it is a competent although rather stiff recital, interesting mainly because the factual content presumably had the approval of Mrs. Roosevelt herself. *The Home at Hyde Park, Together with Sara Delano Roosevelt's Household Book* (New York: Viking, 1950), which Clare and Hardy Steeholm worked on as a labor of love to benefit the Hyde Park village library which Sara Roosevelt had built in memory of her husband, is first a collection of Hyde Park lore, then in its second half reproduces the contents of Mrs. Roosevelt's own notebook in which she jotted down recipes, home remedies for colds, and the like. The most valuable to me was *Gracious Lady: The Life of Sara Delano Roosevelt* by Rita S. Halle Kleeman (New York: Appleton-Century, 1935); since Sara Roosevelt cooperated with Mrs. Kleeman, the volume provides the fullest available account of Mrs. Roosevelt's girlhood, more than amply compensating for the book's rather cloying tone. Again, newspapers were an additional help, and the multitude of clippings tucked away in several of those boxes in the F.D.R. Library vastly simplified the task of searching through old files.

As to the sources of quoted material, "Tut, tut, now!" is from Mrs. Kleeman, p. 25; "Franklin doesn't know everything," Schriftgiesser's *The Amazing Roosevelt Family*, p. 203; "Made by a little girl . . ." Kleeman, p. 41; "Catherine Morrissey . . . our slut of a cook . . ." *ibid.,* pp. 29–30; "Blow, my bully boys . . ." referred to by several writers; "If I had not come then . . ." a letter from Sara Roosevelt to F.D.R., May 8, 1932, quoted in Freidel's *FDR: The Triumph,* p. 216; "James Roosevelt is the first person . . ." used with slight variations by several writers; "He tried to pattern himself . . ." Churchill's *The Roosevelts,* p. 143; "I do hereby appoint my wife . . ." James Roosevelt's will, quoted by Schriftgiesser, pp. 314–15; "His mother was sorry for me . . ." Eleanor Roosevelt's *Autobiography,* p. 38; "Dearest Mama, I have been absolutely rushed . . ." F.D.R. to his mother, December 4, 1903, text from *FDR, His Personal Letters: Early Years;* "I'd like to talk with my mother . . ." Churchill, p. 143; "I got here yesterday at 1:30 . . ." Sara Roosevelt to Frederic Delano, September 2, 1921, quoted by Freidel in *FDR: The Ordeal,* p. 100; "I shall be glad . . ." Sara Roosevelt's miscellaneous papers at F.D.R. Library; "To you we are grateful . . ." Sara Roosevelt's miscellaneous papers; "Who is that dreadful person . . ." Eleanor Roosevelt's *Autobiography,* p. 138; "Young man, I talked to newspapermen . . ." Emmett V. Maum in the newspaper *PM* of September 8, 1941; "Dear Mr. Farley . . ." *Jim Farley's Story,* p. 316.

Jessie Woodrow Wilson

For Jessie Wilson's mature years and for an unvarnished picture of life within the various Wilson parsonages where she brought up her children, the family letters that have been preserved as part of the Wilson Papers are invaluable. Reading these has become wonderfully easy recently, owing to the industry of a team of scholars with headquarters at Princeton; having assembled every known document with any relevance to Wilson's career, they are publishing two unusually handsome and well-edited volumes a year under the general direction of Professor Arthur S. Link, the preeminent authority on Wilson. I am indebted to Professor Link for his allowing me the use of his files to look up data that had not yet appeared in print and for his sparing the time to talk a little about the Freudian furor. For the most part, however, the period in which I was interested was covered more than adequately by Volumes I and II of *The Papers of Woodrow Wilson,* edited by Arthur S. Link (Princeton, N.J.: Princeton University Press, 1966–67). On Jessie Wilson's earlier years, the family reminiscences in the first volume of Ray Stannard Baker's *Woodrow Wilson: Life and Letters* (Garden City, N.Y.: Doubleday, 1927) were helpful, as was Professor Link's *Wilson: The Road to the White House* (Princeton, N.J.: Princeton University Press, 1947). On the Oedipus issue, the main source, of course, was that strange book *Thomas Woodrow Wilson: A Psychological Study* by Sigmund Freud and William C. Bullitt (New York: Houghton Mifflin, 1966). The outpouring of critical reviews, both pro and con, which followed its appearance helped to provide what seems to me a reasonable perspective on the issue; of particular interest were the articles in *The New York Review of Books* of February 9, 1967, by Richard Hofstadter and by Erik E. Erikson. As a reminder that the indoor sport of analyzing Wilson's personality is nothing new, Robert E. Annin's *Woodrow Wilson: A Character Study* (New York: Dodd, Mead, 1924) was interesting. In addition, a visit to the piously preserved Wilson birthplace in Staunton, Virginia, where a goodly assortment of family mementoes is on display, proved valuable in a stage-setting sort of way.

As to specific quotations, "After all, there is a great deal about the Southern people . . ." comes from Jessie Wilson's letter to her first son dated December 1, 1876; "I remember how I clung to her . . ." Woodrow Wilson to Ellen Axson Wilson, April 19, 1888; "My darling Boy, I am so anxious . . ." Jessie Wilson to Woodrow Wilson, May 20, 1874; "P.S. Don't think my signature . . ." Woodrow Wilson to Robert Bridges on November 7, 1879; "Tommy is certainly an unsuitable name . . ." Jessie Wilson to Woodrow Wilson, August 23, 1880; "You tell us nothing about one thing . . ." Jessie Wilson to Woodrow Wilson, November 18, 1879; "I remember thinking . . ." Woodrow Wilson to Ellen Axson, October 11, 1883; "From all I have ever heard . . ." Jessie Wilson to Woodrow Wilson, June 21, 1883.

Louisa Torrey Taft

Family letters included in the Taft Papers in the Library of Congress were the principal sources for this chapter. But to attempt to explore this vast collection without the services of a guide would have been beyond my powers, and I am most indebted to several excellent guides: Miss Kate M. Stewart, manuscript historian at the Library of Congress, whose generous help was by no means limited merely to matters Taftian; Mrs. Willa Beall, formerly of the William Howard Taft Memorial Association; Charles P. Taft, a grandson of Louisa Taft; and Ishbel Ross, author of *An American Family: The Tafts, 1678–1964* (Cleveland, Ohio: World, 1964) who went far beyond the call of duty in sharing some of the contents of her own files with me. Among other sources that provided background material for various periods in Louise Taft's life, the *Centennial History of the Town of Millbury, Massachusetts,* published under the direction of a committee appointed by the town (Millbury, 1915), and Fidelia Fisk's *Recollection of Mary Lyon with selections from her instructions to her pupils in Mount Holyoke Female Seminary* (Boston, 1866) illuminated the early years; some light was shed on later decades by Henry W. Taft's *Opinions Literary and Otherwise* (New York: Macmillan, 1934), Horace Dutton Taft's *Memories and Opinions* (New York: Macmillan, 1942), and Lewis A. Leonard's *Life of Alphonso Taft* (New York: Hawke Publishing Company, 1920). For genealogical guidance, Frederic C. Torrey's *The Torrey Families and their Children in America* (Lakehurst, N.Y., 1929) and Mabel Thacher Washburn's *Ancestry of William Howard Taft* (New York: Frank Allaben Genealogical Company, 1908) were useful. Henry F. Pringle's two-volume *Life and Times of William Howard Taft* (Hamden, Conn.: Archon, 1965) was a valuable supplementary reference. Miscellaneous committee reports and such at the Cincinnati Public Library and the Cincinnati Historical Society, which I visited on July 11–12, 1967, helped to fill in the record, as did a tour of Louise Taft's Cincinnati home which is in process of being restored to its former solid comfort.

Specific quotations in the Taft chapter, all taken from the Taft Papers in the Library of Congress unless otherwise identified, follow: "There is something very delightful to me . . ." Louise to her mother, October 13, 1843; "I have always thought . . ." Louise to her mother, April, 1844; "I think, however . . ." Louise to her mother, undated; "This is owing . . ." Harriet W. Dutton to Susan Waters Torrey, July 1, 1846; "Don't you know that I am rather given . . ." Louise to her mother, January 1, 1846; "that the whole subject be indefinitely postponed," *Centennial History of Millbury,* p. 129; "If Father finds us too expensive . . ." Louise to Delia Torrey, April 26, 1850; "The second difficulty . . ." and "In conclusion he says . . ." Harriet W. Dutton to Louise, undated; "No man was ever more fortunate . . ." Alphonso Taft to Delia Torrey, January 3, 1854; "Oh, Louise, Louise . . ." Delia to Louise, January 18, 1854; "I suppose we might almost as well ask . . ." Delia to Louise, January 15, 1859; "When woman's field widens . . ." Ross in *An American Family: The Tafts,* p. 78; "At half-past nine this morning . . ." Alphonso Taft to S. D. Torrey, February 7, 1855; "I feel as if my hands and feet . . ." Louise to Delia, November 8, 1857; "deeply, darkly, beautifully blue," Louise to Delia, November 8, 1857; "change of diet," Alphonso to Delia, October 8, 1858; "You will perceive . . ." Louise to Delia, December 13, 1858; "I do not believe we can love our children too much . . ." Louise to her mother, February 6, 1860; "What a resource is a cultivated mind!" quoted by Ross, p. 110; "Old age is still old age . . ." quoted by Ross, p. 136;

"You will have the whole Catholic world . . ." Louise to William H. Taft, January 30, 1890; "I hope the man is equal . . ." quoted in Pringle's *Life and Times of William Howard Taft,* p. 286; "I felt certain . . ." Pringle, p. 286; "When do you want to operate?" Horace D. Taft to Pringle, quoted by Pringle, p. 14; "Roosevelt is a good fighter . . ." Louise to William H. Taft, January 21, 1907; "Elihu Root," Pringle, p. 319; "No Taft to my knowledge . . ." Ross, p. 188.

Martha Bulloch Roosevelt

The Theodore Roosevelt Collection housed in Harvard College's Houghton Library contains a rare treasure of documentation for anyone interested in T.R.'s mother. Once one has been passed through its crimson leather portals, one has access to hundreds of family letters, and it was on these that my chapter was based. In addition, a visit to the Theodore Roosevelt birthplace at 28 East Twentieth Street in New York City set the scene for much of Mittie Roosevelt's life. Also helpful were Theodore Roosevelt's *Autobiography* (New York: Macmillan, 1914); Corinne Roosevelt Robinson's *My Brother, Theodore Roosevelt* (New York: Scribner, 1921); and a delightful book embodying the previously unpublished memoirs of the third of Mittie's children who survived to full maturity—*Bamie: Theodore Roosevelt's Remarkable Sister* by Lilian Rixey (New York: McKay, 1963). For genealogical data, *A History of the Genealogy of the Families of Bulloch, Stobo, etc.* by Joseph G. Bulloch (Savannah, 1892) was helpful; Allen Churchill's *The Roosevelts: American Aristocrats* (New York: Harper & Row, 1965) and Karl Schriftgiesser's *The Amazing Roosevelt Family 1613–1942* (New York: Funk, 1942) again proved useful. Much that was of value in filling in the gaps left by letters and family memoirs came from Carleton Putnam's *Theodore Roosevelt: The Formative Years 1858–1886* (New York: Scribner, 1958); and Volume I of Elting E. Morrison's *The Letters of Theodore Roosevelt: The Years of Preparation 1868–1900* (Cambridge: Harvard University Press, 1951) simplified the task of isolating T.R.'s correspondence with his mother. The only published work devoted exclusively to Mittie Roosevelt that I found was a magazine article, "The President's Mother," by Emma Hamilton Bulloch, presumably one of Mittie's relatives; I found it purely serendipitously, pasted into one of Sara Delano Roosevelt's scrapbooks in the F.D.R. Library, with no clue as to the publication in which it had appeared. Competently written and not overly flowery either, it cleared up the mystery of how Mittie got her nickname.

Specific quotations used in my chapter derive from the following sources: "Of all things, I think marriage . . ." Martha S. Bulloch to Mittie, November 21, 1865; "some higher power," Mittie to T.R., Sr., June 9, 1853; "those sofas up at Mary's . . ." T.R., Sr., to Mittie, June 5, 1853; "I am trying to school myself . . ." T.R., Sr., to Mittie, June 10, 1853; "Thee, dearest Thee, I promised . . ." Mittie to T.R., Sr., July 26, 1853; "I love you all I am capable . . ." Mittie to T.R., Sr., August 20, 1853; "I do dread . . ." Mittie to T.R., Sr., December 3, 1853; "When the different servants . . ." Martha S. Bulloch to Susan West, October 28, 1858; "my horror," Mittie to T.R., Sr., June 25, 1873; "I love you and wish to please you . . ." Mittie to T.R., Sr., October 15, 1873; "Generally these Saturdays . . ." from Bamie's unpublished manuscript, quoted by Rixey in *Bamie,* p. 18; "You mustn't feel melancholy . . ." Theodore Roosevelt to Mittie, February 8, 1880, from Morrison's *The Letters of Theodore Roosevelt,* p. 43; "There is a curse . . ." Putnam's *Theodore Roosevelt: The Formative Years,* p. 386.

Eliza Ballou Garfield

Eliza Garfield's autobiographical writings in the Garfield Papers at the Library of Congress were the basis of this chapter. These fragments of various length were supplemented to some extent by direct quotations from her in an effusive campaign biography of her son, *The Life of General James A. Garfield* by Jonas Mills Bundy (New York: A. S. Barnes, 1880); partisan though he was, Bundy took the trouble to spend some time talking with her in Ohio, and his account of what she told him has the ring of authenticity when compared with the recollections she set down in her own handwriting. Otherwise, Theodore C. Smith's *Life and Letters of James Garfield* (New Haven, Conn.: Yale University Press, 1935) was helpful, as was *The Diaries of James Garfield,* edited in two volumes by Harry James Brown and Frederick D. Williams (East Lansing, Mich.: Michigan State University Press, 1967), and Robert A. Caldwell's *James A. Garfield* (New York: Dodd, Mead, 1931). The files of the *New York Sun* from July through September of 1881 were extremely valuable.

As to specific quotations in my chapter, "I will now write . . ." Eliza Garfield's autobiographical fragment dated November 13, 1868; "French pony breed," Smith's *Life . . . of James Garfield,* p. 7; "My mother was a Weaver . . ." Smith, p. 7; "I want you to know . . ." Eliza Garfield, March 31, 1870; "Your father was five feet . . ." Eliza Garfield, March 31, 1870; "So you see we started . . ." Eliza Garfield, November 13, 1868; "Your father took up a piece of land . . ." Eliza Garfield, March 31, 1870; "the Ague," and "shook two weeks," Eliza Garfield, March 31, 1870; "We lived as well as our neighbors . . ." Eliza, February 7, 1869; "Our family Circle . . ." and "but Death . . ." Eliza, November 13, 1868; "I was then brought to exclaim . . ." Eliza, November 13, 1868; ". . . After a while a Disciple Preacher . . ." Eliza, March 31, 1870; "It then seemed . . ." Eliza, March 31, 1870; "Eliza, I have brought you four saplings . . ." Bundy's *The Life of General James A. Garfield,* p. 9; "James A. was the largest Babe . . ." Eliza, March 31, 1870; "did not like work . . ." Eliza, March 31, 1870; "without indignation," quoted p. xiv of *The Diaries of James Garfield,* Volume I; "fighting boy," Smith, p. 16; "I formed the determination . . ." James Garfield biographical note,

1877, quoted Smith, p. 20; "ready to drink in every species of vice," *Diaries,* Volume I, p. 60; "I did not believe that God . . ." and "As I approached the door . . ." James Garfield biographical note, quoted Smith, p. 25; "Give 'em Hail Columbia, boys!" Russell H. Conwell's *The Life, Speeches and Public Services of James A. Garfield* (Portland, Maine, 1881), p. 142; "I cannot tell you how strange . . ." James Garfield to Lucretia Garfield, October 22, 1871, quoted by Smith, p. 891; "Dear Mother, Don't be disturbed . . ." quoted by Smith, p. 1196.

Nancy Hanks Lincoln

Although a great deal has been written about Nancy Hanks Lincoln, this outpouring fits into definite categories. Much of it is almost purely fanciful, and even seriously intended works have to be subdivided further. Since the factual material concerning Lincoln's mother is so very slight, the point of view from which she is regarded makes all the difference. For those whose main objective is the rehabilitation of her good name, Mrs. Caroline Hanks Hitchcock's *Nancy Hanks* (New York: Doubleday & McClure, 1899) is a valuable sourcebook; the most scholarly support for this position is to be found in Louis A. Warren's *Lincoln's Parentage and Childhood* (New York: Century, 1926) and his *Lincoln's Youth: Indiana Years 1816–1830* (New York: Appleton-Century-Crofts, 1959). Adin Baber's *Nancy Hanks of Undistinguished Families* (privately printed, 1960) elaborates enthusiastically on the same theme. However, the weight of dispassionate inquiry seems to bolster the case first presented by Billy Herndon, and his papers in the Library of Congress and the Huntington Library in San Marino, California, have been the basis for my chapter. A good selection of these papers is reproduced in Emanuel Hertz's *The Hidden Lincoln* (New York: Viking, 1938), which I have used along with photocopies of various of the original letters. Other books which I have found valuable include William E. Barton's *Abraham Lincoln* in two volumes (Indianapolis: Bobbs-Merrill, 1925); his *The Women Lincoln Loved* (Indianapolis: Bobbs-Merrill, 1927); and his *The Lineage of Lincoln* (Indianapolis: Bobbs-Merrill, 1929); Benjamin P. Thomas's *Abraham Lincoln* (New York: Knopf, 1952) and his *Portrait for Posterity* (New Brunswick, N.J.: Rutgers University Press, 1947); Carl Sandberg's *Abraham Lincoln: The Prairie Years* (New York: Harcourt, Brace, 1926); David Donald's *Lincoln's Herndon* (New York: Knopf, 1948); and Jesse W. Weik's *The Real Lincoln* (Boston: Houghton Mifflin, 1922). Various innuendo-laden pamphlets such as "The Evidence that Abraham Lincoln Was not Born in Lawful Wedlock . . ." can be seen in the rare book collections of the New York Public Library and other major libraries, but their value is scant; just as, at the opposite end of the spectrum, the sentimental filmstrips and the like exhibited at some of the Lincoln landmarks in Kentucky, Indiana, and Illinois merely warm the hearts of pious patriots.

As to the specific sources for quotations in my chapter, "I was born February 12, 1809 . . ." quoted from Barton's *The Lineage of Lincoln*, p. 9; "Good heavens . . ." Herndon to Isaac A. Arnold, November 20, 1866; "Billy, I'll tell you something . . ." Herndon to Ward H. Lamon, March 6, 1870; "All that I am or hope ever to be . . ." Herndon to Ward H. Lamon, March 6, 1870; "What makes Europe and America love Christ . . ." Herndon to Arnold, November 20, 1866; "castrated, cut, fixed," Herndon to Truman H. Bartlett, September 25, 1887; "The two surprising things about this slender book . . ." Barton's *The Lineage of Lincoln*, p. 128; "The woods are full of them," quoted by Thomas in *Portrait for Posterity*, p. 222; "You set 'em up . . ." *Portrait for Posterity*, p. 222; "There is no fence around the grave . . ." Herndon's memorandum, "A Visit to the Lincoln Farm," dated September 14, 1865.

Abigail Smith Adams

My most valuable source for this chapter was *Letters of Mrs. Adams, The Wife of John Adams, With an introductory memoir by her grandson, Charles Francis Adams* (Boston: Charles C. Little and James Brown, 1840). In addition, I used Stewart Mitchell's collection of *New Letters of Abigail Adams* (Boston: Houghton Mifflin, 1945); *The Adams-Jefferson Letters*, edited by Lester J. Cappon (Chapel Hill, N.C.: University of North Carolina Press, 1959); *The Adams Family in Auteuil*, edited by Howard C. Rice, Jr. (Boston: Massachusetts Historical Society, 1956); and the first four volumes of the Adams Papers, published as the *Diary and Autobiography of John Adams*, edited by Lyman H. Butterfield (Cambridge: The Belknap Press of Harvard University Press, 1961). Other helpful sources included Page Smith's *John Adams* (Garden City, N.Y.: Doubleday, 1962); Janet Whitney's *Abigail Adams* (Boston: Little, Brown, 1947); James T. Adams's *The Adams Family* (Boston: Little, Brown, 1930); Catherine Drinker Bowen's *John Adams and the American Revolution* (Boston: Little, Brown, 1950); Stephen Hess's *America's Political Dynasties* (Garden City, N.Y.: Doubleday, 1966); and Lyman Butterfield's article, "The Papers of the Adams Family: Some Account of Their History," in the *Proceedings* of the Massachusetts Historical Society, Volume LXXI.

Sources for the specific quotations in my chapter, taken unless otherwise specified from the *Letters of Mrs. Adams*, in which they are printed in chronological order, include: "The present is believed to be the first attempt . . ." Charles Francis Adams's introduction to *Letters of Mrs. Adams*, p. xix; "for I really think that your Letters . . ." John Adams to Abigail, quoted by L. H. Butterfield in his article "The Papers of the Adams Family"; "There were many persons . . ." Charles Francis Adams's introduction to *Letters of Mrs. Adams*, p. lxi; "My Friend, I think I write to you every day . . ." Abigail to John Adams, April 16, 1764; "I was struck with General Washington . . ." Abigail to John Adams, July 16, 1775; "I have just returned from Penn's

Hill . . ." Abigail to John Adams, March 4, 1776; "Dearest of Friends, My habitation . . ." Abigail to John Adams, November 14, 1779; "If you had known . . ." Abigail to John Adams, December 23, 1782; "Let me enjoin it upon you . . ." Abigail to John Quincy Adams, June, 1778; "These are times in which a genius . . ." Abigail to John Quincy Adams, January 12, 1780; "It is not giving [her] too much credit . . ." Charles Francis Adams's introduction to *Letters of Mrs. Adams,* p. xlvii; "Why did you not tell me . . ." Abigail Adams, "Diary of Voyage from Boston to Deal, 20 June to 20 July 1784," in Volume III of *Diary and Autobiography of John Adams;* "to put on their Sea Cloaths . . ." *ibid.;* "You who have never tried the Sea" and "To those who have never been at Sea," *ibid.;* "A pretty figure I should make . . ." quoted by Charles Francis Adams in introduction to *Letters of Mrs. Adams,* p. lxxxi; "Nobody ever leaves Paris . . ." Abigail Adams to Thomas Jefferson, June 6, 1785, from Cappon (ed.), *The Adams-Jefferson Letters,* as are the following seven references: "I am for strengthening the federal union," Abigail Adams to Jefferson, July 23, 1786; "This proposition about the exchange of a son . . ." Jefferson to Abigail Adams, August 9, 1786; "I have taken the liberty . . ." Jefferson to Abigail Adams, December 21, 1786; "Miss is as contented . . ." Abigail Adams to Jefferson, June 27, 1787; "I have not the Heart to force her . . ." Abigail Adams to Jefferson, July 6, 1787; "I never felt so attached . . ." Abigail Adams to Jefferson, September 10, 1787; "At this moment she is in the convent . . ." Jefferson to Abigail Adams, October 4, 1787; "I took the earliest opportunity . . ." Abigail Adams to Mary S. Cranch, June, 1789, quoted by Whitney in *Abigail Adams,* p. 232; "always at the right hand of Mrs. Washington," Abigail Adams to Mary S. Cranch, January, 1790, quoted by Whitney, p. 237; "The next question I presume . . ." Abigail Adams to Mary S. Cranch, January, 1790, quoted by Whitney, p. 239; "Providence has been so bountiful . . ." Abigail Adams to Abigail A. Smith, July 31, 1808, from Schlesinger Library, Radcliffe College.

Mary Ball Washington

George Washington's mother has been the subject of more written words based on less reliable information than any other Presidential mother; probably there are few figures in all history who have been as much celebrated on as flimsy a foundation of fact. To separate out the material of any value is no easy task, but I have had the good fortune to follow in the footsteps of a masterly trailblazer. During the 1940's, Douglas Southall Freeman led a team of intrepid researchers through every area that could conceivably shed light on any phase of George Washington's career. His seven-volume *George Washington* (New York: Scribner, 1948–54) contains—quite literally—the reference points from which the seeker of the truth about some particular aspect of Washington's life can proceed intelligently. By studying Freeman's footnotes relating to Mary Washington, one can find expert testimony about various pitfalls to be avoided; and one can also conserve one's strength. For instance, the standard edition of *The Writings of George Washington*, edited by John C. Fitzpatrick (Washington, D.C.: U.S. Government Printing Office, 1931), runs to thirty-nine large volumes. But Freeman's authoritative comments about Washington's limited literary recognition of his mother's existence made it possible for me to concentrate my own investigation on those periods covered by five or six of the Fitzpatrick volumes rather than face the chore of scanning all of them for incidental maternal mentions. This is not to say that I accepted Freeman's judgment as final. Because the scope of his interest was so much broader than mine, I consulted the files of the Library of Congress and various other manuscript repositories as well as dozens of other published works wholly or in some part devoted to the life of Mary Ball Washington—in the hopes of discovering at least a few valid bits of evidence that he had overlooked. If I had no such luck, all of this was still valuable in that it helped me to arrive at my own conclusions. But the fact remains that all we can really know about Mary Washington is based on the grand total of a dozen letters, plus a few paragraphs worth of authentic genealogical data. As for firsthand recollections of her, we have just one source and that is not entirely trustworthy—*Recollections and Private Memoirs of Washington* by George Washington Parke Custis, a grandson of George Washington's wife (New York, 1860). Although Custis could have known Washington's mother only in her extreme old age, his pious chapter about her life comprises the framework for virtually everything else written about her, both mythological and factual. Prominent in the first category is that pre-Custis classic, *The Life of George Washington with curious anecdotes equally honorable to himself and exemplary to his younger countrymen* by Mason L. Weems. Besides an 1809 edition, I also consulted the same work as edited by Marcus Cunliffe (The Belknap Press of Harvard University Press, Cambridge, 1962) and found Cunliffe's introduction exceptionally interesting in its assessment of the importance that such noble frauds have had. Typical of lesser efforts in the Weems genre are a glorification of the Ball family, *The Maternal Ancestry and Nearest of Kin of Washington* (privately printed, 1885) and a British version, *Colonel William Ball of Virginia* by Earl L. W. Heck (London: Sydney Dutton, 1928). Among the seriously intended, if often overpoweringly flowery books about Mary Washington herself, Sara Agnes Pryor's *The Mother of Washington and Her Times* (New York: Macmillan, 1902) is still the best; it provides a helpful account of the efforts by the ladies of Fredericksburg to memorialize Washington's mother. For a scholarly treatment of the life of Mary Washington's daughter Betty, Jane Taylor Duke's *Kenmore and the Lewises* (Fredericksburg: Kenmore Association, 1965) is valuable. *The Diaries of George Washington*, edited by John C. Fitzpatrick (Boston: Houghton Mifflin, 1925) give helpful sidelights. Among other books of some interest are James T. Flexner's *George Washington: The Forge of Experience* (Boston: Little, Brown, 1965); Paul Leicester Ford's

The True George Washington (Philadelphia: Lippincott, 1898); *Letters to Washington and Accompanying Papers,* edited by Stanislaus M. Hamilton (Boston: Houghton Mifflin, 1898); *George Washington* by Rupert Hughes (New York: Morrow, 1922); J. Paul Hudson's *George Washington's Birthplace* (National Park Service Handbook, Series H26, Washington, D.C., 1956); Washington Irving's *Life of Washington* (New York: Putnam, 1856); Benson J. Lossing's *Mary and Martha: The Mother and the Wife of George Washington* (New York: Harper, 1886); and Charles Moore's *The Family Life of George Washington* (Boston: Houghton Mifflin, 1926). In addition, visits to Mount Vernon and to the various sites associated with Mary Washington in and around Fredericksburg were helpful to me on many counts. While old courthouses and new restorations yield no facts about Mary Washington that generations of previous searches have failed to find, they do lead to interesting collateral material, and one learns such fascinating trivia; maintenance expenses for the lovely Kenmore restoration are met in large part by the makers of a ready-mix for gingerbread who have been pleased to describe their product as produced from Mary Washington's original recipe.

As to specific references for quotations in my chapter, "tutelage and government" is from Mary's mother's will, quoted by Freeman in Volume I, p. 45; "The Rose of Epping Forest" from various writers; "but if she should Insist . . ." from Fitzpatrick's *Writings of Washington,* Volume I, p. 73; "Of the mother . . ." the *Recollections* of Custis, p. 131; "trifling objections" from a letter from Robert Jackson to Lawrence Washington, September 18, 1746, quoted by Freeman, Volume I, p. 185; "Hond Madam, I was favored . . ." George Washington to his mother, June 7, 1755, in Library of Congress; "thear was no end to my trouble . . ." Mary B. Washington to Joseph Ball, July 26, 1759, copy provided by Historical Society of Pennsylvania; "In God's name . . ." Fitzpatrick's *Writings of Washington,* Volume XXVI, p. 41; "I never Lived soe pore . . ." Mary B. Washington to Lund Washington, December 9, 1778, copy provided by Historical Society of Pennsylvania; "to relieve her from *real* distress . . ." George Washington to Benjamin Harrison, from Fitzpatrick, Volume XXI, pp. 341–2; "my sincere and pressing advice . . ." George Washington to his mother, February 15, 1787, in Library of Congress; "it is the duty of her relatives . . ." George Washington to Betty Washington Lewis, September 13, 1789, from Fitzpatrick, Volume XXX, pp. 398–9.

Hulda Minthorn Hoover

This is based on a small folder of family letters provided by the Herbert Hoover Library in West Branch, Iowa; and on autobiographical material included in Herbert Hoover's *Years of Adventure 1874–1920* (New York: Macmillan, 1952) and his *A Boyhood in Iowa* (New York: Aventine Press, 1931). Also helpful were David Hinshaw's *Herbert Hoover: American Quaker* (New

York: Farrar, Straus, 1950) and Eugene Lyons's *Our Unknown Ex-President: A Portrait of Herbert Hoover* (Garden City, N.Y.: Doubleday, 1948).

As to quotations, "She was such a gifted girl" is from a reminiscence of her niece Agnes Minthorn Miles provided by the Hoover Library; and "Remember me . . ." from a letter from Hulda Minthorn to Miranda Stowe, dated 1st day, 3d month, 1863, also in the Hoover Library.

Victoria Moor Coolidge

Sources include Calvin Coolidge's *Autobiography* (New York: Cosmopolitan Book Corp., 1929); Claude M. Fuess's *Calvin Coolidge* (Boston: Little, Brown, 1940); Edward Connery Latham's *Meet Calvin Coolidge: The Man Behind the Mystery* (Brattleboro, Vt.: Stephen Green Press, 1960); and William Allen White's *A Puritan in Babylon* (New York: Macmillan, 1938).

As to quotations, "The greatest grief . . ." Coolidge's *Autobiography*, p. 13; "Do you know . . ." Coolidge statement to Frank Stearns quoted by White, pp. 24–5; "She was of a very light and fair complexion . . ." and "There was a touch of mysticism . . ." Coolidge *Autobiography*, pp. 12–13.

Phoebe Dickerson Harding

The most valuable source here is the Ray B. Harris Collection in the Ohio Historical Society in Columbus; this large assortment of manuscripts and miscellaneous material was the basis for the late Mr. Harris's article "Background and Youth of the Seventh Ohio President" in the *Ohio State Archaeological and Historical Quarterly* of July, 1943, and for an unpublished biography of Warren G. Harding, the manuscript of which is also included in the collection. A brief manuscript that is also of interest is "President Harding's Story of His Mother," by Frank M. Warwick, one of Harding's associates on the *Marion Star;* this is also at the Ohio Historical Society's library. In addition, *Incredible Era: The Life and Times of Warren G. Harding* by Samuel Hopkins Adams (Boston: Houghton Mifflin, 1939) is helpful.

As to quotations, "Phoebe Dickerson is no more . . ." is from the Ray B. Harris Collection described above; "We are all well and hearty . . ." Phoebe to Thomas Dickerson, January 13, 1863, copy in Harris Collection; and "Warren, it's a good thing . . ." from Adams, p. 7.

Nancy Allison McKinley

The Stark County Historical Society in Canton, Ohio, provided me with a privately printed work on the McKinley family by Herbert T. O. Blue, and Mr. Blue's *History of Stark County* (Chicago, 1928) also was helpful. Other books of interest were William T. Kuhn's *Memories of Old Canton* (Canton, 1937); H. H. Kohlsaat's *From McKinley to Harding* (New York: Scribner, 1923); Margaret Leech's *In the Days of McKinley* (New York: Harper & Row, 1959); Charles S. Olcott's *The Life of William McKinley* (Boston: Houghton Mifflin, 1916). The *New York Sun* and *The New York Times* for the week of McKinley's inauguration also proved useful.

As to specific quotations, "Oh, God keep him humble," is from Kohlsaat, p. 54; "Mother, this is better . . ." *Canton Repository* quoted by Leech, p. 113; and "Those who knew her best . . ." *Canton Repository* of December 13, 1897, reproduced in Blue's *History of Stark County*, Volume I, p. 808.

Ann Neal Cleveland

At the Library of Congress I was told that there might be some material pertaining to Grover Cleveland's mother in his miscellaneous papers, which fill eighty-five large manuscript boxes; these have not yet been indexed. Being unequal to this search, I have relied here on *Grover Cleveland* by Allan Nevins (New York: Dodd, Mead, 1932), the *Letters of Grover Cleveland,* edited by Professor Nevins (Boston: Houghton Mifflin, 1933), and Robert T. McElroy's *Grover Cleveland* (New York: Harper & Row, 1923). *A History of Presidential Elections* by Eugene H. Rosebloom (New York: Macmillan, 1964) also was helpful.

As to quotations, "Ma! Ma!" is from Rosebloom, p. 273; "Do you know . . ." is from a letter from Grover to William M. Cleveland, November 7, 1882, printed in *Letters of Cleveland,* pp. 17–18.

Elizabeth Irwin Harrison

Here I did go through the John Scott Harrison Papers in the Library of Congress to no great purpose, and I also visited the Benjamin Harrison home in Indianapolis. However, I did not attempt to duplicate the extensive combing of Harrison archives carried out by Harry J. Sievers, whose *Benjamin Harrison: Hoosier Warrior* (Chicago: Henry Regnery, 1952) is an excellent biography. *America's Political Dynasties* by Stephen Hess (Garden City, N.Y.: Doubleday, 1966) also was useful.

As to quotations, "I pray for you daily . . ." Elizabeth Harrison to Archibald and Benjamin Harrison, July 24, 1848, quoted by Sievers, p. 29; "I hope you will be prudent . . ." quoted by Sievers, p. 43; "Grandpa's pants . . ." Hess, p. 233.

Malvina Stone Arthur

The *New York Sun* of September 21, 1881, was my main source here. Other material of interest came from *A History of Franklin and Grand Isle Counties, Vermont,* edited by Lewis Cass Aldrich (Syracuse, N.Y.: D. Mason & Co., 1891); from George Frederick Howe's *Chester A. Arthur* (New York: Dodd, Mead, 1934); and from Herbert Eaton's *Presidential Timber* (New York: Free Press of Glencoe, 1964).

"The evidence upon which this theory . . ." is from the *New York Sun* of September 21, 1881.

Sophia Birchard Hayes

There is a superabundance of material about this lady; at the Rutherford B. Hayes Library in Fremont, Ohio, the first of the separate Presidential libraries, several hundred letters in her own hand are available, along with many times that number of letters written by close members of her family. This treasure, which I mined as expeditiously as I could during a two-day visit in July of 1967, is naturally my basic source. Two useful supplements were Harry Barnard's *Rutherford B. Hayes and His America* (Indianapolis: Bobbs-Merrill, 1954) and Hamilton J. Eckenrode's *Rutherford B. Hayes* (New York: Dodd, Mead, 1939).

As to specific quotations, "Did you ever observe . . ." is from a letter from Fanny Hayes Platt to Rutherford B. Hayes, July 10, 1849; "She is grand company . . ." R. B. Hayes Diary, quoted by Barnard, p. 35; "Had we not better support . . ." Sophia Hayes to Sardis Birchard, February 5, 1838; "Dear Rutherford . . . Seventeen years . . ." Sophia Hayes to Rutherford Hayes, July 20, 1839; "Well, verily, Mother . . ." Fanny H. Platt to Rutherford Hayes, July 22, 1839; "My only support and comfort . . ." Sophia to Rutherford Hayes, June 17, 1856.

Hannah Simpson Grant

The most valuable source here is *The Papers of Ulysses S. Grant,* Volume I, 1837–1861, edited by John Y. Simon (Carbondale, Ill.: Southern Illinois University Press, 1967). Also helpful are the *Personal Memoirs* of U. S. Grant (New York: C. L. Webster, 1885–86); *Letters of Ulysses S. Grant to his Father and Youngest Sister,* edited by Jesse Grant Cramer (New York: Putnam, 1912); *Captain Sam Grant* by Lloyd Lewis (Boston: Little, Brown, 1950); *Letters from Lloyd Lewis Showing Steps in His Research for His Biography of U. S. Grant* by Lloyd Lewis (Boston: Little, Brown, 1950); *A Personal History of*

U. S. Grant by Albert Deane Richardson (Hartford, 1868); *The General's Wife: The Life of Mrs. Ulysses S. Grant* by Ishbel Ross (New York: Dodd, Mead, 1959); *Early Records of Simpson Families in Scotland, North Ireland and Eastern United States* by Helen A. Simpson (Philadelphia: Lippincott, 1927); and *Meet General Grant* by W. E. Woodward (New York: Liverwright, 1928).

As to specific quotations, "as much the deportment of a woman," Mrs. Sarah Hare Simpson quoted by Lewis in *Captain Sam Grant*, p. 14; "Backwoodsman, sir . . ." Richardson, pp. 53–4; "Why, Mrs. Bailey . . ." Richardson, p. 76; "Ulysses, you've grown straighter . . ." Richardson, p. 91; "She thought nothing you could do . . ." Lewis in *Captain Sam Grant*, p. 14; "Dear Sister King . . ." Hannah Grant, March 2, 1880, from Library of Congress.

Mary McDonough Johnson

The record here is slim indeed, and I have relied on Robert W. Winston's *Andrew Johnson: Plebian and Patriot* (New York: Henry Holt, 1928), and to a lesser extent on Lloyd Paul Stryker's *Andrew Johnson: A Study in Courage* (New York: Macmillan, 1929). Wilfred E. Binkley's *American Political Parties* (New York: Knopf, 1962) was also helpful.

As to quotations, "ghouls and hyenas" is from an open letter by Andrew Johnson, dated October 15, 1845, in Library of Congress; "a wild, harum-scarum sort of boy," Selby quoted by Winston, p. 9.

Elizabeth Speer Buchanan

The bulk of the Buchanan Papers were given to the Lancaster County Historical Society in Pennsylvania, and, uncatalogued, have been deposited in the society's vault for safekeeping; thus they are of use, for all practical purposes, only to the scholar specializing in Buchanan research. For my purposes, the works of two such scholars had to suffice—Philip S. Klein, who published *President James Buchanan* (University Park, Pa.: Pennsylvania State University Press, 1962); and George Ticknor Curtis, who produced an authorized *Life of James Buchanan* much earlier (New York: Harper, 1883). In addition, I was helped by the fact that a few random maternal papers turned up at the Historical Society of Pennsylvania, which made copies available to me.

As to quotations, "Monarchs, we envy . . ." is from an undated manuscript in the Historical Society of Pennsylvania's collection, attributed to Elizabeth Buchanan; "the giddy dance" is from the same source; "My dear Mother, I can now write . . ." James Buchanan to Elizabeth Buchanan, July 3, 1833, copy from Historical Society of Pennsylvania.

Anna Kendrick Pierce

A similar situation applies in the case of the Pierce Papers at the New Hampshire Historical Society in Concord. Being unable to devote many months to searching for maternal references there, I have relied on *Franklin Pierce* by Roy F. Nichols (Philadelphia: University of Pennsylvania Press, 1958); two older biographies—Nathaniel Hawthorne's *Life of Franklin Pierce* (Boston, 1852) and B. W. Bartlett's *Life of Frank Pierce* (Auburn, N.Y., 1852); and several local histories—*History of Concord, N.H.*, edited by James Lyford (Concord, 1896), *History of the Town of Amherst, N.H.* by Daniel F. Secomb (Concord, 1883), and *History of Hillsborough, N.H.* by C. Waldo Browne (Manchester, N.H., 1921).

As to quotations, "She was a most affectionate . . ." Franklin Pierce to John McNeil, December 14, 1838, quoted by Nichols, p. 10; "At this early period . . ." Hawthorne, p. 17.

Phoebe Millard Fillmore

An autobiographical sketch by Millard Fillmore dated February 8, 1871, fragmentary as it is, provides most of what is known about this President's mother; a copy of this was made available to me by the Huntington Library in San Marino, California. Robert J. Rayback's *Millard Fillmore* (published for the Buffalo Historical Society by Henry Stewart, Buffalo, 1959) also was helpful, and in addition I consulted two contemporary biographies, Ivory Chamberlain's *Millard Fillmore* (Buffalo, 1856) and "The Life and Administration of Ex-President Fillmore" from Walker's *Statesmen's Manual* (New York: Edward Walker, 1856).

Sarah Strother Taylor

Besides Zachary Taylor's autobiographical manuscript dated 1826 from the Library of Congress, the following were helpful: *Zachary Taylor: Soldier in the White House* by Hamilton Holman (Indianapolis: Bobbs-Merrill, 1951); *Old Rough and Ready* by Silas Bent McKinley and Silas Bent (New York: Vanguard, 1946) and *Zachary Taylor* by Brainerd Dyer (Baton Rouge, La.: Louisiana State University Press, 1946).

"I was born . . ." is from Zachary Taylor's 1826 manuscript in the Library of Congress.

Jane Knox Polk

The best source here is "The Boyhood of President Polk" by Albert V. Good-pasture in the *Tennessee Historical Magazine* for April, 1921. Other helpful material came from *James K. Polk, Jacksonian* by Charles Grier Sellers, Jr. (Princeton, N.J.: Princeton University Press, 1957); *James K. Polk* by Eugene I. McCormick (New York: Russell, 1965); and *The Polk Family and Kinsmen* by William Harrison Polk (Louisville, Ky., 1912).

As to quotations, "Mother unto death Jane Polk," is from a letter from Jane Polk to James K. Polk dated January 5, 1828, the only such letter in the Polk Papers in the Library of Congress; and "Mother, I have never . . ." is from Goodpasture's article.

Mary Armistead Tyler

The only clues concerning this lady that I was able to find came from Oliver Perry Chitwood's *John Tyler: Champion of the Old South* (New York: Appleton-Century, 1939) and *And Tyler Too* by Robert Seager II (New York: McGraw-Hill, 1965). On their evidence, it seemed fruitless to look any further.

Elizabeth Bassett Harrison

Visiting Berkeley, the Harrison plantation, on April 19, 1967, was most helpful here. Books of some value were Freeman Cleaves's *Old Tippecanoe: William Henry Harrison and His Time* (New York: Scribner, 1939) and Dorothy B. Goebel's *William Henry Harrison* (Indianapolis Historical Bureau of Indiana State Library, 1926). Eugene H. Rosebloom's *A History of Presidential Elections* (New York: Macmillan, 1964) was also pertinent.

"Old Tip he wears . . ." is from Rosebloom, p. 122.

Maria Hoes Van Alen Van Buren

The resources of the Columbia County Historical Society in Kinderhook, N.Y., provided a much appreciated supplement here to the local history resources of the New-York Historical Society and the New York Public Library, but none of these was able to provide much of moment about this mother. Material of most use to me came from Edward A. Collier's *History of Old Kinderhook* (New York: Putnam, 1914); William Emmons's *Martin Van Buren* (Washington, 1835); Will S. Kline's *Kinderhook, N.Y., The Village Beautiful* (privately printed, 1911); Denis Tilden Lynch's *An Epoch and a*

Man: Martin Van Buren and His Times (New York: Liverwright, 1929); Harriet C. Peckham's *History of Cornelis Maessen Van Buren* (New York: Tobias A. Wright, 1913); and Martin Van Buren's *Autobiography*, edited by John C. Fitzpatrick (Washington, D.C.: U. S. Government Printing Office, 1920). *Columbia County at the End of the Century* (Hudson Gazette, 1900) was of some interest, too.

As to quotations, "she was regarded . . ." Van Buren's *Autobiography*, p. 10; "utterly devoid of the spirit of accumulation . . ." *ibid.*, p. 10; "a common country lawyer . . ." *New York Herald*, May 3, 1837, quoted by Collier, p. 415.

Elizabeth Hutchinson Jackson

The Jackson Papers in the Library of Congress include a manuscript, "The Jackson Family," which is neither dated nor signed; this is typical of the kind of documentation available here. Of most use to me were such works by Jackson specialists as *Andrew Jackson and Early Tennessee History* by S. G. Heiskell (Nashville, Tenn., 1920); *Andrew Jackson: The Border Captain* by Marquis James (Indianapolis: Bobbs-Merrill, 1933); *Andrew Jackson* by James Parton (New York, 1860); *Andrew Jackson* by Robert V. Remini (New York: Twayne, 1966); and *Andrew Jackson* by William Graham Sumner (Boston: Houghton Mifflin, 1883).

As to quotations, "Andy, never tell a lie . . ." W. H. Sparks, quoted by James, p. 30; "fresh-looking," "very conversive," "she could spin . . ." *National Intelligencer* of August 1, 1845, quoted by James, p. 13; "Andrew Jackson was . . ." Parton, Volume I, p. 104.

Elizabeth Jones Monroe

Various efforts in Virginia to find any further information about this mother came to naught, and I have had to rely on fragmentary references in James Monroe's *Autobiography*, edited by Stuart Gerry Brown (Syracuse, N.Y.: Syracuse University Press, 1959); and in David W. Eaton's *Historical Atlas of Westmoreland County* (Richmond, Va.: Dietz Press, 1942); and on a few pertinent documents in the University of Virginia Library.

As to quotations, "very amiable and respectable woman," is from Monroe's *Autobiography*, p. 21; "undertaker in architecture," *William and Mary Quarterly*, Volume XV, p. 52; "allowing my nephew . . ." Will of Joseph Jones in University of Virginia Library.

Nelly Conway Madison

James Madison by Irving Brandt (Indianapolis: Bobbs-Merrill, 1941–61) and the long sequence of letters between James Madison and his father in the Library of Congress were the main sources here. Horace E. Hayden's *Virginia Genealogies* (Washington, D.C.: Rare Book Shop, 1931) was also helpful, as were Margaret Bayard Smith's letters in *The First Forty Years of Washington Society,* edited by Gaillard Hunt (New York: Scribner, 1906), and Katharine Anthony's *Dolly Madison* (Garden City, N.Y.: Doubleday, 1949).

As to quotations, "Hon^d Sir: The spectacles . . ." James Madison Jr. to James Madison Sr., May 13, 1784, Madison Papers in Library of Congress; "She lacks but 3 years . . ." Margaret Bayard Smith to Mrs. Samuel Boyd, August 12, 1828, quoted in *The First Forty Years of Washington Society,* p. 236.

Jane Randolph Jefferson

Such documents as the wills of Jane Jefferson and of her husband can be seen in the University of Virginia Library, but to acquire any precise impression of this mother is virtually impossible. Among the works I have consulted toward this end were Thomas Jefferson's *Autobiography,* with an introduction and notes by Paul Leicester Ford (New York: Putnam, 1914); Volume I of *The Papers of Thomas Jefferson* edited by Julian Boyd (Princeton, N.J.: Princeton University Press, 1950); *The Domestic Life of Thomas Jefferson* by his great granddaughter Sarah N. Randolph (New York: Harper, 1871); *Thomas Jefferson and His Unknown Brother Randolph,* edited by Bernard Mayo (Charlottesville, Va.: University of Virginia, 1942); Volume I of *Jefferson and His Time* by Dumas Malone (Boston: Little, Brown, 1948); *Thomas Jefferson* by Nathan Schachner (New York: Yoseloff, 1957); *The Randolphs* by H. V. Eckenrode (Indianapolis: Bobbs-Merrill, 1946); and *William Randolph of Turkey Island . . . and his immediate descendants* by Randolph Wassell (Memphis, Tenn., 1949).

As to quotations, "My mother died . . ." quoted by Schachner, p. 88; "They trace their pedigree . . ." Jefferson's *Autobiography,* Volume I, p. 4; "His mother, from whom . . ." Sarah Randolph, pp. 21–2; "but ah, we saved your fiddle," Sarah Randolph, p. 43; "She was crazy as can be," a Shadwell neighbor to author.

Susanna Boylston Adams

The bibliographical material listed for Abigail Smith Adams also applies in this lady's case, with only a few exceptions. Only a handful of additional references of any interest pertain specifically to the mother of John Adams; among these are Nina F. Little's *Some Old Brookline Houses* (Brookline, Mass., Historical Society, 1949) and *Henry and Mary Lee Letters and Journals,* edited by Frances Rollins Morse (Boston, 1926).

As to quotations, "How a whole family . . ." and "M. seems to have no Scheme . . ." from John Adams's Diary, December 30, 1758, quoted in *Diary and Autobiography of John Adams,* edited by Lyman H. Butterfield (Cambridge: The Belknap Press of Harvard University Press, 1961); and "the islands, the rivers . . ." John Adams to Nicholas Boylston, August 10, 1820, quoted in *John Adams* by Page Smith (Garden City, N.Y.: Doubleday, 1961), p. 11.

Index

Abilene, Kansas, 39–40

Adams, Abigail Smith, xi, 146–61, 238; published volume of letters of, and extracts from, 148, 149, 152, 153, 158, 161; influence of, over public conduct of husband, 148, 149, 157–58; as source of strength and inspiration for husband, 149; possessed of something close to genius in accomplishing her objectives, 149; background and early training of, 149–50; marriage of, to John Adams, 150–51; birth of five children to, 151; begins making politics her business, 151–52; perfectionist zeal of, concentrated on son John Quincy, 153; children of, 153–54, 159; supervision of family's material wealth by, 154, 160; and American Philosophical Society, 154; sea-trip diary of, 154–55; with husband in London, 154–57, 238; friendship of, with Thomas Jefferson, 156–57; as Mrs. Vice President, 157–59; as First Lady, 159–60; folklore of laundry hung up to dry in the East Room of White House, 160; as grand old lady in retirement in Quincy, 160–61; death of, 161; notes and bibliography, 251–52

Adams, Charles, 154, 159

Adams, Charles Francis, 148, 159

Adams, Deacon John, 237

Adams, Henry, 159

Adams, John, 148, 150, 151, 152–53, 154, 158, 159, 236, 237–38; influence of wife on public conduct of, 148–49, 157–58; administration of,

159–60; extracts from diary of, 235–36; mother of, see Adams, Susanna Boylston

Adams, John Quincy, 153, 159; mother of, see Adams, Abigail Smith

Adams, Nabby, 153, 159

Adams Papers, 237

Adams, Susanna Boylston, 150, 155, 235–38, 263

Adams, Thomas, 154, 159

Algonac estate of the Delanos, 65, 66, 67, 68, 69, 70

American Philosophical Society in Philadelphia, 154

Anti-Masons, 214

Armistead, Robert, 219

Arthur, Chester A., 193–94; mother of, see Arthur, Malvina Stone

Arthur, Malvina Stone, 193–94, 257

Arthur, William, 193–94

Axson, Ellen Louise (Mrs. Woodrow Wilson), 88

Bailey, Joseph W. ("Silver-toned Joe"), 7

Baines, Joseph Wilson, 3–5, 12

Baines, Rebekah, see Johnson, Rebekah Baines

Ball, Joseph, 164

Ball, Mary, see Washington, Mary Ball

Ball, William, 164

Ballou, Eliza, see Garfield, Eliza Ballou

Ballou, Mehitabel, 124

Barton, William Eleazor, 140, 141

Bassett, William, 219

264

ABOUT THE AUTHOR

Doris Faber was a reporter for *The New York Times* until she married one of her colleagues, who has since become an editor at the *Times*. While raising two daughters, she has written more than a dozen books for children and teen-agers, in the process becoming interested both in motherhood and history; this book is the result. She lives with her family outside of New York City.